D0059616

ADVANCED
BACKPACKING

A TRAILSIDE GUIDE
BY
KAREN BERGER

Illustrations by Ron Hildebrand

A TRAILSIDE SERIES GUIDE

W. W. NORTON & COMPANY

NEW YORK   LONDON

Look for these other Trailside® Series Guides:
Bicycling: Touring and Mountain Bike Basics
Canoeing: A Trailside Guide
Cross-Country Skiing: A Complete Guide
Fly Fishing: A Trailside Guide
Hiking & Backpacking: A Complete Guide
Kayaking: Whitewater and Touring Basics
Parents' Guide to Hiking & Camping: A Trailside Guide
Rock Climbing: A Trailside Guide
Snowshoeing: A Trailside Guide
Winter Adventure: A Complete Guide to Winter Sports

Trailside: Make Your Own Adventure is a registered trademark of New Media, Inc.

The text of this book is composed in Bodoni Book with the display set in Triplex
Page composition by Tina Christensen
Color separations and prepress by Bergman Graphics, Incorporated
Manufacturing by South China Printing Co. Ltd.
Illustrations by Ron Hildebrand

Book design by Bill Harvey

Library of Congress Cataloging-in-Publication Data

Berger, Karen, 1959-
Advanced backpacking: A Trailside guide/ by Karen Berger:
illustrations by Ron Hildebrand
p. cm. — (A trailside series guide)
Includes bibliographical references and index.
ISBN 0-393-31769-2
1. Backpacking. I. Backpacking — Equipment and supplies. 3. Trails.
I. Title. II. Title: Trailside, make your own adventure III. Series.
GV199.6.B47   1998   796.51—dc21   97-43849

W. W. Norton & Company, Inc., 500 Fifth Avenue, New York, NY 10110
http://web.wwnorton.com
W. W. Norton & Company Ltd., 10 Coptic Street, London WC1A 1PU

2 3 4 5 6 7 8 9 0

C O N T E N T S

INTRODUCTION

Imagine simplicity.

Harder than it sounds, isn't it? Well, of course it is, when you've got bills to pay and dates to keep and a job to do and calls to return and a lawn to mow and that leak in the gutter that needed to be fixed last year.

But try.

Imagine a day during which you have only three decisions to make: How far to walk. What to eat. When to sleep.

A wall of time grows higher every day, separating you from the complexities back home until even the memory of everyday hassles melts away like alpine snow under a strong summer sun. Your mind, freed of clutter, opens to observe the world around you. You watch spring creep up a mountain a hundred feet a day. A day-old elk fawn follows its mother on stilt-like, uncertain legs. A marmot basks in the sun. Your lungs expand to feel mountain air that cleanses from the inside. Your eyes shift their focus from the harried hustle of the city to quiet, faraway vistas. You find yourself staring, enraptured, as a single hawk catches a thermal current and rides it in hypnotic spirals.

The author hikes along the 2,638-mile Pacific Crest Trail, one of North America's four super-long footpaths.

Its tough terrain, remoteness, and unpredictable weather make the highcountry among the most rewarding and demanding for trekkers.

The purpose of hiking? In the words of Benton MacKaye, Appalachian Trail founder: "To walk. To see. And to see what you see."

Simplicity has been in the news a lot lately, but it's not news to hikers. Backpackers of all stripes — from weekend hikers out for 20 miles to expeditionists out for 2,000 miles — know that the backcountry is rejuvenating simply because it takes us away from all of the unimportant emergencies that make up so much of modern life. But those who strike out for longer periods of time or to more remote and untrammeled wildernesses find a life stripped to its very essentials.

Longer hikes, more difficult terrain, and extreme conditions offer special rewards: There is the intensity of a southwestern desert or an exposed alpine slope. There is the satisfaction of being one of only 300 people who complete the Appalachian Trail in a given year. There is the solitude that you find when you climb a little higher, walk a little farther, or leave the well-trod trail behind. But these kinds of hikes also require a special set of skills.

This book is for those hikers and backpackers who find themselves constantly looking to see what's over the next ridge. It's for people who have wondered what it would be like to hike the Grand Canyon, backpack across cirques of exposed alpine scree, live outdoors when the temperature plummets below zero, hike across foreign countries, or perhaps embark on the trip of a lifetime — a thru-hike of a multi-thousand-mile hiking trail.

To get the most out of this book, you don't have to be an expert, but I do assume that you already know a little bit about backpacking. If you don't, Trailside's earlier guide, *Hiking & Backpacking*, covers information about basic gear selection, general safety, first aid, and how to use a map and compass. In this book I'll try to expand your hiking universe. With that in mind, Part I covers the basics of expedition planning, including scheduling, route selection, and food and gear resupply. Part II examines the special gear and skills you need for a variety of situations, including rain, winter, high mountains, deserts, and foreign travel. And Part III offers a wish list of destinations (along with contact information) with descriptions of hikes that ramble over every conceivable type of terrain and ecosystem, from saguaros to sequoias and cactus to krummholz.

This book is also for hikers who may not be interested in difficult or extreme conditions, but who want to learn how to maximize their comfort in the backcountry. What long-distance hikers have learned mile after mile and day after day can help make any backpacker's trip more enjoyable: How to make every ounce you carry into the wilderness work for you. What to pack, what to leave home, and how to make a 40-pound load meet your every need. Which gear lasts through many lifetimes' worth of use and abuse.

My own backpacking experience spans five continents and well over 12,000 miles, including the Appalachian Trail, the Pacific Crest Trail, and the Continental Divide. But that's not all I've relied on to write this book. My husband, Dan Smith, is one of America's premier wilderness walkers, who has worn out dozens of "lifetime warranties" during more than 35,000 trail miles, and much of what I know about the backcountry I've learned from him. I've also learned from dozens of cohorts, especially those who are members of the Appalachian Long Distance Hikers Association. ALDHA's annual "Gathering," usually held over the Columbus Day weekend, draws several hundred of America's most experienced, trail-hardened, and enthusiastic hikers. These are people who have camped next to Icelandic geysers or bushwhacked through Peruvian jungles. They've climbed Kilimanjaro or trekked in the Himalayas. Most of them have spent 6 months on the Appalachian Trail. And their cumulative hiking experience can be numbered somewhere in the millions — yes, *millions* — of miles. I've attended their talks and slide shows, argued over gear with them, and picked up more than a few tried-and-true trail tricks.

But maybe the most important thing I've learned from my friends in

The author and her husband Daniel R. Smith atop Checo Mesa in the rugged, arid country of northwestern New Mexico during their 3,000-mile-long trek along North America's Continental Divide.

ALDHA is that anybody can inject adventure into their lives. I'm inspired by what my fellow hikers have done and by who they are — people just like you and me. Sure, a few of them could read for the role of Grizzly Adams. But far more of them look a lot like the folks next door. They are students, doctors, retirees, construction workers, teachers, lawyers, ministers, firefighters, and the gainfully, gleefully unemployed. Their ages range from under 20 to over 80, and the person answering questions about a 500-mile hike could be someone who looks like your grandmother, your nephew, or your accountant. Some of my hiking pals are much stronger than I am; some are not. Some are faster, some slower; some older, some younger; some fitter, some fatter. What they have in common is that they followed a dream.

Whether your goal is to take the vacation of a lifetime, attempt a thruhike of a multi-thousand-mile mega-trail, or stretch your experience to alpine altitudes, the snowy seasons, or foreign shores, this book offers suggestions and techniques that will pave the way for safer, more comfortable, more skillful and confident enjoyment of the backcountry.

As Emma Gatewood, who at the age of 67 became the first woman to thru-hike the Appalachian Trail, was fond of saying, "Hiking takes more head than heel."

LONG-
DISTANCE
BASICS

The term "long-distance hiking" is more an idea than a set definition. Someone who's just finished a first-ever 50-mile hike is likely to think she's walked to the ends of the earth. Other folks set out on a 500-mile jaunt without thinking twice. And then there are the thru-hikers: those who take on America's most famous long-distance paths, such as the 2,160-mile-long Appalachian Trail, the 2,638-mile-long Pacific Crest Trail, and the 3,100-mile-long Continental Divide Trail.

For me, a long-distance hike is one that takes me away from my everyday life for long enough that the journey *becomes* my everyday life.

Other hikers think of a long-distance hike as one that requires them to replenish some of their supplies (usually food) while en route. Still others use mileage as a yardstick.

However you define it, a long-distance hike is an intense experience that will teach you a lot about yourself, about backpacking, and about the natural world. You might learn that you can push harder than you ever thought possible. That spring blooms one flower at a time. That you can walk in the rain, sleep in the cold, wear the same clothes day after day and be perfectly content. That something as simple as a trailside store serving ice cream can

careers. The mega-trails take 5 or 6 months to hike: Who *are* these people who have all that time?

Some have dreamed about a long hike for years; for others it's a spur-of-the-moment decision. Many long-distance hikers are people in the middle of some sort of life transition: finishing up college or graduate school, making a career change, coping with a divorce or the death of a loved one. These major

A thru-hiker completes a southbound trek of the Applachian Trail at Amicalola Falls State Park in western Georgia.

make you deliriously, ridiculously happy. That perfect strangers with huge hearts will show up just when you're in need of help or a friendly smile.

Of course, the truth is that for many of us, it's not quite that easy to find exorbitant blocks of free time to go gallivanting about in the woods. We have families, responsibilities,

upheavals can give people both the time and the motivation to pursue a long-held dream — such as hike the Appalachian Trail. In recent years, there's been a surge of retired people hiking long trails, a reflection of the fact that senior citizens are living longer, healthier, and more active lives; are celebrating their freedom in fine style; and, in the process, are setting an example for the rest of us.

But other people simply save time and money, take long vacations, arrange leaves of absence, or (in an era where "corporate downsizing" means that the average worker has many different employers during his or her career) take time for themselves between jobs. A three-week vacation isn't enough to hike the Appalachian Trail, but it's long enough for the John Muir Trail in California or the Long Trail in Vermont. There are plenty of other long trails — and no rule that says you have to hike them all in one go. And, assuming you have the gear and can arrange the time, hiking is relatively inexpensive. The trick, I think, is convincing yourself that your dreams are worth the same kind of effort you put into your work and your responsibilities.

Choosing a Hike

Choosing a trail is a lot like choosing a vacation. If you're going away for a quick weekend getaway, you might not spend too much time plotting out every detail to be sure you get the best deal on the best bed-and-breakfast. But if you're going to be spending a week or two somewhere, you want it to be really special. And if you're planning a trip that is going to take 6 months of your life, you'll want to be sure that it's just about the thing you most want to do in the world. But as soon as you start reading up on hiking trails, you're sure to be dumbfounded by all the possibilities. Somehow, you've got to choose: The Grand Canyon or Yellowstone? The Himalayas or the Alps? The Continental Divide or the Pacific Crest?

HOW LONG A HIKE? For your first long hike, a couple of weeks is a good length: long enough to be a major adventure in its own right, and an ideal shakedown for you and your gear if your ambitions are leaning to longer expeditions. It's also enough to be worth a plane trip: If you're going to spend two weeks hiking, you may as well go to the most spectacular place you can think of.

Often, the hike you choose is at least in part determined by how much time you have, so you'll need a sense of your average mileage in order to determine whether it's feasible to do the hike in the time you have available. Hikers who are fit before they hit the trail might start on moderate terrain at about 8 or 10 miles a day and, after 3 or 4 weeks, work up to 15 or 20 miles a day. If they are stronger than average, they can start commensurately faster. As a general rule (which will vary drastically according to terrain and fitness), 100 miles a week is a fair estimate for fit, trail-hardened hikers; 60–70 miles a week is a better guess when you're just starting out. Strong hikers often do considerably higher mileage, but this is something you have to learn from your body — not from a book. Until you've logged quite a bit of trail expe-

which to enjoy high elevations. If you don't care for summer heat, you'll want to gain some elevation well before the summer solstice ticks by. You also need to be thinking about regional patterns like storms (July and August in the Southwest are the so-called monsoon season); pests (mountain snowmelt in June and July heralds the start of mosquito season); and not-to-be missed seasonal highlights (the

Above treeline in the Bugaboo Mountains, British Columbia, Canada. Such highcountry concentrates many challenges, including steeps, boulder fields, glaciers, capricious weather (often with lightning), and exposure.

rience, it's better to be conservative than enthusiastic.

WHICH SEASON? Don't only look at your calendar for the answer to this question: Altitude and latitude make a difference, too. If you hate snow and ice, you have a narrow window in rhododendrons in an Appalachian June, the New England foliage in autumn, the wildflower bloom of the summertime Rocky Mountains).

WHAT KIND OF TERRAIN? The swamps of Florida or the deserts of Arizona? The wooded ridges of the

Appalachians or the sky-scraping passes of the Pacific Crest Trail? Eye-popping views or subtle loveli-nesses? Trails offer astonishing variety. In the 100-mile to 200-mile category, you can hike most of the length of the Grand Canyon (Tonto Trail), run the ridgelines of Vermont's Green Mountains (Long Trail), cir-cumnavigate Mount Rainier (Wonder-land Trail), or meander in any season through the deciduous forests of cen-tral Pennsylvania (Susquehanna and Black Forest Trails).

CHARACTER OF HIKE Does your ideal backcountry scenario contain other people in it? The answer to this ques-tion can affect the trail you choose, the season you hike in, and even the direction of travel. Start the Appalachian Trail (AT) on April 1 down in Georgia, and you're in for a rollicking road trip the likes of which you haven't seen since college spring break. You'll meet everyone from nuclear physicists to high school dropouts, either of whom might go by a nickname like Stinkbomb, one or two people who stretch the definition of sanity, and folks who will become the friends of a lifetime. Flip the trip to a southbound hike, start in August in Maine, finish as the first snows hit Dixie, and you'll come home won-dering why no one has discovered the world's most famous trail. On shorter hikes, the same applies: During hol-iday weeks, the number of people out on the trails multiplies; after Labor Day, everyone goes home. And in the dead of winter even an overcrowded RV campground like Grand Teton National Park's Jenny Lake can be a desolate, isolated, lunarlike landscape.

INTERACTIONS WITH LOCALS Some trails pass through towns and villages and offer the opportunity to interact with local folks. A trail that fre-quently crosses roads and passes through towns will provide several opportunities to sample regional cuisines and learn about different lifestyles; by contrast, in some western wildernesses, you can walk for 100 miles without seeing a power-line, a telephone pole, or a slice of pavement. In foreign countries, trails that pass through towns and villages offer the best of both worlds: a back-country experience and cross-cultural interaction at the same time — not to mention the delights of sampling local food and wine.

TRAIL CONDITIONS Trails exist in dif-ferent stages of completion. Some are marked frequently and consistently. Some are marked inconsistently, some infrequently, and some incom-petently. Unfinished trails like New Mexico's segment of the Continental Divide Trail or the Pacific Northwest Trail (from Glacier National Park to the Pacific Ocean on the Olympic Peninsula) string together existing trails, abandoned and deteriorating roads, and trailless sections of cross-country travel. Sometimes the trail builders have run into local opposi-tion or land use problems, and they haven't yet figured out where the trail

Sunrise on the Appalachian Trail, Mount Hight, White Mountains. Solitude is important to many long-distance hikers, and it can be found anywhere, even on the busy Appalachian Trail.

is going to go, so you'll have to devise your own route, which may require permission from local landowners. The challenge of relying on your skills in a remote area where you're unlikely to run into other hikers can be exhilarating. On the flip side, navigating and cross-country travel are a tricky business, and if you get really good and lost, it can take hours to get back on track.

Long-Distance Ethics and Aesthetics

Hikers prize qualities like independence and value the freedoms of the trail. It shows in the mantra of the long-distance community: "Hike your own hike."

But as soon as hikers take their first steps, they learn that there are, in fact, many ways to hike a trail. You can spend every night on the trail in your tent, or you can take a break in hotels as often as your schedule and your budget allow. You can follow every inch of the official trail from one end to the other (hikers call this "white-blazing" after the AT's signature blazes) or you can wander off-trail to take side trips to interesting spots, climb to the summits of nearby peaks, or take advantage of shortcuts — also called "blue-blazing," because on the AT side trails are most often blazed in blue. You can carry your pack every step of the way or you can allow a friend with a car to shuttle it up the trail for you (called "slackpacking"). Does staying

THE TRIPLE CROWN

If you've got your sights set on an ultra-long hike, the nation's three long north-to-south national scenic trails offer three entirely different backcountry experiences.

APPALACHIAN TRAIL

LENGTH: 2,160 miles from Spring Mountain, Georgia, to Mount Katahdin, Maine.

NUMBER OF THRU-HIKERS: 1,200–2,000 start per year; 200–400 finish.

TERRAIN: Don't be misled by the wooded ridgelines and the modest elevations. This trail boasts 470,000 feet of elevation gain (and loss).

HOW MARKED: 2-inch x 6-inch white paint blazes, often within sight of each other, usually no more than a $1/4$ mile apart. Double blazes show change of direction. Most often painted on trees; blazes may also be on highway signs, trail junction signs, buildings, rocks, and cairns (piles of rocks) above treeline.

DIFFICULTY OF FOOTWAY: Varies from easy trails rarely exceeding a 10 percent grade (Shenandoah National Park, Virginia) to difficult 20 percent grades and occasional rock scrambling (New Hampshire and western Maine). The trail is designed for foot traffic only. Mountain bikes are not permitted, and stock use is allowed only in Great Smoky Mountains National Park.

RESUPPLY: The trail frequently crosses roads and passes near towns. Most AT hikers carry about 5 days of food at a time.

COMMENTS: More than 200 lean-tos provide shelter for hikers along the trail. Tent camping is also permitted, although some areas (especially Baxter State Park in Maine, Great Smoky Mountains National Park on the Tennessee–North Carolina border, Shenandoah National Park in Virginia, and the White Mountain National Forest in New Hampshire) restrict where and under what circumstances tenting is permitted. It is possible to hike the AT in either direction, but most thru-hikers go northbound starting in Georgia in March or April.

PACIFIC CREST TRAIL

LENGTH: 2,638 miles from Campo, California, on the Mexican border to Manning Provincial Park in British Columbia, Canada.

NUMBER OF THRU-HIKERS: About 300–500 people have thru-hiked the entire trail, most of them in recent years. The number of thru-hikers is growing quickly, but is

continued on page 18

still fewer than 100 a year.
TERRAIN: The PCT crosses six of
North America's seven ecological
zones. Altitude ranges from near
sea level (at the Columbia River
on the Oregon-Washington border)
to 13,180 feet (Forester Pass,
High Sierra).
HOW MARKED: Ax blazes, cairns,
and chevrons nailed into trees
mark the way, although not as frequently as on the AT. The maps in
the PCT guidebook are adequate.
DIFFICULTY OF FOOTWAY: The
Pacific Crest Trail is designed to
be a single-track footway passable
by stock as well as hikers, so the
grades tend to be gentle, and usually don't exceed 10 percent.
RESUPPLY: The longest section

between roads — about 200
miles — is in the High Sierra,
but a few backwoods lodges near
the trail will help hikers resupply
by receiving and holding boxes of
supplies hikers mail to themselves. In addition, some hikers
take side trails out to resupply. On
the rest of the trail, convenient
resupply points are spaced an
average of 6–10 days apart.
COMMENTS: Thru-hikers need to
average higher mileage because
their hike is bookended on both
sides by snow: spring snowmelt in
the Sierra and new winter snow in
the North Cascades.

CONTINENTAL DIVIDE TRAIL
LENGTH: 3,100 miles from the
Antelope Wells border station on
the Mexican–New Mexico border
to Glacier-Waterton Lakes Interna-

in a hotel instead of a hostel make
you "less" of a hiker? Does "blue-
blazing" or "slackpacking" mean
you're a "cheater"? It sounds like a
stupid issue when you're reading
about it in the comfort of your home,
but don't be surprised if some rainy
night in a lean-to you find yourself in
passionate argument with someone on
the other side of the line.

Does any of this matter? Depends
on whom you ask. Some of my fellow
hikers adhere to the slippery slope

theory: The slightest deviation from
your intended route is only the first
step that ultimately leads to your abandoning your goals, losing motivation,
taking all kinds of shortcuts, and
maybe even sticking out your thumb,
cadging a ride 100 miles up the trail,
and ultimately becoming that most-
looked-down-upon specimen of a
fallen hiker: a "yellow-blazer" (named
after the yellow line in the middle of
the highway).

What may very well be true is that

tional Peace Park on the Montana-Alberta border.

NUMBER OF THRU-HIKERS: A handful every year.

TERRAIN: Similar to the Pacific Crest Trail, the CDT passes through six eco-zones from desert to alpine tundra. Highlights include the Gila Wilderness, Rocky Mountain National Park, Yellowstone National Park, the Wind River Mountains, the Bob Marshall Wilderness, the Weminuche Wilderness, and Glacier National Park.

HOW MARKED: Inconsistently. About 2,000 miles of trail exist. The rest is in various stages of planning and implementation. Even where trail exists, it is usually not blazed with specific CDT markers. Map and compass skills are essential.

DIFFICULTY OF FOOTWAY: Varies from high-grade gravel roads to two-track jeep roads to cut hiking trail to cross-country travel.

RESUPPLY: There's a resupply opportunity about every 7 days. The longest roadless stretch is the arc around the headwaters of the Rio Grande in the San Juan and Rio Grande National Forests, from Wolf Creek Pass to Spring Creek Pass: 120 miles. From these two passes, it's a 30-mile hitch to the nearest towns.

COMMENTS: In Montana and Colorado, much of the trail is in place. In northern Wyoming, the route exists as a combination of backroads and cut foot trail, but most of it is not marked with the CDT emblem. Southern Wyoming is in the initial planning stages. New Mexico is a mess.

the sense of accomplishment you feel at the end of your journey will be in some measure related to how well you stuck to your ideals — whatever they were. Is there a rule that says you have to carry your pack up Katahdin at the end of the Appalachian Trail, when you're just going to come right back down the same way you went up? Of course not — unless you say there is.

But it's worth remembering that your goals are your business — not someone else's. And vice versa.

The Cost

Good news! Once you've got your gear, long-distance hiking is one of the most inexpensive addictions you can develop.

Some averages: Long-standing trail lore (bolstered by a few surveys) says that it costs $1.00 to $1.50 a mile to hike the Appalachian Trail, not including gear or transportation to and from the trailhead, and assuming that you've bought much of your food beforehand. The figure also assumes that you'll usually opt for hostels or campgrounds over hotels during your town stops and won't detour to the nearest restaurant every time the trail crosses a road. Most of that money will be spent on town expenses: hostels, campgrounds, the occasional motels, restaurant meals, laundry, replacement supplies, and extra trail food. Couples traveling together can share some expenses and lower their bills for lodging. If you frequently stay in hotels and take every opportunity to eat in restaurants, you might find yourself spending twice as much as your more frugal compatriots.

CHALLENGES AND DIFFICULTIES

There's a lot to love about long-distance hiking: the wilderness lifestyle, the beauty of forests and mountains, the utter lack of the kind of nonessential clutter that manages to worm its way into the lives of even the best adjusted of us. Almost without exception, thru-hikers will tell you that the experience of hiking a long trail was a lifetime highlight. But very few of them will say that it was easy. And that's because it isn't — not at all. If it were easy, the dropout rate among potential AT thru-hikers wouldn't be close to 90 percent.

Part of the reason that the AT has such a high attrition rate is that it's a high-profile trail. Well-known, well-marked, well-maintained, and fre-

quently in the media, it attracts a lot of people who show up at Springer Mountain, Georgia (the southern terminus where most people start), with brand-new gear still in its packing boxes. More remote, less celebrated long trails seem to attract hikers who already have quite a bit of experience and know what they're getting into — but even so, the dropout rate is well over 50 percent.

The reasons people drop out vary. Some don't know what hiking is all about and are surprised at how much effort it takes to haul a 40-pound pack over a 4,000-foot mountain. Injuries, boredom, homesickness, family emergencies, and running out of time or money also cause people to quit. Even exceedingly fit hikers who show no signs of physical strain sometimes simply lose motivation. Two thousand or 3,000 miles is a very long way, and few people can predict in advance how they'll hold up. It's interesting that the word "quit" is usually not used among long-distance hikers, who are more likely to say that someone "got off." Deep down, perhaps, is the realization that it could happen to anyone.

What Makes a Long-Distance Hiker?

It's tempting to think that a long distance hike is just lots of short hikes strung together. Actually, there's a huge difference between doing forty 50-mile hikes and one 2,000-mile hike. It boils down to day-in, day-out exposure without recovery time in between.

One of the most common questions asked of distance hikers is "What about safety?" Usually, the questioner has something in mind on the order of bears or lunatics or rattlesnakes or avalanches, the kinds of big-ticket dangers you'd see on a television rescue show. The fact is that most of the problems distance hikers face fall into the niggling-little-annoyance category and most hikers who quit long trails don't do so because of big dramatic events. What can elevate a minor irritation into a major problem is constant daily exposure. Hikers quit when they can no longer make themselves cope with all of the little things — rain, gnats, poison ivy, heat, wet socks, and gimpy knees — that can add up, until finally, like the camel with the broken back, the poor beleaguered hiker says "Enough!" Often, however, knowing about the challenges in advance can help a backpacker completely avoid a problem.

Blister care at a stream crossing on the Appalachian Trail in Maine. If you feel the vaguest hint of a blister coming on, STOP instantly and treat the tender spot.

Blisters and Boots

The common little blister is one of the problems that bedevils hikers, forces some of them off the trail — yet is almost completely avoidable.

Over the years I've become a bit of an expert (and more than a bit of a fanatic) on the subject of avoiding blisters. But my obsession has paid off: I didn't have one on the entire Appalachian Trail.

If there's one thing you can do to ensure your hiking comfort, it's to take the threat of blisters seriously. Forget about being bitten by a rattlesnake or chased by a bear or confronted by a lunatic or struck by lightning. Instead, worry about what you can do to break in your boots and get your feet ready for the journey ahead.

• Put 50 miles on new boots before you start a major expedition. Walk to the grocery store. Wear them around the house. Go for a few dayhikes or a casual overnighter. Even lightweight boots need some breaking in if you want to be sure you won't get blisters. Breaking in a pair of well-fitting boots before you hit the trail is the most important thing you can do to ensure your comfort (and success) on a long trail.

• Wear wicking sock liners and cushy wool or wool-plus-synthetic socks. No cotton! It absorbs sweat and guarantees blisters.

• Pre-treat places on your feet that always give you trouble. Use Band-Aids on toes, moleskin for big-blister areas like the back of your heel.

• If your boot chafes, check for grains of sand, grass seeds, dirt, and sock wrinkles.

• If the chafing seems due to a tight spot, rub the inside of the boot where it's bothering you with the handle of your spoon or some other blunt object. This will give you a smidge more room, which may make all the difference.

• You can refine the fit of your boot in the field by trimming the insoles in places where you need more room, and by taping moleskin inside the boot as extra padding. If it's a seam that's causing problems, put a patch of duct tape over it.

• Most important: If you feel a blister coming on — even the tee-niest tiniest hint of one, even if your hiking partner is begging you to please stop dithering and start walking — STOP immediately. Don't even try to walk to a bench 100 yards away! It doesn't matter if you're "tough enough to put up with it for a while longer." That's entirely beside the point. Think of that little nagging, almost inconsequential, barely noticeable pinch as a bomb waiting to explode.

• If a blister does develop, use Second Skin (a blister treatment from Spenco) to treat it. It's a dressing that has roughly the consistency of almost-frozen Jell-O. It soothes the pain and absorbs any further rubbing between boot and skin. Simply put the dressing over the blister and hold it in place with waterproof athletic tape.

• Plan easy mileage your first few days out.

Physical Ailments

The Appalachian Trail's 470,000 feet of elevation gain is the equivalent of 400 trips up and down the Empire State Building. Sort of. On the AT, you don't have nice even steps, you have rocks and roots and boulders and bogs and steep slippery mud and ice and rain.

Or think of it this way: 2,160 miles is 82.5 marathons — with a pack on your back, and up and down those mountains.

The wear and tear on the body is enormous. Knees and ankles take the brunt of the abuse — so much so that ibuprofen (hikers call it "vitamin I") is part of some hikers' daily diets! An Ace bandage has become part of my standard first aid kit because of all the bandages I've had to buy on previous trips when I didn't have one. I also own a sturdier, special knee brace that I can take on gnarly trails. But by far the most effective thing I do to keep my knees working is ruthlessly pare down my pack weight and use two adjustable, shock-absorbing walking sticks (made by Leki), which take tons (literally) of pressure off my knees every day.

choose a boot that has good, stiff lateral support — usually, this means a high-cut all-leather boot.

Working out before your hike will pay big dividends, especially during your first weeks on the trail.

Ankles are another problem area. Common problems like over-pronation can put extra stress on your ankles. If you've had ankle problems in the past, it might be worth a visit to a podiatrist, because sometimes a simple solution like custom-made orthotic footbeds can take pressure off your ankle joints by correcting the way you walk. Also

Alpine hiking in the Bugaboo Mountains, Canadian Rockies. Without the support of rugged high-top mountaineering boots like these, such a leap combined with the weight of a full backpack could strain your ankles.

Some hikers claim that the rigors of long-distance backpacking are so extreme that the only way to prepare for it is to actually do it. (And I have to reluctantly admit that I rarely am in peak condition in the frantic work-filled months just before a long trip.) But there's no question that the fitter

on your muscles and joints. Finally, if you're concerned about your knees, consider doing exercises before your hike to strengthen your hamstrings, quadriceps, and calf muscles.

Water

If you've ever read a health and fitness magazine, you know that one of the most effective ways to keep your body running smoothly is to drink enough water. But let's face it: Most of us ignore this simple rule. When was the last time you drank the rec-

A sign left on the Appalachian Trail in Virginia during a dry summer. Thru-hikers form a tight-knit community in which each member looks out for all of his comrades.

you are, the fewer aches and pains you'll feel during that initial breaking-in period. Remember, if you're overweight, those extra pounds around your waist perform exactly the same as extra pounds in your pack: They slow you down and put pressure ommended eight glasses of water a day?

On the trail, adequate hydration is doubly important. It affects everything from how efficiently your muscles work to how susceptible you are to hypothermia and altitude sickness.

Unfortunately, it's no longer possible to simply dip your canteen into a clear running stream, gulp down a cup of fresh-tasting mountain water, and hike on. In today's backcountry, many streams and springs are contaminated with pesticides, herbicides, fertilizers, and minerals. Not to mention organic parasites like *Giardia lamblia* and *Cryptosporidium*.

If these sound like creatures that belong in a science fiction film, think again: These microscopic monsters can stop even the hardiest hiker in his tracks.

Of the three methods of purifying water, filters are most effective. Boiling takes too long and is impractical during the day. And iodine does not remove *Cryptosporidium*. Unfortunately, long-distance hikers detest filtering and filters. They resent the need for it. They complain about the time it takes; they question whether it's really and truly essential; they cite anecdotal evidence from fellow hikers who never treat any water as justification for their decisions; and they throw up their hands in frustration when their filter clogs or jams or squirts water back in their faces. Water filters are the most reviled equipment on long trails, and hikers are as likely to send them home as keep them throughout their entire hike.

Experienced hikers know that not all backcountry water will make you sick. The trick, however, is sorting out which source is contaminated and which is safe. The truth is, there's no foolproof way. To decide whether to treat water, I look at the location of the source (above treeline? in a populated area?). I consider the ecology (any beaver dams nearby? cow pastures?) and the type of source (an underground spring or a stream?). And still, I know that I'm taking a risk whenever I succumb to the temptation to drink "wild water."

Lately, I've been treating a lot more water than I used to. Partly this is conservatism that comes with age and experience (mostly other people's). And partly it's because filters have improved. My recommendation, based on thru-hiker interviews and personal experience, is the PUR Hiker. It's not completely hassle free, but it is lightweight and easy to handle. You'll find yourself more willing to filter all your water if you don't have to make a major production out of the process.

As important as treating water is some semblance of backcountry cleanliness. Some intestinal ailments can be contracted through shared eating utensils and unclean pots and dishes, and one study found little difference between the rates of illness experienced by hikers who filtered their water and those who didn't. My own anecdotal experience supports the conclusion that there is more than one way to get sick in the backcountry: On a recent trip in Europe, I contracted a violent intestinal illness, even though I treated all of my water. One of my hiking partners suffered a similar problem only several days before I did. It's entirely possible that I caught the bug from him, not from the water.

Weight Loss

I have a friend who once, many years ago, wanted my opinion on a new outfit. "Do you think I look too skinny?" she asked. (Now there's a question I've never felt compelled to utter.) Like many other long-distance hikers, I regard weight loss as a pleasant fringe benefit of thru-hiking. But if you're the kind of person who can't seem to keep weight on, thru-hiking presents a very real health danger: excessive weight loss and malnutrition.

Friends of mine of the perennially skinny variety say that snacking often, carrying nutritional supplements such as protein powder, popping vitamins, and eating well in town all help keep weight on. One strategy for hikers with runaway metabolisms is to stop in towns as frequently as possible. If you're only going five days between towns rather than seven or eight, you can carry more food per day. And more frequent town stops give you more frequent opportunities to eat heartily in restaurants.

Emotional Stress

On our 1994 Appalachian Trail thru-hike, Dan and I planned an extra-slow 7-month pace to take advantage of the time we had available. Being enthusiastic winter hikers, we started in January. Our schedule had us arriving in Vermont in late June and finishing at Katahdin on Labor Day. I was certain that this schedule would eliminate the problems I most wanted to avoid: namely, blackflies in New England and the heat wave that catches many northbounders in Pennsylvania and New York in July.

We missed the blackflies. But the heat chased us down and knocked us out. In June, the temperatures climbed to 100 degrees. The humidity bogged down at 95 percent. We kept walking. We sweated it out (and up and down). And I was miserable. Those 3 weeks were hands-down the worst time I've ever had hiking — come to think of it, they're among the worst times I've ever had anywhere. But for some reason, we kept going. One day Dan commented that we hadn't seen any other hikers for a while. No one had passed us: It was like there was a huge monster just behind us on the trail devouring all the hikers behind us.

It wasn't a monster; it was common sense. Other hikers had some. They holed up in motel rooms. Or cut down on their mileage. Some of them went to the beach. In retrospect, the only regret I have about my thru-hike is that I didn't exhibit the same good judgment during those 3 weeks.

If you find you're at the end of your rope, stop. Take a day off, or two or three. Decrease your mileage. Stay in town until the sun comes out or the heat wave breaks or the snow stops or you feel like going on.

AT thru-hikers have a saying: "No rain, no pain, no Maine." This may be true, but there's no reason to wallow in the difficulties. Most hikers plan a $5^{1}/_{2}$- or 6-month pace, and that gives you plenty of slack time for rest days — plenty of time to wait for a change in weather. Taking a day off when you need it pays big dividends because the extra rest will help you get through the tough spots.

Hiking Partners

Hiking partners can be a source of emotional support or the worst irritation you can imagine. Twenty-four hours a day, day after day after day is not an arrangement most partnerships can withstand.

There's no question that long hikes can strain relationships. Before you put your friendship or marriage to this test, you need to sit down and have an honest discussion about your physical and emotional compatibility and your goals for the hike.

I plead guilty to stereotyping here: By far the most common partnership problem is that male hikers are stronger and want to go faster than their female partners. Chapter 7, "The Highcountry," offers some hints on how to deal with this problem on the biggest battlefield of all: the long uphill.

But the potential for conflict unfortunately outlasts a single mountain. On a long-distance hike, you need to discuss your overall mileage goals and expectations. Even if you are physically mismatched, you'll need to agree on just about everything: how far to go, when to get up in the morning, what to eat, which route to take, whether to stop before the last big mountain when there's a thunderstorm rolling in or to press on ahead. Chores need to be divvied up, like who has to crawl out of a snug and cozy sleeping bag in the morning to make coffee, or who has to walk that extra $^{3}/_{10}$ ths of a mile to get water for camp. Often, compromise will seem one-sided — for instance, if the stronger hiker always has to slow down because the weaker hiker simply can't do any more. You and your partner need to take a good hard look at the realities of your particular partnership and figure out a way to travel together that will make both of you happy. Unfortunately, without realistic expectations of what each of you can expect from the other, many hiking partnerships — both friendships and romances — don't survive a long trail.

When the going gets tough it helps to remember why you're out there: to enjoy yourselves — not to have a running argument from one end of the country to the other. Besides, survival is bound to enhance your ability to compromise. Taking a break, listening to your partner, and taking turns accommodating each other's idiosyncrasies will help ensure that you enjoy your hike — and your partner.

SECTION HIKING

What if you simply can't get away for 6 months at a pop? You've got kids. Or a mortgage payment. Or your own business or a professional practice that can't sustain a 6-month absence while you're off communing with nature. Or hiking is important to you — just not important enough to put the rest of your life on hold for half a year. You can still hike a long trail — one section at a time.

In 1995, my husband, Dan, walked into Appalachian Trail headquarters in Harper's Ferry, West Virginia, having just completed a project he had begun 18 years earlier — hiking the entire trail a week at a time during peak foliage in the autumn.

The reason? Dan is an insatiable lover of the Appalachian Trail: He's hiked the whole trail five times, and some parts of it many more. But autumn captured his imagination. He says, "One fall in New Hampshire, I looked across the flaming hills and red and gold woods, and I thought how odd it is that people call the Appalachian Trail the Long Green Tunnel. I decided that I'd like to see the whole AT in autumn."

Hundreds of people hike long trails one section at a time. Many of them don't have the slightest intention of hiking a whole trail when they start out, but as they meet other hikers and learn more about the trail, the idea grows on them. They start taking longer trips to trailheads farther and farther away. Completing the trail becomes part love affair, part goal, part hobby. When they climb the last mountain, sometimes many years later, it is often the culmination of what has become one of the most cherished projects of their lives. And talk about a project that can last a lifetime: One section hiker took 61 years to finish hiking the entire Appalachian Trail!

In addition to being more practical for people with limited vacation time, section hiking offers some distinct advantages:

You can hike each trail segment at the best time of year. Thru-hiking a long trail puts you at the mercy of seasonal patterns. Take the Pacific Crest Trail: A successful thru-hike requires high daily mileage (20 miles a day isn't an unusual average) because of the limited snow-free window of the highcountry. And even so, hikers often tackle the High Sierra's 12,000- and 13,000-foot passes before the snow has melted and then must race through Oregon and Washington to beat winter to the North Cascades.

Section hiking is quite the opposite: Section hikers can hike the High Sierra in July if they like. They can traverse California's desert valleys in the cooler months, unlike thru-hikers, who sweat their way through in May and June. And while thru-hikers slog through the Cascades' fall rains and early winter storms, section hikers can just say no — and cheerfully plan their hikes for sunny August.

Ridge walking, Jewel Basin Hiking Area, northwest Montana. Set in the enormous Flathead National Forest (230,350,508 acres), Jewel Basin is especially beautiful with its 25 lakes and 35 miles of trails. It is but a small corner of a vast and spectacular land that includes the Bob Marshall Wilderness Area, perhaps the nation's grandest with more than a million acres and thousands of miles of trails.

Section hiking is easier on the body. The repetitive strain of long-distance hiking — month after month of hauling heavy packs over high mountains — is physically grueling. Some people develop injuries, especially to feet and knees.

It's easier to include family members in a section hike. It's almost impossible for people in average physical condition to join thru-hikers on a long trail: After a month or so, thru-hikers simply go too fast. But section hikers travel a little slower, so family members can keep up. A non-hiking spouse can take part in the experience by meeting the hiker at road crossings. And section hikes can be planned so that children can participate, too, depending on their age and abilities.

The trail becomes part of your everyday life. You'll find yourself reading up on your trail, eagerly planning your next hike as you string together sections you've completed. Having a long-term goal like completing a major trail can keep you motivated to stay fit and take the time to hike, even when your life is busy with other commitments. And section hikers often feel more connected to the trail than single-season thru-hikers because their commitment lasts over many years.

Planning Your Section Hike

The first rule is, there are no rules.

Snowshoeing on the Appalachian Trail in Maine. Appreciated by very few, winter trekking offers unique rewards, among them a stripping away to bare essentials and untold solitude and peace.

How you hike a long trail is completely up to you. You might choose a theme, as Dan did, and see the entire trail during your favorite season. Or you might hike the sections in order, from end to end, just like a thru-hiker, but over a longer period of time. The advantage to this is that you see your progress in an ever-growing line of forward motion. The disadvantage is that your vacation schedule may not coincide with peak season — for instance, your summer vacation is in July, and you've worked your way up to steamy Tennessee on the Appalachian Trail. The length of your hikes can vary from several large sections of several hun-dred miles at a time to a series of many short weekend hikes. On trails that cross roads frequently, like the Appalachian Trail, the Ohio Trail, and the Northcountry Trail, you can arrange to have a friend or a spouse meet you so that you don't even have to carry a pack.

Planning and transportation are probably the two biggest problems with section hiking, especially when you're hiking far from home. You've got to get yourself to the trailhead — which might be several hundred miles away — and then when you've finished your hike, you've got to find a way back to your car. Many hikers find that to section hike a long trail, they're also putting tens of thousands of miles in at the driver's seat as they shuttle cars from one trailhead to the other.

One way to minimize your car time is to plan so that you take your longest hikes on those sections of trail farthest from your home. Also, try to plan these hikes so that the next one begins where the last one left off. Jumping around can leave you with a little undone section many miles from home. (For example, say you go from A to B on one hike, and from C to B on a subsequent hike. Now imagine that you have to leave the trail early on that second hike because of inclement weather or an injury: You might end up with a 20-mile "hole" 500 miles from home.)

Local shuttlers — people who offer (usually for a fee) help with transportation logistics — can help get you and your car from one trailhead to the other. Check with the trail-maintaining organization or club; they often have lists of people who offer shuttles. Traditionally, hikers leave their car at the trailhead where they expect to finish the hike, and the shuttler drives them to the starting trailhead. But in recent years, it's become unwise to leave cars at trailhead parking lots because of vandalism. Sometimes, the person who shuttles you will agree to keep your car until the end of your hike and deliver it on the day you plan to come out. Or a business near the trail will allow you to park in their parking lot. If you do leave your car at a trailhead, be sure to check with the local trail club, local police, or land management agency to find out whether there has been vandalism at that site. (Lots of litter or a pile of broken safety glass is a sure sign of trouble.)

Finally, keeping in good physical shape between hikes needs to be part of your overall plan, because as a section hiker, you need to "break in" each time you go out. Most distance hikers agree that the breaking-in period — the first couple of weeks when desk-bound, citified bodies reacquaint themselves with the realities of gravity, footway, and exactly what it means to walk 10 miles up a mountain — is the most difficult. The better shape you're in between hikes, the more you'll enjoy section hiking (but you already knew that, right?).

Flip-Flops and Yo-Yos

A traditional thru-hike is a one-way event: You go from one point to the other in a single, continuous journey. But there are a few variations on the thru-hiking theme. Take the following example: You've taken your sweet time and smelled a bower of roses, and now, 80 percent of the way along the AT, you realize that if you don't do 20 miles a day through western Maine, you will end up arriving at Katahdin on Thanksgiving. There are two problems with this. First, almost nobody can hike 20 miles a day in western Maine; the terrain is simply too rough. And second, by Thanksgiving, Katahdin is accessible only to winter mountaineers. Rather than kill yourself trying to do the impossible, you "flip" up to Katahdin and "flop" — start hiking south, planning to end your hike where you left off. Flip-flopping is simply doing a thru-hike that is continuous in time, but not in your direction of travel. The variations are endless; depending on how creative you are, you can use flip-flops to avoid certain sections of trail in inclement seasons.

Yo-yoing is another thing altogether. Get this: After hiking 2,160 miles from Georgia to Maine, some people turn around and start walking back. The reasons for such an undertaking usually involve physical challenge, for instance trying to set some kind of a record. But it is also true that going in a different direction during a different season results in

This book assumes you've got basic back-packing skills, but that's not to say that all of us can't stand to learn a little more. Here, four of my favorite books that cover the most important aspects of backpacking.

● THE COMPLETE WALKER, by Colin Fletcher (*Knopf*) Sure, gear has changed since Colin Fletcher last updated his classic, encyclo-pedic volume in 1984. But his voice is as fresh today as it ever was, his common sense as uncommonly perceptive, and his passion as fierce. This book not only tells you how to do it, it teaches you how to think about it. And that transcends trends, fashions, and techno-talk.

● MEDICINE FOR MOUNTAINEERING, edited by James A. Wilkerson, M.D. (*The Mountaineers*) First aid in the back-country differs in one important respect from first aid in everyday life — even if

you've got a cell phone in your pack, you may not be able to call for help. This book tells you how to deal with injuries in the backcountry, including hypothermia, falls, bleeding, and evacuation.

● BE EXPERT WITH MAP AND COMPASS, by Bjorn Kjellstrom (*Scribners*) The squiggles and lines on a contour map can seem inde-cipherable, but if you're heading out to one of the long trails that hasn't yet been com-pleted, you're going to need to know how to make sense of them. This book shows you how.

● WILDERNESS ETHICS, by Guy and Laura Waterman (*Countryman Press*) If you love the outdoors, sooner or later you'll get around to thinking about your role in it. Beautifully written, thoughtful, and original, this book explores the intersection where backpackers meet the wilderness.

an entirely different experience. The only thing that needs to be said about this is that it is considered generally bad form to announce that you are doing a yo-yo at the beginning of your journey. Beyond that, if you're considering a yo-yo, you probably don't need to be reading this book.

EXPEDITION
PLANNING

One of the matrices of the popular Myers-Briggs personality test (used by psychologists, career counselors, and human resources managers) divides people into those who like to plan and make decisions and those who like to leave their options open to the very last minute. I belong, firmly and irrevocably, to the latter category. That works fine on the trail, where flexibility and a willingness to "go with the flow" are distinct advantages. But as every hiker knows, even a short hike starts with a plan. Somebody has to locate the maps, figure out the best season to go, get the right gear together, and make the transportation arrange-

ments. Fortunately, I'm married to a fellow hiker who happens to be firmly rooted in the fraternity of the planful — and I cheerfully admit that much of the contents of this chapter I learned from him.

PLANNING ISSUES FOR BIG TRIPS

If your hiking experience has so far been limited to short trips, the first thing you'll notice about planning a longer expedition is that it poses a whole slew of new questions. On a weekend hike, you assume your boots won't blow out. Not so on an expedition: Chances are something is going

Trip planning can be difficult on some routes, such as the Continental Divide Trail in New Mexico's mesa country where there is neither a marked trail nor a guidebook. Map and compass skills are a must.

planning process involves figuring out how you're going to arrange to resupply and calculating how long you're going to take to get from one resupply point to the next. There's a lot to be said for starting your long-distance hiking career on a trail where information is readily available. On the venerable Appalachian Trail, some 2,000 people each year declare their intention to thru-hike — far more than on any other major long-distance trail. One of the reasons might be that the Appalachian Trail Conference publishes or distributes several books on how to plan a thru-hike. Information is available regarding everything from the names of trail shelters to the zip codes of towns to which you might want to send yourself a box of supplies.

On the other end of the spectrum are trails like the Continental Divide National Scenic Trail, which in some places is nary more than a wish. Guidebooks that describe a proposed (and hikable) route for the CDT in Colorado, Wyoming, and Montana have been published by the Continental Divide Trail Society, but in

to break, tear, or wear out. On a 40-mile loop hike, you don't have to take into account the changing of the seasons. But if your route goes through a hot desert and cold mountains, will you be able to use the same 20-degree sleeping bag for both? And then there's food: How much can you carry? How do you resupply?

Before you can even begin to address those questions, there are the basic issues of your route and your schedule, the twin pillars of the planning process.

Some trails — those with a clear route and a good guidebook — lend themselves to easy, methodical planning. Take the 470-mile Colorado Trail for an example. The weather dictates that you'll probably be doing the hike in the summer. As far as a route is concerned, all you've got to do is buy the latest guidebook, which comes complete with maps. Your some cases the guidebook route conflicts with the official CDT route as designated by the Forest Service. A new series of guidebooks is being published by Westcliffe Press, but so far, only one is available (for Colorado). As for New Mexico, there's no guidebook at all, in part because public land managers have yet to agree on a route. Confused? A thru-hike of the CDT can require months of planning — including contacting dozens of individual ranger stations and buying and marking a route on hundreds of topographic maps.

Trails Illustrated maps (bottom) are detailed enough to be useful where routes are poorly marked. Topographic maps combined with profile maps (below) allow for an added measure of trip planning in which elevation gain can be factored in (see page 42).

Trail Status and Maps

Trail status may be the most important (and most elusive) piece of information in the entire planning process. The sad truth is that many of our long trails, including most of those in the national scenic trails system, are nowhere near completed. Before you can even consider hiking a trail, you need to find out its condition. Is it finished? Is it blazed? Is it described in a

North Cascades
National Park
Washington

NATIONAL GEOGRAPHIC MAPS
TRAILS ILLUSTRATED
•Topographic Map
•Waterproof / Tearproof
•100% Plastic Material
•Revised Regularly

Crater Lake
National Park
Oregon
Hiking Guide with Road Trails
Visitor Information
TRAILS ILLUSTRATED
Waterproof TOPO MAPS
Tearproof
100% Plastic Material
Revised Regularly

guidebook? Is it located correctly on USGS or Forest Service maps? (Be extremely careful here: USGS maps are revised even more infrequently than trails are built and relocated: In one case, we ordered a topographic quadrangle from the USGS and received a map that was surveyed by the War Department in 1918 — and not revised since! More commonly, you can expect topos to be 20 or 30 years old.) Can the trail be hiked with only a guidebook, or does it require maps? Some trails are marked so well that you follow blazes and cairns the whole way (although you should always carry a map for information about water sources, elevation gain, campsites, and side trails that you could use in case of emergency). Other trails are marked only sporadically and inconsistently, requiring the hiker to consult maps and guidebooks for directions every time the route crosses a dirt road.

Trail Clubs

Trail organizations and land management agencies are the best places to find specific up-to-date trail information. Chapter 10 lists resources and organizations for the trails described there. For similar information about other trails, two good places to start looking are the list of organizations belonging to the American Hiking Society. Many hiking clubs also have sites on the World Wide Web. Check GORP.com; from there, you can cyberhike virtually anywhere. Be aware that some hiking organizations are professionally run by paid staff; some are all-volunteer efforts, and some are one- or two-person operations. The quality of information you get will differ. (Also make sure the information on the Web comes from an official source.)

Some trail organizations publish information that addresses the special needs of long-distance hikers, like resupply opportunities. Many publish or sell guidebooks (a new trend is the "guidebook" available in a CD-ROM format, which is cheaper to produce and to keep up-to-date — a huge benefit — but less convenient

---

WHICH MAP?

1:25,000 These maps are good for difficult cross-country terrain, especially if the terrain doesn't have dramatic, easy-to-locate geographic features. They are published by the USGS (United States Geological Survey). These maps are identified by name (for instance: Massacre Mountain, New Mexico). To help you locate the ones you need, the USGS publishes state indexes. Each index features an overview map that gives the name and location of each topographic map in the state. 1:50,000–1: 62,500 This scale is perfect for situations where you expect to have to use maps to find your way, but you don't expect the work to be too difficult: trails that mostly exist, may be described in a guidebook, but may not be well-marked or well-maintained on the ground. Commercial maps like those produced by Trails Illustrated and government maps produced for some wilderness areas generally use scales in this range. 1:100,000–1: 130,000 This is the scale most often used in Forest Service maps. These maps are useful as a general overview if you are traveling well-marked, maintained trails. They are also useful

to actually use, because you need to print a hard copy). In addition, most major trail organizations maintain Web sites, where they post trail conditions and weather news. Trail clubs also publish newsletters, where they keep members up-to-date about relocations and other trail-related information. It's a good idea to join the association of any trail you plan to hike. The modest dues support the trail, and the information you'll receive is well worth your small contribution.

Direction of Travel

Most guidebooks are written one-way: That is, the author hikes, and describes, the trail going in one direction only. Usually, the direction the author takes is based on what most hikers do, which may be governed by tradition or (most often) seasonal factors. There's one additional reason to hike in the same direction as the guidebook narrative: *backwards use to frustrating and difficult are guidebooks.*

Direction of travel is especially important when a trail involves more than one season, lots of elevation change, or different climate zones. Seasonal variations affect mileage (*i.e.*, snow slows you down) and gear (do you need an ice ax or extra clothing?). They also affect feasi-

---

as backups or for sudden changes of plan: If, for instance, there's a forest fire and you have to get out some other way than you had planned. If there's a snowstorm. If someone is injured. They can augment a guidebook that contains poorly reproduced, hard-to-read maps. But the lack of topographic detail makes them incomplete for off-trail navigating.

1: 250,000 This is the scale used in the DeLorme Atlas and Gazetteer Series. Don't use these to hike with — they don't offer enough detail. But they can be extremely helpful for planning food resupplies and town stops or if you need

to come up with an alternate or emergency route.

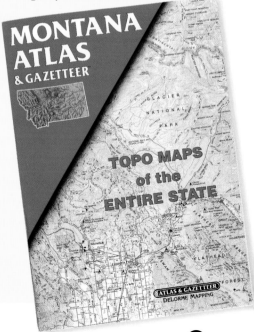

Double-checking the route on the topo map, Mount Gould, Glacier National Park, Montana.

bility. (Unless you've got mountaineering experience — and maybe even if you've got it — the high mountains of the northcountry are no place to be when winter roars in.)

To see the effect of the direction of travel on a thru-hike, consider the Continental Divide Trail. Knowing that the northern Rockies are snow-clogged until early July, you decide to hike northbound from New Mexico in order to avoid slogging through snow in Montana. You choose an April 1 start date at the Mexican border because you know that New Mexico is hot and arid, and you want to be well north by the time the real heat sets in. So far so good. Figuring 15 miles a day for 750 miles, including your days off, you learn that you'll be crossing into Colorado on May 20. You know from your maps that the trail in Colorado averages more than 11,000 feet in elevation. A call to the San Juan National Forest confirms what you expected: The highcountry of Colorado will be snow-choked in May. Time to revise your plan: Either take more time in New Mexico, start a little later, or work out how your schedule plays out if you start southbound from Canada in late June.

Scheduling

Your schedule is a matter of mathematics. To make one, you need to know your average daily mileage, and you need to decide how often you want to resupply. You'll also need to guess how many rest days you'll want to take.

Average mileage varies — sometimes drastically — from trail to trail (or from section to section on a trail), so be careful about making assumptions based on your past experience on other trails. PCT hikers, for instance, tend to log more miles daily than AT hikers because the PCT, despite its higher elevations, is better graded. Other factors come into play: In a desert, mileage is determined by water sources, not personal preference. In high mountains, traverses across lingering ice slopes can be slow and hazardous and if you are postholing in melting slush, your pace can slide down to a mile an hour. Finally, unfinished trails like the Continental Divide and the Pacific Northwest Trail test not only endurance, but navigating skills as well, and navigating (not to mention getting lost) takes time.

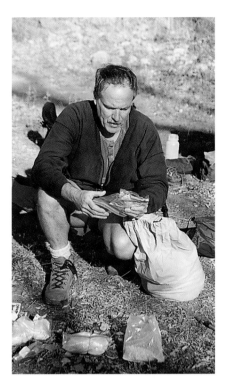

Resupply along the Arizona Trail, arid country where the amount of water you can carry and the location of the water sources determine your schedule and pace.

How often you resupply also affects your schedule. Having more town stops means carrying a lighter pack — but it also means hopping on and off the trail a lot. On trails where towns are close to the actual hiking route, some people prefer to keep pack weight down by resupplying often. But on other trails, resupplying might require walking out several miles on a side trail, hitchhiking many miles to and from the nearest town, then walking several miles back in. Is the lighter pack worth the time and effort? Each hiker has an opinion.

Long-distance hikers typically try to maximize their town time by trying to go as far as they can the day before so they arrive in town early in the morning, giving them a full day to pick up mail and supplies at the post office, do laundry, clean selves and gear, arrange for the repair of any broken equipment, and pick up last-minute additions to their larders. They usually spend the night in a hostel, hotel, or campground, then hike out in the morning. A town day isn't really a rest day since there are numerous chores to be done, so many hikers also schedule in the occasional 0-mileage day, which means two nights off the trail and a full day off their feet.

Once you know your mileage and you have decided how many days of food you're willing to carry, you can start planning your way through guidebooks and maps. Figure a slow

ABOUT MILEAGE

Knowing some statistics might help you in your planning.

● The average Appalachian Trail hiker completes the 2,160-mile walk in $5^{1}/_{2}$ to 6 months, which means that daily mileage (including days off) is 12–13 miles a day (2,160 miles divided by 165–180 days).

● Most hikers take off about one day a week for in-town chores, resupplying, and rest.

● Thru-hikers tend to carry 5-8 days' worth of food.

● For a more accurate picture of how long the average full day of hiking is, take the days off-trail out of the equation: Using the $5^{1}/_{2}$-month example, hikers take 1 day in 7 off, so they're actually hiking for only 141 of the 165 days they are on the trail. Dividing 2,160 by 141 gives you an average daily hiking mileage of 15.2. If you have less than $5^{1}/_{2}$ months available, you'll need to walk faster.

● Mileage varies over the length of a thru-hike. Figure that you'll be doing lower mileage at the beginning when you're not yet in peak condition.

● Changes in terrain affect mileage. A few examples from my experience: On the Continental Divide, we averaged 20 miles a day in central New Mexico, but in Colorado, our average mileage plummeted to 14 miles a day. On the Appalachian Trail, hikers tend to log high mileage in Virginia (18–20 miles a day is not unusual) and scale way back in New Hampshire and western Maine, where the terrain forces even strong hikers to slow down to 10-12 miles a day.

● Don't forget to factor in elevation. Count the contour lines on your topo maps, study the profile maps, and, most important, learn what "a lot of climbing" means to you. My scale when I'm really trail-hardened: Under 2,000 feet is an easy day; 3,000 is average; 4,000 is work; 5,000 is really work; and 6,000 is no longer any fun. During the early days of a long-distance hike, however, I find that 3,000 feet of climbing is quite enough for one day.

Water stop at an alpine lake in Idaho. In such highcountry water is plentiful, yet elevation gain, a brush with altitude sickness, or having to pick your way across tricky scree fields can profoundly affect your pace.

start for the first week or two — maybe 10 miles a day. Let's assume you want to carry between 5 and 8 days' worth of food on any given stretch. That means you'll be looking for a town near the trail somewhere in the 50- to 80-mile range. Some guidebooks recommend towns for resupply. In other cases, you'll need to look at maps (maps on the scale of 1:250,000, like those in the DeLorme Atlas and Gazetteer Series, are useful for this purpose). When you locate the town, *voilà*: You have identified your first resupply point. Now all you have to do is repeat the process until you've moved 2,000 miles up the trail! Don't forget to think about how your mileage will change as you get

stronger and the terrain and seasons change.

In moderate terrain with lots of campsites and water sources, there's no need to plan a day-to-day schedule (although some hikers like the security of a detailed plan). As long as you stick to approximately your intended average mileage and don't raid your food supply, you should make it to town before your last Snickers bar is gone.

More careful planning does have advantages on more difficult trails (lots of steep climbs, gnarly terrain without many places to camp, or arid country with few water sources). For example, say you want to average 15 miles a day. But the mileage between water sources is 8 miles, 14 miles, 10 miles, and 12 miles. Either you're going to have to do two big-mileage days or you're going to have to carry water and "dry-camp." (See Chapter 8, "Deserts.") If neither of those choices sounds good, you're going to have to decrease your mileage. The

THE MILEAGE-ELEVATION CONNECTION

How many miles should you plan to hike in a day? That depends on (1) the kind of miles and (2) how hard you want to work. This chart rates the difficulty of different combinations of mileage and elevation.

LEVEL 1: A couple of days like this will help you break in and remain comfortable.

LEVEL 2: Faster hikers should bring a book — they'll be done by midafternoon. If you're a little slower, don't worry: You'll be in camp in plenty of time for dinner. If you've adhered to the 50-mile rule, you can start at this level.

LEVEL 3: Veteran hikers find this range a nice balance for smelling the flowers while covering some distance. Newer hikers can do the mileage without hating themselves for overreaching — once they are in shape. But you'll want to break in at Level 1 or 2 before you start covering this kind of distance.

LEVEL 4: You're not a fanatic, but you are in good aerobic shape. You don't mind pushing a bit. You don't smell too many flowers.

LEVEL 5: No lollygagging for you. You're a serious backpacker, a regular exerciser, and you're broken in to the trail. Make sure you know what you're getting into: These kinds of days aren't for everyone.

LEVEL 6: You are a marathon runner, a long-distance hiker, or a masochist. Maybe all three.

ELEVATION GAIN (FEET)	Less than 8	8–10	11–13	14–17	More than 17
Less than 1,000	1	1	2	3	4
1,000–2,000	1	2	3	4	4
2,000–3,000	2	3	3	4	5
3,000–4,000	3	4	4	5	5
4,000–5,000	4	5	5	6	6
More than 5,000	5	5	6	6	6

M I L E A G E

choice you make affects the amount (and weight) of the supplies you'll have to carry.

A warning about scheduling, terrain, and season: Don't try to use common sense to "figure out" the vagaries of regional climate. You might think that January in Georgia will be a sunny winter warm spot (not true — temperatures in the southern Appalachians can hover around 0 degrees). Or that May is a good time to hike in the Sonoran Desert (wrong again — the Tohono O'odham Indians call May and June the "painful months"). Or that you'll enjoy a June hike in Maine (good luck — the woods belong to the blackflies). There are too many variables that affect hiking seasons — weather, pests, snowmelt, local climate patterns, as well as local highlights you shouldn't miss — and there's no way you can know them all. Once you've come up with a schedule, call someone in a local hiking organization, a fellow hiker who knows the trail and the terrain, or the agency that manages the land. Run your plan by them.

Hitchhiking

With all this talk about resupplying, you might be imagining that long-distance trails frequently go through towns. The truth is that towns may be quite some distance from where the trail crosses the road. Long-distance hikers love hiking — but they uniformly hate walking "extra" miles, especially on roads, to get into and out of towns. Even a mile or two from trail to town will elicit some grumbling. If it's more than that (and sometimes it can be quite a bit more), hikers often turn into hitchhikers.

Fortunately, local people near major hiking trails know that grungy, unshaven characters carrying worn-out packs are more likely to be upstanding citizens on vacation than dangerous sociopaths on the rampage. Rides in these areas tend to be frequently offered. But in our society, the fact remains that accepting rides from strangers is not risk-free. (Nor is picking up strangers and offering them rides, which is why so many cars will pass you by.) There are a few things you can do to make your hitchhiking both safer and more successful.

● Hitch with one other person (two others at the most — more than that and the chance of getting a ride drops to nil).

● Men hitching with women have much better luck getting rides than men hitching alone or with other men. A woman hitching with a male companion is safer than a woman hitching alone or with other women. Neat-looking older people have better luck getting rides than grungy youngsters. There's not much you can do about the age factor (except, perhaps, beg an older hiker to let you hitch with him), but you can make yourself more presentable by putting on a clean T-shirt.

● If you're at or near a trailhead, try making conversation with people

Hitchhiking into towns to resupply is a regular part of a thru-hiker's routine along the 2,160-mile Appalachian Trail.

driver. And drivers of pickups stop far more often for hitchhikers than drivers of automobiles or recreational vehicles. Unfortunately, riding in the back of pickups is now illegal in some states.

● Keep money, valuables, and your camera on your person. I keep my "wallet" (really a zipper-lock plastic bag) in a small, cheap, lightweight fanny pack, which I always store in the same place in my pack. Before hitching, I get it out and slip it around my waist.

● You can make a sign on the back of your topo map to let drivers know that you just need a short ride to the next town.

● If your gut says no, decline the ride.

starting and ending their hikes. People using trails are (almost by definition) sympathetic to hikers. Often, an explanation of what you're doing will lead to the offer of a ride (or you can ask outright). And a short conversation gives you the chance to assess a stranger before you get into a car.

● The same strategy works to get out of town: Ask the waiters at the diner you're eating breakfast in (or the clerk at any business you are patronizing) if they know anyone heading up to the pass. Or you can offer to pay someone.

● Be friendly to everyone you meet on the trail: A dayhiker just out for a short walk might offer you a ride into town. Plus, you might feel more comfortable getting into the car of someone you've seen on the trail.

● Riding in the back of a pickup truck is safest for you — and for the

Route Planning on Unfinished Trails

If you're going to hike a trail that is finished, blazed, mapped, maintained, and described in a guidebook, route planning means buying said guidebook. But in some cases — usually when the trail is unfinished or not yet mapped — you will need to map out your actual route. The key

The author and her husband Dan Smith at the summit of Mount Katahdin, Maine, having completed a thru-hike of the Appalachian Trail. Ninety percent of those who start the trek do not complete it. Those who succeed plan carefully, leaving little to chance.

to this process is gathering as much information as possible. Remember that maps are frequently out-of-date. Roads and trails that show up on a 30-year-old map may be impossible to find, let alone to hike.

Say you've read about a new trail (let's use a hypothetical Great Discovery Trail). There's a lot of hype from trail organizers, but no guidebook. A photocopied handout from the fledgling trail organization tells you where the trail will go when complete, and that 500 miles currently exist and are open to the public. It also gives you the addresses of the national forests through which the trail passes (or will pass). You write to the various national forest offices for maps and more information about where the trail goes in their jurisdictions.

The first ranger district the trail passes through sends you a pamphlet telling you that 10 miles of the Great Discovery Trail are finished and marked and follow the route of old Ridgeline Trail #100. You look at the Forest Service map. There's no sign of a Great Discovery Trail, but you see Ridgeline #100. Easy enough: You highlight it on the map.

But, like all good things, Ridgeline #100 eventually comes to an end. In the next ranger district, you learn that the Great Discovery Trail was newly constructed and completed in 1995, but the route (quite logically) doesn't show up on the 1990 Forest Service map or the 1976 USGS topos. The information officer you talk to promises that the trail is so well marked that a blind person could follow it in the dark. Don't believe it! First of all, no trail is foolproof. (I've even been temporarily befuddled on the Appalachian Trail, and I figure that if someone with many thousands of miles of backpacking can get turned around on the dot-to-dot AT, anyone can get mixed up — if only momentarily — anywhere.) Second, trail markings aren't permanent: Trees can fall and block key junctions or vandals might take down a trail marker. And third, a map provides essential information about water sources, possible campgrounds, elevation gain, and the distance you've yet to cover.

In this case, you've got to find someone who can tell you where the new Great Discovery Trail goes. Usu-

THRU-HIKER GLOSSARY

Put together a group of people and an intense experience, and what do you get? A new language. Looking like a thru-hiker isn't enough: You also have to sound like one.

BLUE BLAZE (N.): The painted blazes often seen on maintained side trials. Blue-blaze (V.): To take trails other than the official white-blazed trails, usually because the alternatives are shorter or easier.

FLIP-FLOP (V.): To do a long-distance hike that is continuous in time but not in direction.

POWER HIKER (N.): A hiker who hikes long distances every day.

PURIST (N.) (also WHITE-BLAZER, N.): A hiker who sticks to the official route no matter what.

SLACKPACK (V.): (a) To hike without your pack by letting friends with a car shuttle it up the trail for you. (b) To take your time and do much slower, lazier miles than your fellow hikers.

TRAIL ANGELS (N.): Strangers who befriend long-distance hikers just because they think what you're doing is cool.

TRAIL MAGIC (N.): The generosity hikers find along the way.

TRAIL NAME (N.): Nicknames hikers adopt for themselves when they are on the trail.

WHITE BLAZE (N.): The white blazes are the Appalachian Trail's signature markers. White-blaze (V.): To follow all of the trail's official route.

YELLOW-BLAZE (V.): To hitchhike instead of to hike.

YOGI (V.): After Yogi the Bear because of his habit of making off with other people's picnic baskets. Thru-hikers "yogi" when they get someone to give them something they need (or want) without actually asking for it.

YO-YO (N.): A round-trip on a long-distance trail.

ally the best way to do this is to ask a trail planner to mark the route on a map for you, noting any water sources or good campsites along its route. Some persistence might yield a planning document that shows the route of the trail. (If it's a trail on government property, such a document exists, undoubtedly in triplicate.)

This accomplished, you move on to the next trail segment, which passes through BLM land. Here, you decide that the biggest challenge about hiking the Great Discovery Trail is discovering where it goes. The first three people you talk to haven't heard of it. When you finally find a trail manager, you learn about "alignments" and "easements" and some rancher who owns an in-holding and doesn't want hikers trespassing on his property. Now is when you need to start getting creative to figure out your own route. Your choices: Look for existing trails on the maps. Try to link together old jeep roads. Or do a little bushwhacking, taking care to avoid the irascible rancher's property. (Not only is your presence uninvited, but it could make the rancher feel even less disposed to enter into future negotiations regarding a right-of-way for trail use. Forest Service and BLM maps indicate property ownership; USGS topo maps do not.) The temptation in these segments is to just road-walk around the problem, but careful map work usually yields a far superior, more aesthetically enjoyable (if longer and more difficult)

backcountry experience.

Trail building, it sometimes seems, is one great unfinished symphony. Here are some other variations on the theme:

The trail's route "temporarily" follows a dirt road — but since the routing is temporary, the road isn't marked as part of the trail.

A clear-cut has decimated the dirt road and the surrounding area — and because the dirt road is not part of the permanent trail, the loggers weren't required to flag a path for hikers through the mess.

There is a huge sign at the trailhead parking lot — but once you get into the woods, you find that key junctions aren't marked and you can't follow the route without a map.

The trail's route has been added to the most up-to-date maps — but construction has not yet been completed. You follow the map and end up at a dead end with a heap of trail-building equipment.

Unfinished trails aren't for everyone. But they do offer advanced hikers a special pioneer experience. Rather than following along on the assembly line, hikers on an unfinished trail are often making their own unique route. There's lots more decision-making, and usually a few wrong turns. But it's a process that is both rewarding and challenging — and, one could argue, more in keeping with the idea (and the ideal) of a true wilderness adventure.

● LONG-DISTANCE HIKING: LESSONS FROM THE APPALACHIAN TRAIL, by Roland Mueser (*Ragged Mountain Press*) This unique book is based on an extensive, exhaustive survey Roland Mueser, a retired scientist, did on his 1989 thru-hike of the Appalachian Trail. Nothing escaped the author's attention: He covers hiker diets, mileage, gear, attitudes, techniques, and feelings. The result is readable, intriguing, sometimes surprising, and educational. Whether you're a weekend hiker or an aspiring expeditionist, you can learn a lot from the experiences of a group of people who cumulatively hiked more than 250,000 miles!

● WALKING THE APPALACHIAN TRAIL, by Larry Luxenberg (*Stackpole Books*) What's it like to walk 2,000 miles? Who does it? What happens along the route? Larry Luxenberg conducted hundreds of interviews of Appalachian Trail thru-hikers to write this book, which looks at every aspect of the thru-hiking experience.

● THE APPALACHIAN TRAIL READER, edited by David Emblidge (*Oxford University Press*) The Appalachian Trail may be the most beloved long trail in the world. This book examines its appeal through the voices of people who have written about the trail and the lands through which it passes. Included among them are historic figures like Thomas Jefferson, Herman Melville, and Henry David Thoreau, who lived before the trail was founded, but who loved its landscape. Also included are the words of trail founders, including Benton MacKaye's original article proposing a trail along the skyline of the Appalachians, and the contemporary voices of trail workers, well-known writers, and unknown hikers.

● THE PCT HIKER'S HANDBOOK, by Ray Jardine (*Adventurelore Press*) If you're interested in aggressive, big-mileage long-distance hiking, and you like to travel fast and light, you'll find this book packed with suggestions and advice. Not all of the author's ideas will gel with your hiking style, but this book will get you thinking—and maybe arguing. Some of the advice is controversial (like trading in your hiking boots for running shoes, or making your own backpack), but there's no rule that says you have to incorporate all of it. Recommended for hikers who have enough miles under their boots to be able to evaluate the safety implications of unorthodox decisions.

F O O D
&
R E S U P P L Y

One of the most frequently asked questions on long-distance trails is "What do you eat?" The simple answer is: what any other backpacker eats, just more of it.

Lots more: A master's degree study by Appalachian Trail thru-hiker Karen Lutz concluded that hikers need between 4,000 and 6,000 calories a day to put back in what they work off. (The average recommended intake for an adult is 2,000-2,500 calories.) Lutz also concluded that it was impossible to carry this amount of food over the long haul. Carrying additional food means burning more calories, which requires even more food, and so on. The bottom line: Most long-distance hikers lose weight during their journey. In a trail town, you can easily recognize someone who's been out for 1,000 miles. As a waitress told me: "You're the ones who walk funny, look gaunt, and are on a fourth pass through the all-you-can-eat buffet."

Nutrition

The criterion for good hiking food is the same whether you're going to be spending a few days in the woods or a few months: Food needs to be conveniently portable — that is, long-lasting, lightweight, and compact.

The biggest difference between weekend hikers and long-distance

Bagels and cream cheese for lunch on the Appalachian Trail in Virginia. The monotony of typical trail food can be dispelled with treats purchased during resupply stops in towns along the route.

mixes, instant rice and potatoes, and mac and cheese — may be lightweight and easy to prepare, but they are less nutritious than unprocessed fresh foods. Some hikers take vitamins to compensate or load up with power bars or other specially formulated snacks developed for athletes. Other hikers (many of them vegetarians and health-food enthusiasts) spend months dehydraing meals that they prepare in advance at home. A less time-consuming strategy is to pack supplies with an eye to variety and try to make up the shortfall in towns.

hikers (appetite aside) is that the latter need to be concerned with nutrition. Weekend hikers can survive on just about anything, come out of the woods, and head for the nearest restaurant. But long-distance hikers depend on their daily meals for their energy *and* health. The longer you're out, the more important the selection of food becomes. There might not be a gold medal waiting at the end of a long trail, but the long-distance backpacker has the same nutritional needs as an elite athlete who spends hours a day training for a competitive sport. But unlike that athlete, who may dine on specially prepared, nutritionally balanced meals at the end of the day, the hiker has to make do with what he has been able to carry on his back.

Unfortunately, the mainstays of backpackers' diets — prepackaged foods like Lipton noodles and sauce

While nutritionists disagree on the exact makeup of an optimal trail diet, they agree that hikers, like athletes, need a high-carbohydrate, lowfat diet. Figure about 60 to 70 percent carbos, 10 to 15 percent protein, and 15 to 30 percent fat. Few hikers actually count grams of fat in the woods, since they're operating on a calorie deficit and will generally eat anything that doesn't run away. But when you're planning your food drops, you might want to keep those numbers in mind.

Paying attention to variety will

help minimize nutritional deficiencies and keep your taste buds happy. Come up with a dozen different dinners (you'll find lots of suggestions in outdoor magazines and hiker cookbooks). Throw in a couple of freeze-dried meals every once in a while, some home-dehydrated meals, and your own concoctions using grocery store staples (pastas, tomato sauce, gravy mixes, Parmesan cheese, small cans of meat or fish, bags of TVP). Pay a visit to local specialty shops, foreign markets (especially Oriental and Caribbean markets), and health-food stores. Do remember, however, to try out new brands and flavors before you buy multiple quantities to take on your hike.

And don't forget snacks — lots of snacks. Nuts, fruits, and whole-grain-based snacks will give you more staying power than candy bars, but there's room for a few sugary snacks in your pack, too — especially for a quick burst of power on a steep hill.

Flipping flapjacks, winter trek in Glacier National Park. A high-carbohydrate, low-fat diet is considered best for hikers.

FOOD RESUPPLY

The mileage you can cover without resupplying varies according to how strong you are, the terrain, the season, and how long you've been out. Figuring about 2 pounds of food a person a day (2½ pounds for high-mileage hikers, hikers whose body weight or metabolism makes them prone to malnutrition, or winter hikers), most people find that carrying about 8 days of food and supplies is getting up near the "comfort limit." (Although very experienced, very fit long-distance hikers can carry twice as much.) Multiply the days of food you can carry with your average mileage and you'll come up with your range — the distance you can cover before you need to come off the trail to resupply. Usually, it's somewhere around 100 to 120 miles for a fit hiker, although on occasion I've carried supplies for more than 200 miles. On the other hand, if you find that your route takes you right past a grocery store midway through a 100-mile hike, it seems only sensible to cut your pack weight down and take advantage of the convenient resupply.

There are two ways to resupply on the trail. Some hikers simply arrive in a town and shop for supplies as they go. Others send themselves "food drops" — a box of supplies they've pre-packaged and pre-measured for the next stretch of trail.

Both methods have their advantages and disadvantages, but money isn't one of them: Neither method is necessarily cheaper or more expensive. It's not an either-or choice, and most hikers do some combination of food drops (usually sent to one-store towns) and shopping en route (in larger towns with a better selection).

do all that work. You can make up your schedule as you go along. If you develop a taste for some regional specialty, you can eat it every day for a month. If you get sick of a popular trail food, you don't have to buy it again. But all this free-wheeling flexibility has a price. If the town's only store — a one-aisle mini-mart — just sold its last box of macaroni and cheese to the hiker ahead of you, you could be out of luck. Finally, buying as you go means added work on the trail. When you come into town dripping wet after 3 days of rain and exhausted from that last big climb, you might appreciate having all the buying, counting, and organizing for the next leg of your trip already done.

Buy As You Go

This is the seat-of-the-pants approach: no planning, no fussing, no hours spent taping and addressing boxes months in advance. The advantages are obvious: You don't have to

Food Drops

This is a strategy for people who like to plan. It's by far the best approach if you are resupplying in tiny towns with limited supplies, especially if the towns are far apart. You can plan for

SHOPPING LIST

BREAKFAST

Coffee (coffee bags are best — they give you a precise measure, they don't spill, and they taste more like the real thing than instant) and tea (bags, of course). Cocoa. Instant cereal (oatmeal, farina, Cream of Wheat, and so on; take two packets per hiker per day). Boxed cereal (granola, muesli, and the like are a little heavier than instant, but add variety; add some powdered milk, and hot or cold water; figure on 2–3 ounces per hiker per day). Ramen noodle soup (the Japanese eat soup for breakfast; some hikers do, too).

more variety. (If you buy as you go, you could end up having to buy a huge box of mashed potatoes and then trying to figure out five different potato dinners for the next 5 days.) You get the right amounts of the foods you like. On the downside: Mail drops can limit your spontaneity — for example, you might find yourself having to do high mileage to get to a town before the post office closes on Saturday morning for a long holiday weekend. And it takes an incredible amount of time to prepare, pack, and ship several months' worth of groceries. Nonetheless, Dan and I usually (but not always) go the food-drop route — mostly because Dan is willing to do the planning. I'm used to a living room that looks like a food distribution warehouse, with hundreds of packages of instant soup, instant oatmeal, instant rice, instant freeze-dried dinners (are you getting the picture here?), along with the inevitable boxes of mac and cheese, spaghetti and whatever, Lipton noodles and sauce mixes, crackers, cereals, and candy.

If you're using food drops, you can also throw in a few supplies that are sometimes difficult to find in small towns (at least in the brands and quantities you may prefer). Examples: sample- or hotel-sized containers of personal toiletries (toothpaste, soap, shampoo); health items (replacement medications, vitamins); cleaning supplies (a zipper-lock bag full of laundry detergent means you don't have to depend on a small-town Laundromat for supplies; a small tube of boot wax can prolong the life of your boots). Other suggestions: sunscreen, bug repellent, journals, map and guidebook pages for the next leg of the trip, the occasional paperback book, new film, new matches, extra socks, replacement insoles for boots, and a stash of zipper-lock bags.

Other Resupply Options

LOCAL BUSINESSES Businesses near trails sometimes hold hiker packages, usually in a good-natured bid for hiker business. Some trail guide-

SHOPPING LIST

LUNCH

Cheese lasts outdoors for a longer time than you would expect. So does salami. Crackers don't go moldy; bread can. (Crackers keep better if stored in their original boxes.) Mustard lasts (get packets from fast food places). Peanut butter is a favorite. Some hikers swear by sardines. Alternatives: Just-add-water mixes for refried beans, hummus, and tabbouleh are popular with the health-food crowd (they're light to carry, but low in fat).

Food resupply and visit at the Corner Diner in Bastion, Virginia, along the Appalachian Trail. Storekeepers near the trail become accustomed to thru-hikers; some will hold hiker's food boxes mailed ahead.

instance, will accept only UPS shipments. Some charge a flat fee, some by the box, and some by the number of days they hold it for you. Some waive their fee if you'll be a paying guest. If you use a local business as a food drop, do make an effort to eat a meal there or buy something you need: It stores up goodwill for the next hiker.

books include this information. Check first to make sure the business is still accepting packages. Some wilderness lodges charge a fee for holding packages, because they have to pick up the boxes in town and drive them out themselves. (The Muir Ranch on the Pacific Crest Trail actually brings in hiker resupply boxes on mule-back!) Be sure to check to see whether the business has any requirements: Some, for

DELIVER YOUR OWN MAIL This is more feasible for shorter hikes. If you're driving to the trail and your route takes you past some of your resupply points, it may be worth a detour to hand-deliver your package yourself. You can't, however, hand-deliver a package to a post office

SHOPPING LIST

BEVERAGES

Coffee and tea. Powdered beverages like Kool-Aid and Crystal Light. Electrolyte-replacement beverages like Gatorade are excellent, particularly in hot weather, but the mixes are surprisingly heavy. Crystal Light is excellent for camouflaging the taste of chemically purified water. Hot chocolate is a nighttime favorite. Another choice: hot liquid Jell-O.

without paying postage! Some ranger stations, restaurants, shops, or hotels near the trail will hold packages (call first). A hotel where you have a reservation is a safe bet. Advantages: You'll know your package arrived safely — and you'll save the cost of shipping. Disadvantages: Delivery takes time. And some hikers feel that driving to a place you're going to walk into takes some of the sense of adventure out of your trip.

DRAFT YOUR FRIENDS Non-hiking friends or a non-hiking spouse might delight in taking part in your trip. They can arrange to meet you at trailheads and dayhike for a stretch — and when they show up, they can deliver your next food drop to you right on the trail.

This is a great way to share your adventure, especially if your friends or family express an interest but are not up to hiking with you.

CACHES

I've only used backwoods caches a couple of times. The reasons: They require a car, which I usually don't have at my disposal if I fly somewhere to hike. They take a lot of time. More convenient options are usually available. (Most of the time, if you can drive in to place a cache, there's a business within a couple of days' walk or a road from which you can hitch to a town.) And from a purely neurotic perspective, I'd

SHOPPING LIST

SNACKS

Depending on how many miles you cover, you'll need two to six snacks per person per day. Most hikers find that it's important to keep eating small amounts throughout the day to keep their energy and blood sugar up. Some suggestions:

Nuts (check out your local food co-op). GORP (the ubiquitous "good old raisins 'n' peanuts" plus whatever else you add: fruit chunks, coconut, M&Ms, chocolate chips). Beef jerky (also try chicken or turkey jerky; if you have a dehydrator, you can make your own). Granola bars, Snickers, Kudos, Fibars, fruit leather: Trade with your hiking partners. Power bars and pemmican bars (expensive but great for an energy boost; they're available at your local outfitter). Fresh fruits like apples and oranges last well but are heavy. If you can carry the extra weight, they make a delicious treat.

rather carry an extra 5 days' worth of food to the next sure food drop than leave a bag hanging from a tree and spend the next few days worrying whether a bear got his paws on it!

Nonetheless, there are certain times when caches are advisable. In desert, for example, the terrain is often accessible to an automobile or a truck, and a well-placed cache can solve the problem of long food carries, water shortages, and long detours to civilization.

If you decide to go this route, it's worth remembering that the word cache derives from the French *cacher*, which means to hide.

To deter inadvertent human interference, leave a note on your cache saying that a hiker will be depending on these supplies and giving the dates, so that someone who stumbles on your cache knows that the supplies aren't left over from some long-ago abandoned trek. A more serious problem is vandals; fortunately, they're easily foiled. Simply put the cache out of reach. Go off the beaten track, away from the roads, out of sight, anywhere it's the least

FOOD-DROP TIPS

● Try before you buy. Make sure you really and truly like something you're going to buy in bulk, or you might learn the hard way that you detest freeze-dried sweet and sour shrimp, pilot biscuits, or plain oatmeal.

● Throw in a treat. Something that isn't part of your daily diet spices up the routine and relieves the tedium of a trail-food diet. Anything that lasts and doesn't weigh too much is a candidate, from a can of anchovies to a bar of imported chocolate.

● If your favorite backcountry meal is pasta-plus-whatever, vary the kind of pasta you buy: Spinach-, carrot-, and beet-fla-

vored pastas are all available. But stay away from the thicker noodles, which take longer to cook, and opt for angel hair instead.

● Clarified butter is available from backcountry food distributors in plastic packages.

● Bouillon cubes make a quick pickup on a cold day. So do tea bags.

● Read directions before you buy something you haven't tried before. It may take too long to cook or require too many fresh ingredients.

● Finally, a use for that fruitcake your grandmother gives you every Christmas: trail food! It lasts, it's dense, it doesn't dry out or fall apart, and with all those ingredients, it's very nutritious.

bit difficult to get to. Go to a little effort, then go to a little more. Problem solved.

Animals, now that's a different story. Animals are resourceful. And hungry. It's a much more effective combination than immoral and lazy (*i.e.*, human vandals).

Animal-proofing your cache begins with what's in it. Choose foods that don't have strong odors — better a sealed plastic tub of peanut butter than a hunk of salami. At the same time, you need to minimize the packaging because you're going to have to pack out everything in your cache. So remove bulky cardboard and plastic and replace them with sealed zipper-locking bags.

Then there's the matter of where to stash your cache. One answer — the answer in bear country — is up in the air, in a standard bear-bag.

In deserts, however, there aren't likely to be trees. One solution is to make an animal-proof container using a net made of fine wire mesh

Phoning home from Damascus, Virginia, near the Appalachian Trail. Resupply stops offer a chance to revive the spirit (as well as the body) with calls to loved ones.

(so-called hardware cloth). First, minimize food odors with zipper bags. Then line your food sack with a

SHOPPING LIST

STAPLES

Dried milk, sugar, honey, Parmesan cheese (makes everything taste better). Spices (suggestions: salt, pepper, Louisiana hot sauce, dried garlic, oregano, onion flakes, lemon-pepper mix, soy sauce; pack them in tiny bags or plastic containers available from outdoor shops). Packets of clarified butter (they don't need refrigeration). Sun-dried tomatoes and dried mushrooms. For fresh flavor and variety, an onion, several carrots, and a clove of garlic last well.

An Appalachian Trail thru-hiker at a Virginia hostel repackages the contents of his mail drop before beginning the next leg of his trek.

plastic garbage bag. Finally, make a lightweight animal-proof container by improvising an envelope out of the wire mesh. Fold it over and sew the three sides together with wire. But, again remember, you'll have to pack the wire mesh out.

Finally, there's the issue of cementing the location of your cache in your memory. It might seem simple enough when you're hiding your stash of food and water behind that really big cactus. But several days, dozens of miles, and a thousand giant cacti into your hike, you'll need to know, specifically, how to single out the one that has your food and water stashed behind it. There's no one right way, except to realize

that mix-ups are possible and to use every tool at your disposal to prevent confusion. Take time to look — really look — at the area. Jot down some notes about natural features. Take a few compass bearings to notable landmarks. If you've got a GPS, take a reading.

If it's possible to mix up where you yourself left a stash, imagine how easily you can get confused if a friend or an outfitter brings your resupply in and caches it for you. In general, the best advice is don't. Why? You'll be depending on someone else to give you directions to a place you've never been in the middle of a wilderness, and if these instructions are anything other than crystal clear, you'll be going without dinner until you can get yourself out of the woods. Still need convincing? Consider how poorly most people give simple street directions. Your life might depend on finding your cache — your comfort and enjoyment of the backcountry certainly will.

Repackaging Food for the Trail

After you pick up your food drop, you'll need to repackage your supplies. Get rid of all those boxes, tubes, and jars. They weigh too much and take up too much space in your pack. Especially, get rid of glass (it shatters; for this reason, it is actually illegal to carry glass containers in some national parks). The exception to the repackaging rule is crackers, which need to stay in their protective boxes unless you don't mind a lunch of crumbs and cheese instead of crackers and cheese.

Zipper-lock bags protect your food from moisture, spills, and dirt. They also prevent a mess if a container of liquid explodes due to changing air pressure when you climb 4,000 feet up a mountain. In the case of easily confused items like sugar and salt, or Parmesan cheese and powdered milk, label the plastic bags. These kinds of powdered foods can get stuck in the closing mecha-nism of a zipper-locking bag, so use two bags. Wrapping a rubber band around the package will help hold things together even if the zipper locks do separate.

As you're repackaging, try to put the ingredients for each meal together, along with any directions. This not only makes finding what-goes-with-what easier in the back-country, it helps ensure that you won't run out of food. On long stretches, you can also pack your food supplies in a few small stuff sacks, each containing all the rations

MAILING TIPS

Address the box with:
  Your Name
  c/o General Delivery
  Town, State, Zip
and write on the box "please hold for hiker arriving on or about. . ." and the date.

● Use a sturdy box in good condition. The extra-strong boxes from liquor stores are tough enough to protect glass bottles, so they work well for food drops. They're the right size, too.

● General delivery usually holds packages for 10 days, but post offices near major trails are used to dealing with hikers and may hold the box longer if you specify the date of your anticipated arrival on the box.

● If you're hiking in an area where you suspect there isn't a lot of trail traffic, postmasters may not routinely deal with hikers. Send them a note (or call) to ask if they will hold your package until you arrive. On occasion, you'll learn that a remote rural post office can't hold packages; they'll usually tell you, however, the nearest post office that will.

● Write your return address on the box in case your plans change. Remember, first-class and priority mail can be forwarded or sent home at no charge. Forwarding or returning parcel post mail will

continued on page 60

MAILING TIPS
continued from page 59

cost you extra.

- Over long distances, priority mail or first class costs virtually the same as parcel post. Parcel post is much cheaper over short distances.
- Never use UPS or any other private carrier to send a mail drop to a post office or a post office box. A post office will not accept private carrier mail.
- Some businesses hold boxes for hikers (especially if you state that you will be a patron when you're in the area). If you are using a business as a food drop, check to see how to send your box to them. Many proprietors of rural businesses specify UPS or Federal Express because the post office doesn't deliver to them out in the boonies. Rural mail is often held for pickup in post offices that can be many miles from the actual address.
- Before you leave, write up a list of mail-drop addresses and any specific mailing instructions for each one. This way, your friends can send you letters and trail treats.
- Include a padded envelope and some tape in the resupply box to send home spent film, used maps, and the odd piece of gear.
- Leave food in its original packaging for its journey to the trail town: Your supplies need all the protection they can get. Pack plenty of zipper-locking bags so you can repackage supplies for the trail.

for 2 or 3 days. This will help you keep track of your food supplies — and resist the temptation to "eat just a little more" from tomorrow's rations.

GEAR RESUPPLY

In addition to planning their food drops, hikers on long trails need to replace gear as climate and conditions change or as equipment breaks or wears out. Since you can't count on finding quality (or sometimes any) gear in Outer Nowhere, you'll need to think about your equipment down to the tiniest detail. For instance, the popular Petzl headlamps use a type of battery that isn't widely available — even a general outdoors store may not carry it, although a serious backpacking store usually does. You can send yourself replacement batteries somewhere up the trail or try to find out where and when you'll pass through a town with a backpacking

store. Some-
times guide-
books will have
this informa-
tion. If not,
your best bets
for finding an
outfitter
include large
cities, college
towns, and
vacation desti-
nations.

Cooking dinner on an MSR Whisperlite at Walnut Mountain Shelter on the Appalachian Trial in North Carolina. This stove is one of the most popular among thru-hikers (see page 64).

Here's another strategy for dealing with those essentials that wear out or get used up at an unpredictable rate (socks, sock liners, batteries, boot insoles, mosquito repellent, personal hygiene supplies, and even T-shirts): Pack a box that bounces from post office to post office as you travel up the trail. Put in it all those items that are hard to replace and impossible to live without, and ship it up ahead. When you arrive in town, the box will be waiting for you along with the rest of your resupply. You retrieve what you need, add anything to the box that you haven't been using and want to save, and ship it to yourself in care of a post office a couple of weeks up the trail.

SHOPPING LIST

SOUPS

Most hikers start dinner with instant soup. In fact, some consider soup the best part of dinner, especially on a cold day. It's easy to make, easy to clean up, and it helps fill the empty spot at the bottom of your stomach. Ramen noodles are a big favorite. I ate them for 200 days in a row on the Appalachian Trail and — this is not an exaggeration — never got sick of them. Salt replenishment is important, and packaged soups are high in sodium. Knorr and Lipton offer a wide selection; make sure you buy the no-cook, just-add-water selections. Miso soup (avail-able at your local health-food store or co-op) is another good choice.

DINNER

Freeze-dried meals, Lipton side dishes, macaroni and cheese, home-dehydrated meals. Or concoct your own on the spot by using what I call the Chinese-menu approach: A carbohydrate from Column A + a meat and/or vegetable from Column B + a sauce or flavoring from Column C, and you've got yourself a meal. (But pay attention — not everything goes with everything.)

BASE (A)	PROTEIN AND VEGGIES (B)	FLAVORING (C)
Instant potatoes	Small cans of:	Tomato paste
Rice	tuna	Tomato sauce mix
Pasta ($^1/_4$–$^1/_3$ pound/person;	turkey	Gravy mix
angel hair cooks quickest)	chicken	Onion or mushroom
Stovetop stuffing mix	TVP*	soup mix
Couscous		Parmesan cheese

* Textured vegetable protein for the uninitiated: can be used to make veggie burgers or to add bulk to one-pot dinners.

There's also seasonal gear to consider. At the very least, you'll have to change your layering system as the seasons and the altitude change. The same goes for sleeping bags, if you own more than one. Other seasonal gear might include ice axes and crampons for highcountry in early summer, a rope for hanging food in bear country, and a tarp instead of a tent in dry, warm weather.

Plan gear swaps for towns with post offices, because you may not be able to send out the supplies you're finished with from a remote mountain lodge or a campground.

If you pack a little mailing tape in with your food drop, you won't have to worry about whether the local general store sells tape — and you won't have to buy 100 yards of it when all you need is 100 inches. You can usually purchase boxes at the post office (or reuse your food-drop boxes).

PART II: EXTREME GEAR & ADVANCED SKILLS

GEAR
FOR THE
LONG HAUL

Count up the listings in a year's worth of outdoor catalogs, magazines, and advertisements and you'll find thousands of items: tents, backpacks, sleeping bags, stoves, boots, air mattresses, watches, cameras, and assorted accessories. If you're looking to this information to help you make up your mind about what to buy, good luck. The sheer number of choices might make you wonder how it is that hikers claim the "simple life" as one of backpacking's great attractions.

There have been lots of times I've come close to a state of paralyzed confusion when confronted with all those choices. But when you spend a little more time with gear,

you learn that the trail makes lots of decisions for you. In fact, long-distance hikers — people who use their gear day after day for months on end — come to extraordinary (not, however, unanimous) consensus on the subject of equipment. In a national park campground, you'll see dozens of different makes and models of tents — everything from teeny little bivy tents to those palatial fabric condominiums that can house an entire family. But at a gathering of long-distance hikers, two basic designs — both ultralight tents weighing 5 pounds or less — dominate (see page 87). And despite the fact that more than 60 stoves are on

Leki sticks are telescoping, adjustable, and have nifty little springs that help absorb shock.

the market, in a survey I did of 60 Appalachian Trail thru-hikers, 40 used the MSR Whisperlite. Of the remaining 20, 6 used the Whisperlite's "big brother," the MSR XGK-II multifuel, and 6 used the similarly designed Peak I Apex II — which means that of 60 hikers, 52 used three models of stoves by just two manufacturers. (It's interesting to note, however, that there is far less consensus about stoves on the PCT, where many hikers prefer compressed-fuel cartridge stoves.)

It's as if the trail whittles down everything extraneous until hikers are left with only the essentials. The best way I know to equip yourself for the long haul is to get out there and talk to the people who slide their packs down an ice chute, ford streams in their boots, sleep out in the snow, filter water from a beaver pond, drop their stoves on a sand beach, and complain when their gear breaks down after 3,000 miles. Ask them what they'd buy next time. Hikers are a talkative lot, and their favorite subject (well, maybe second favorite:

there's always food) is gear. Hiker babble, a friend of mine calls it, the incessant chatter about delaminating boot soles and snapped clevis pins and clogged water filters that runs like an undercurrent beneath hiker conversations.

So what kind of consensus is there? The keywords are *lightweight*, *durable*, and *functional*. LIGHTWEIGHT because every extra pound is going to have to be hefted and hauled — as many as 6 million steps, if you're challenging one of the megatrails. That's why you so rarely see a long-distance hiker on a three-season trip carrying fancy tents. Manufacturers can add on all the nifty extras and gizmos they like, and equipment reviewers can wax euphoric about organization pouches and extra vestibule space, but hikers who intend to carry their tents for hundreds or thousands of miles will happily abandon all that to shave off a few unnecessary ounces. It's impossible to overestimate the importance of hiking light. Heavy packs make for debilitating climbs, aching feet, damaged joints, and heavy spirits. Without food and water, I try to keep my three-season pack weight down to around 20 or 25 pounds. Water weighs in at 2 pounds a quart, and I figure about 2 pounds of food per day, which means that an average 5-day load will be in the neighborhood of 32 - 37 pounds, less if I'm hiking with a partner. Sometimes (as in winter) the terrain and climate require a heavier pack.

DURABLE because the day you take the last of those 6 million steps, you are going to be just as dependent on your stove to light, your tent to shed rain, and your water filter to work as you were on the first day of your trip. One long-distance hike can put a lifetime's worth of normal use on a piece of equipment — which gives you new insight into that common promise, "lifetime guarantee."

Hiking in Olympic National Park, Washington. Not everyone uses one walking stick, let alone two, but two-stick hikers (like the author) are fanatic on the subject of how much a pair of sticks helps with knees and balance.

Durability is found in the details — but not too many of them. Look for strong construction, tough materials, and finishing touches like taped seams. Pay special attention to any place where one component is joined to another, because these are the places that tend to blow out first. Finally, seek out simplicity.

Remember, Murphy's Law works in the woods. Seams, grommets, gizmos, straps, adjustments, toggles, panels, and patches not only add weight, they also tend to be weak spots that tear or break under heavy use. Be sure you need all the features you're paying for.

FUNCTIONAL because you need different equipment to do different jobs in different conditions. Rain gear is a whole lot more important to an Appalachian Trail hiker than it is to an Arizona hiker. Sleeping bag quality isn't nearly as critical in summer as it is in winter. You need a bomb-proof tent in winter conditions (and yes, that's going to set you back more than 5 pounds), whereas a tarp might keep you perfectly comfortable below treeline in the summer. Good rain gear is necessary in the high-country and in fall or spring hiking. In temperate climates during the summer, a poncho could do the trick.

A Word about Cost

Good gear is expensive, but you get value for the price. My Northface tent has weathered at least a thousand nights. My four-year-old Dana Design pack has well over 7,000 miles on it and looks as good as new. Ditto for Dan's Gregory Denali pack. If you're looking for gear for serious hiking, buy the best you can afford.

Gear is important: At times, it's what you will depend on for comfort and safety. I take pride in occasionally being regarded as something of an anti-trend iconoclast, so it pains me to admit that in the world of backpacking, shopping for name brands makes a lot of sense. I'd take a lot more pleasure in scrambling onto a didactic mountaintop and proclaiming that you can make your own gear or modify inexpensive army-surplus store equipment to meet most any backcountry need — and who knows, maybe *you* can. But I lack either the time or the talent, probably both. Now that I'm thoroughly addicted to the backpacking way of life and have stomped my way through several lifetime guarantees, I've learned, to both my satisfaction and my surprise, that in outdoor equipment the name on the pack (or tent or whatever) means something. Well-established major manufacturers with good reputations are staffed by outdoor enthusiasts and they honor the guarantees they make with excellent service. That's part of what you're buying when you buy the designer label.

But that doesn't mean that the right answer is always the most expensive item available. To the contrary, a $30 tarp may meet your needs better than a $300 tent! In the following discussions, I include the names of gear manufacturers whose products are frequently seen on long trails. Many of them are top of the line, but some lower- or medium-priced brands offer remarkable value, and I've included them as well. If you're on a budget, three tricks will help you make the most of your gear-buying dollars.

First, spend them where they count. My priorities: boots, packs, and rain gear (probably in that order). For three-season conditions, you can save money on sleeping bags and tents because in these categories there are excellent values among lower-cost products. Someone who shows up at a national park campground on the Fourth of July weekend with a $600 mountaineering tent has simply wasted $600. I'd go so far as to say that anyone who spends $600 on a tent for anything that resembles typical three-season use has wasted his or her money.

Second, check out house brands such as REI, EMS, or L.L. Bean. These companies often make scaled-down versions of high-end products, but they use quality materials and offer good warranties.

Third, go for simplicity. If you're buying a mid-range pack, for instance, avoid flimsy models with extra features and choose instead a straightforward, solid pack with good seams, tough materials, and enough padding in the shoulders and waist.

Lifetime Guarantees

It's important to realize that the lifetime guarantees offered by most major manufacturers cover defects in materials or workmanship, not wear and tear. This opens up a big gray area because in backpacking, wear and tear is the name of the game. Equipment that can't stand up to normal use is defective. But what is normal use? That's where the debate begins. Backpacking equipment is designed to be rugged — and it is certainly advertised as such (how many ads have you seen trumpeting that a particular pair of boots or type of foul-weather gear was tested on Mt. Everest?). The fact is that most backpacking gear spends most of its life in someone's closet and never gets near worn out before being replaced by something newer and trendier. But for people who really use their gear, season after season, mile after mile, the issue of lifetime warranties is important.

High-end manufacturers generally stand by their word, and the quality of customer service offered by many of these manufacturers wins them customers for life. And even though they probably weren't thinking of thru-hikers' lifetimes when they offered lifetime guarantees, manufacturers often go the extra mile to help long-distance hikers stranded in the field with a defective or broken piece of equipment. Partly, this is public relations. Many thru-hikers give advice to beginners they meet on the trail, and a large number go on to lecture or teach classes in backpacking. I've recommended dozens of packs and pairs of boots to friends who were taking up backpacking, and I always recommend companies like Dana, Gregory, The Northface, and Marmot, which produce good products and service them well.

Premium gear does cost more — but you're paying for service, and if you do your research to identify which companies stand by their products, you'll get it. Three places to start your research: Other hikers, *Backpacker* magazine's annual gear guide, and your outfitting store. *Backpacker* publishes an annual gear guide every March. Be sure to read the fine print at the bottom where the editors share some of their personal evaluations. (Do remember, however, that most of the editors are not long-distance hikers, so they can't address the issue of durability on a thru-hike.) At your local store, tell the salesperson how you plan to use the gear you're buying. If you're buying a lot of gear at once for a big trip, ask to speak with the store manager, and find out what the store's guarantee policy is. (Many good stores have their own warranty programs, which can double the protection you get from the manufacturer's warranty.) If you're looking at equipment made by a particular manufacturer, ask what the manager thinks about the manufacturer's service.

Some hikers take advantage of

the goodwill of equipment makers by expecting them to replace (free of charge) boots that have gone 1,500 miles or 20-year-old packs that have done their job with honor. If you think that your gear has not performed up to standard, by all means say so — but be fair. Split seams, delaminating soles, snapped tent poles, and torn grommets are all problems that shouldn't happen with high-quality equipment. But worn-out zipper sliders, webbing that has been rubbed smooth, and worn-down boot soles are usually not results of defects, but of wear and tear.

If you do have a problem, call the manufacturer. (Jot the phone numbers in your address book. *Backpacker*'s annual gear guide lists manufacturers and their numbers.) Typically, manufacturers prefer that you return the item and then, after examining it, they'll repair or replace it.

But most customer service reps understand that if you're on the trail, you can't sit around for a month waiting for a repair. Usually, you can arrange to have the manufacturer ship out a replacement or a loaner, and you are expected to ship back the defective item. They may ask for a credit card number to guarantee that you do, in fact, return the item. If the problem is due to gross abuse (say you dropped your pack off a 500-foot cliff) there may be a fee for repair, but the fees are reasonable.

BOOTS

Funny thing about hiking boots. Every aspect of their design is intended to protect your feet, yet boots actually cause more foot problems than anything else.

True, hiking boots keep your feet safe from myriad lurking dangers. Rugged Vibram soles provide traction on slippery ground. Gore-Tex linings and gusseted

From left: the Merrell Wilderness, EMS Classic, and OneSport Moraine are three very popular midweight yet tough boots among thru-hikers.

tongues help keep feet warm and dry. Scree collars repel pebbles and rocks. Good leather uppers protect ankles from twisting on every protruding root.

But while tough-as-nails hiking boots are good watchdogs, they don't do their job gently. The result can be fierce blisters that make you wonder why anyone invented hiking boots in the first place.

The reason: Like most marriages, the mesh between boot and foot is not always a perfect match. If you look at

GETTING A GOOD FIT

There are all too many opportunities for feet and boots to have screaming arguments on the trail. As in any successful partnership, foot and boot must eventually come to compromise.

Even if you've worn the same size shoe for 20 years, have your feet measured by a Brannock device before trying on boots. If one foot is bigger than the other, fit the boot to the larger foot: Unless your feet are drastically different sizes, you can compensate by wearing thicker socks or using a thicker insole for the smaller foot.

Try on boots with the socks you're going to wear on the trail. And, if you prefer cushy insoles to those provided by the manufacturer, try the boot with the insoles

continued on page 70

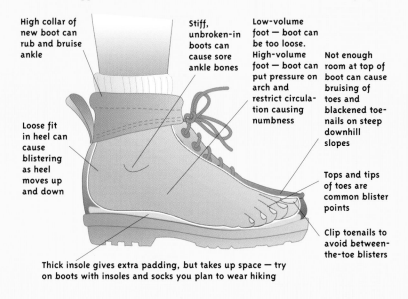

High collar of new boot can rub and bruise ankle

Loose fit in heel can cause blistering as heel moves up and down

Stiff, unbroken-in boots can cause sore ankle bones

Low-volume foot — boot can be too loose. High-volume foot — boot can put pressure on arch and restrict circulation causing numbness

Not enough room at top of boot can cause bruising of toes and blackened toenails on steep downhill slopes

Tops and tips of toes are common blister points

Clip toenails to avoid between-the-toe blisters

Thick insole gives extra padding, but takes up space — try on boots with insoles and socks you plan to wear hiking you plan to use. (Superfeet is a popular insole model.)

To see if the boot is the right length, before lacing the boot scrunch your toes toward the front. You should just barely be able to cram your index finger down the back of the boot. When you lace the boot up, you should be able to wiggle your toes without feeling the front of the boot. Next, try flexing the boot by going uphill (a good outfitter will have a ramp especially for this purpose). If your heel comes up more than about ¼ inch, you need a different size or a different model. This is important: The back of the heels are a common blister point, and going uphill is work enough without the irritation of an ill-fitting boot.

In addition to length and width, you also need to consider the volume of your foot. Basically, the volume refers to how much space your foot takes up. There really isn't an accurate measure for it except for how the boot feels. Boots are cut on different "lasts" by different manufacturers, so try on different makes and models. In general, look for an all-around supportive fit, with no tight spots. If there's a part of your foot that always seems to blister, pay special attention to how the boot feels in that area. If you have a small-volume foot, look for boots that have a hook near the instep that is set back farther than the other hooks and eyelets; this hook gives you the leverage to pull the boot snug around your instep when you lace it up.

A good store will encourage you to keep the boots on for a while — maybe even while wearing a weighted pack. Walk around and check out all the nifty new gizmos. Read the magazines by the checkout counter. The longer you spend in the boots, the more you'll get a sense of how they really fit.

the feet of several people, you'll undoubtedly see a range of bumps and bunions, arches and anklebones — all of which are encased in the same hard leather cage. It takes a little bit of time, accommodation, and softening for boots and feet to settle into comfortable routine.

I polled a few manufacturers about boots for long-distance hiking and found consensus on one crucial point: Choosing the right boot for the right job and the right fit for your foot are *the* two most important decisions you will make in gearing up for your hike. "Over time, foot discomfort can actually damage your feet," said a spokesperson for OneSport, makers of the popular Moraine boot, which tests out well on long-distance trails. The impact of these decisions will last the length of your hike and will be a crucial factor in your success, as well as your enjoyment.

The boot-buying public has been riding a crazily swinging pendulum over the last decade or so, alternating between heavyweight, intractable, seriously ugly-looking waffle-stompers and trendy, snazzy, not to mention lighter, cheaper, and far more comfortable fabric-and-leather featherweights. Long-distance hikers have been riding the swing, too, in search of the elusive ideal: a boot that is at once lightweight and durable.

Boot Durability

Rule Number 1: Do not plan to hike a major long-distance trail in one pair of boots.

Manufacturers are loathe even to guestimate how many miles a pair of their boots will survive before wearing out. The reason: Differences in gait, body weight, pack weight, foot physiology, and hiking style can mean a difference in boot longevity of hundreds of miles. If you're a Mack truck kind of hiker who carries a lot of weight and kicks every rock in your path, your boots are going to wear out faster than if you were a little lighter on your feet. Durability

also depends on where you hike. The Appalachian Trail, for instance, with its rocks, bogs, mud, and steep ups and downs, is much harder on boots than a trail that goes through gentler terrain and drier climates. In my survey of 20 AT thru-hikers, only 4 reached the end in the same boots they started with. (Two were Vasques, one was OneSport Moraines, and the other was a pair of Redwing workboots.)

Not surprisingly, hikers have more problems with their footwear than any other piece of equipment, and bootmakers have the most uneven reputations of all for customer service. Customer service representatives at both Vasque and One-Sport (both are companies that offer a good selection of boots for serious hikers) commented that thru-hikers often buy boots that don't fit correctly, or choose boots not designed for the job. That may be true, but it begs the question: How is the consumer supposed to know which boots are long-trail worthy and which aren't when they all come with brightly colored tags trumpeting that they were tested on rough, rugged, rocky, rubbly, ruinous terrain and are made of five-syllable high-tech components that sound like materials you'd use to build a rocket ship? Even the heaviest-footed thru-hiker on the gnarliest trail has the right to boots that perform as advertised.

One strategy is to go straight to the manufacturer. After you try on

The author's husband Dan waxes his boots during a trek in Nepal. The more remote your destination, the more important it becomes to maintain gear to prevent blow-outs.

boots and are 100 percent convinced that they fit exactly, precisely right, go home without buying them. Call the manufacturer and speak to a customer service representative. Discuss your hiking plans and which boot model you are considering purchasing and ask what they think of your choice. Often, retailers will carry only one or two boots from a particular maker. The service rep will know if the company has a boot better suited for your needs. Be as specific as possible about what those needs are. If you have consistent foot problems (a wide forefoot, a high arch, pronation, or a consistent blister spot), mention these as well. Finally, get the rep's name and ask about customer support in the field. Going through this

process sounds time-consuming, but you'll get good advice — and if the boot should fall short of your expectations, you'll know whom to talk to about getting service or a replacement.

How far can you reasonably expect a pair of boots to go? During his 1989 thru-hike of the AT, Roland Mueser, a retired scientist, conducted a detailed survey. In *Long-Distance Hiking: Lessons from the Appalachian Trail* (Ragged Mountain Press, Rockport, Maine), he reports that a total of 136 hikers wore out a total of 238 pairs of boots on the Appalachian Trail. Among his findings: A pair of running shoes (an option used by only 4 people in his survey) lasted 700 miles; lightweight fabric-and-leather boots lasted 1,000; midweight boots (either all leather or reinforced fabric and leather) lasted 1,050; and heavyweight full-grain leather lasted 1,600. My own survey of 20 Appalachian Trail hikers found that the average hiker used and just about wore out two pairs of boots on the 2,160-mile thru-hike, a finding that is consistent with Mueser's survey and my own long-distance experience. These data aren't fail-safe — there's a lot of room for what statisticians call "margin of error" — but they do represent more than 300,000 miles of backpacking experience. If your gait, weight, and hiking style are anywhere on the long-distance hiker's bell curve, a decent pair of boots ought to last you 1,000–1,500 miles — and you may be able to get them resoled. Less than 1,000 miles, and you can probably get some satisfaction (*i.e.*, repair or replacement) from the manufacturer or the retailer where you bought your boots.

Lightweight versus Heavyweight

While sturdy all-leather middleweight boots are the clear thruhiker choice on the rugged and rock-strewn Appalachian Trail, many experienced distance hikers choose the lightest boot that will do the job, especially on western trails like the PCT, which aren't quite as tough on footwear. Your choice is going to depend in part on the length of your trip, the requirements of the trail you are hiking, and your own preferences.

LIGHTWEIGHTS (UNDER 2.5 POUNDS)
Lightweight fabric-and-leather boots are popular on well-graded footway like the Pacific Crest Trail. They won't last as long as heavier all-leather boots, but if they fit and don't give you blisters, you might happily trade durability for comfort. Boots made of fabric and leather are lighter (hence easier to lift) than all-leather boots, but they have a major weak spot: lots of seams that can split under prolonged use. There is a huge difference between upper-end lightweights and lower-end boots made (and used) primarily for dayhiking. Don't go bargain hunting. Although price is not always an indication of quality, you can be fairly well guaranteed that very inexpensive lightweight boots are not going to stand up to prolonged abuse. They tend to be too flimsy to provide the necessary support, and in horrendous conditions (think Vermont in April: freezing rain, snow, and mud) they perform miserably. But there are always exceptions: I once got about 1,000 miles out of a pair of $75 Nike boots. Those were mostly dry, easy western miles, but still, 1,000 miles is 1,000 miles. For more rugged adventures, I've done well with better-quality Gore-Tex-lined lightweights like the Vasque Skywalker IIs, an excellent choice for three-season use on a variety of terrain. But they don't hold up as well as all-leather boots in miserable freezing

rain and wet snow conditions. Finally, many of these boots have molded soles that must be replaced by a specialist — not every cobbler has the right materials and glues. MIDWEIGHTS (2.5–5 POUNDS) For serious backpacking, a sturdy mid-weight all-leather boot is the all-around favorite. Here's why: Leather — in addition to offering good ankle support — is water-resistant and breathable. Leather boots have fewer seams, so you'll have fewer problems with leakage and splitting. And they have replaceable soles, so when the Vibram starts looking as smooth as dancing pumps (figure about 1,000 miles) you don't have to replace your by now beloved and broken-in boots, but can have them resoled.

Warning: As with lightweight boots, some midweight leather boots like the OneSport Moraine have molded soles that need to be resoled by the manufacturer or by a factory-authorized repair facility that uses specific glues. Your local cobbler might think he can do the job, but this is something you need to check with the manufacturer first.

A few leather models to check out, listed in order of heftiness from light to heavy: the EMS Classic, Vasque Sundowners, Vasque Super-hikers, OneSport Moraine, Merrell Wilderness. HEAVYWEIGHTS (MORE THAN 5 POUNDS) In general, stay away from anything this heavy. These boots simply weigh too much, considering

how many times you're going to have to pick them up and set them down. But for some people in some circum-stances, they may be appropriate. Like if you're hiking off-trail and need a lot of ankle support. If you're going to the bona fide back-of-beyond (say, walking across Mon-golia) where there's no way you could get equipment help. If you expect to do a lot of step-kicking on ice slopes. If you're going to need to use cram-pons frequently. If you are extremely hard on boots and have had dura-bility problems with a variety of lighter models. Even so, choose the lightest boots that'll do the job and give yourself plenty of time to break them in.

The Running-Shoe Debate

You've probably heard that 1 pound on your feet equals 5 pounds on your back. Some backpackers abandon hiking boots altogether. Indeed, on portions of the Pacific Crest Trail, wearing running shoes has become something of a trend. If you think this is something you might want to try, experiment with wearing running shoes on a shorter hike first.

I've backpacked for a few hun-dred miles in running shoes, and it's not a bad choice under certain conditions:

DRY TERRAIN Running shoes work best in dry terrain, where you don't have to slosh through bogs and pud-dles. If it's wet and muddy, you'll be tempted to walk around, rather than through, mud puddles on the trails. This violates minimum-impact principles because it widens the treadway. Also, running shoes don't have the same kind of traction as hiking boots, so they don't handle wet leaves or slick rocks as well.

DRY WEATHER A combination of waterproof boots, gaiters, and rain pants will help keep your feet dry in moderate rain; running shoes will not. (But remember, in a spell of day-after-day downpour, it doesn't much matter — dry feet are an impossible dream.) I find, however, that wet boots feel drier than wet running shoes.

WARM WEATHER In hot weather, your feet will sweat less in running shoes.

But in colder places, you should remember that good hiking boots, even when wet, will keep your feet warmer than running shoes.

GOOD TRAIL Hiking boots keep out scree, dirt, cactus needles, and grass seed. If you're hiking off-trail in running shoes, you'll find yourself stopping at annoying frequency to remove junk from your shoes. And on very rocky trails, the thinner soles of running shoes can make each step acutely painful.

EASY TRAIL If you're climbing on steep talus or have to rock-scramble, you need better traction than a running shoe can provide.

ROAD-WALKING Here's where running shoes are a great choice. Road-

BACKUP BOOTS

Because the evidence is overwhelming that you'll need two pairs of boots to complete a really long trail, it's a good idea to buy an extra pair *and break them in* before you go on a long hike. Two pairs of good-quality midweights (either fabric and leather or all leather) should survive a major trail. These days, I always have at least one backup pair of newish, broken-in boots sitting in a box at home so that I can have them sent to me if there's a blow-out on the trail.

When buying backup boots, consider that many hikers find that their feet get a little bigger on very long hikes (an average of $1/2$ to 1 size). This most often happens on a backpacker's first thru-hike. (Maybe there's a limit to how big a foot can get!) So buy your boots a touch on the roomy side. A good way to plan for a slightly expanding foot is to wear thick socks and cushy insoles when you try on boots. If your foot does expand a bit, you can trade the thick insoles for ones that take up less space in the boot.

walking on hard surfaces is brutal on the feet, especially the heels. The extra cushioning in the heels of running shoes helps absorb the impact of some of the extra weight backpackers carry. Some trails, like the American Discovery Trail, the North-country Trail, or the Ohio Trail, frequently follow bike paths and country roads; on those sections, seriously consider running shoes rather than hiking boots.

LIGHT PACK Human ankles are designed for walking, but they're not

WHEN THE BOOT BREAKS

The most common boot breakdown is when two boot parts formerly joined split asunder. Blown stitching is one example — maybe in the welting that joins boot to sole, or the stitching that joins fabric to leather — and an argument for buying boots with the fewest seams possible. Once the seams start to go, there isn't much you can do in the field. For a fraying seam, try covering the area with a seam sealant, which might give the stitches a last gasp of life, at least for a while. If the seam splits, you can try holding it together with trusty old duct tape.

Another example is delaminating soles: That's when the glue that holds the soles together gives out and the soles start peeling like banana skins. This is far more serious, because it can make walking dangerous if not, in severe cases, impossible. Delaminating boots can be held together with a urethane-based glue, although the conditions most hikers find themselves in prevent the proper application (and therefore, best results). The process is to wait until the boot is thoroughly dry, then sand the parts of the sole that need to be glued together. Apply an adhesive compound like barge cement or Shoo-goo. Using duct tape as a "clamp" tape the repair together and allow it to cure for 48 hours.

If you can't spend the time to do it right, the repair won't last. But a slipshod glue job might be better than nothing. Held together with a lot of duct tape (you'll need to reapply it about every 15 miles), your boots might survive to the nearest cobbler without your breaking your neck.

Finally, clean your boots regularly and apply a leather treatment to them. Most manufacturers include care advice with their boots, and you should follow it. Using some compounds on some leathers can actually cause damage and may void your warranty.

designed for walking under a 40-pound pack. If you're carrying a big pack on tricky, uneven terrain, you need the support of a stiffer boot. YOUR ANKLE STRENGTH Many hikers need the lateral support of a boot on rocky ground, especially under a heavy load. And some hikers are much more prone to ankle injury than others. I happen to be blessed with strong ankles — in all the years I've been backpacking, I've never strained or sprained one (knees, however, are another story) — so I find running shoes an appealing option. But I hesitate to recommend them to anyone who isn't sure of his or her ankles.

Finally, if you opt for running shoes, wear them with wicking sock liners and wool socks — not cotton running socks, which will absorb sweat and give you blisters. This means you'll need to buy running shoes about a half size to a size larger than usual.

Thru-hikers do not necessarily agree that internal-frame packs are superior. The byword: find the best fit for your body and needs.

PACKS
The success with which you marry your back to your pack is second only to the relationship between your boots and your feet as far as overall step-by-step comfort (or discomfort) is concerned. A pack that distributes its weight correctly can actually feel more like a hug than a load. But the opposite is painfully true. Trouble is, it's hard to tell in the store how a pack is going to feel

10 miles down the trail.

The first decision you'll have to make puts you smack in the middle of one of backpacking's longest-running debates: whether to choose an internal frame or an external frame. Get ready to take sides.

Conventional wisdom says that external frames are good for basic backpacking, and that internals are best for rock scrambling, off-trail, and winter use. But in the long-distance hiking community, there's fairly strong, although not unanimous, consensus in favor of internal-frame packs. In a 60-person survey among Appalachian Trail thru-hikers, I found that 50 hikers used internal-frame packs, and, of those, 32 packs were made by higher-end manufacturers: Dana, Gregory, Lowe, and Mountainsmith. One model stood out: The Dana Design Terraplane was used by 10 hikers in the survey. Of the external-frame packs, the Kelty Super-Tioga (a load-monster pack that works best on big backs) was the clear winner, with 4 users.

Among long-distance hikers, there were few complaints about packs. The most common pack problems (aside from a bad fit) were split

PACKING FOR TRAVEL

● Pack protection. An inexpensive duffel is the best way to protect your pack from those who would harm it. Buy one that's big enough for *everything*, including your hiking boots, air mattress, and a flat shipping box. Why the box? When you get where you're going, put the duffel and your street clothes into the shipping box and send them home. Or send them, food-drop style, to a post office at the end of your trip, so your pack can travel home in safety, too (and you can wear your old street clothes home on the plane and marvel at how much weight you've lost).

● Garbage bags. If you must go without a duffel, at least use a garbage bag — or several. Remove any straps and buckles that can be removed from the pack. Buckle and tighten everything else and wrap the whole thing in garbage bags with so much duct tape and rope that you'll swear at yourself when the time comes to remove it all.

● Wrap it in plastic. The change in air pressure in the baggage compartment of a plane causes liquids to expand. To prevent your mosquito repellent from exploding onto your peanut butter, put all liquids and semi-liquids into a sealed zipper-lock bag and secure the bag with a rubber band. The rubber band will help keep the package together even if the bag pops open.

● Luggage tags. Use them. Include a local contact (or the hotel you'll be staying in your first night) so that if your luggage is lost, it can be returned promptly. Also put a tag inside your pack somewhere.

● Locks. Small combination locks will deter theft — and you won't have to worry about losing the keys.

seams (especially at pressure points), broken hardware (mostly on external-frame packs), and the fact that after a few months on a hiking trail, some people had lost so much weight that their waist belts no longer fit! A few well-chosen fix-alls in your repair kit can save the day: heavy-duty needles and thread (wire is also a good idea), oversized safety pins with snaps that lock them in place, and backup hardware like clevis pins, split rings, belt buckle parts, and Fastex snaps.

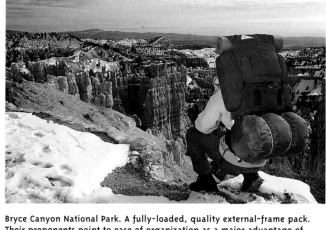

Bryce Canyon National Park. A fully-loaded, quality external-frame pack. Their proponents point to ease of organization as a major advantage of these many-pocketed packs.

What to Look for in a Pack

SIMPLICITY Like boots, the more seams, the more problems. The more things that can break, the more things that will break. If you've never been above treeline, do you really need an ice-ax loop or crampon guard? Have you ever used those leather thingamabobs to attach anything to your pack? And do you really want to be fussing with all of those straps in a snowstorm? Admittedly, some hikers are more enamored with gadgets and variations than others, but most distance hikers come down on the side of simplicity.

QUALITY Good padded areas in shoulders and waist belts are worth their weight in comfort. True, cushier pads and beefier belts weigh something, but it's weight that's working for you. Each ounce of padding and suspension can help a pound or two of clothing, tents, and food seem to disappear.

FIT The best-made pack in the world will add nothing to your trip but misery unless it fits well. It's difficult to measure and fit yourself, especially if your pack has an adjustable backstay (designed to be custom-bent to fit the curvature of your spine). If you live near a reputable outfitter, that's where you should buy — and fit — your pack. Many good packs come with exchangeable parts, so, for instance, if you've got a small waist and a long back, you can buy a small waist belt and a long pack frame.

SIZE Pack capacity is measured in

cubic inches. The manufacturer of my pack says it holds 5,800 cubic inches of stuff, and I have to admit that, so far, I've been content to take their word for it. The measurement is useful by way of comparison: If the zippers of said pack are groaning and threatening to burst open under the strain of 7 days of food and winter gear, I know that I need a pack that can hold more cubic inches (or socks, sweaters, and candy bars) for a more serious expedition.

I've found the 5,800-cubic-inch size perfect for three-season hiking. It's a little cramped if I'm going on a long trip in the dead of winter, when I carry a warmer (i.e., bigger) sleeping bag and more clothes,

accessories, and food. On a short summer hike, it has space for rent, so I sometimes take off the top "bonnet" (the lid where most people stow their rain gear and lunch) because I don't need all that room and can save a few ounces on weight.

Avoid getting a pack that's too big for the average load you carry. Packs are designed to ride best when they're full — and if you have extra space, be assured that there will always be a hiking partner around who has just one thing that doesn't fit right into his or her pack!

ORGANIZATION Some long-distance hikers stay loyal to their external-frame packs for one reason: ease of organization. External-frame packs

BEFORE YOU GO

● Give your gear one last once-over. Do you really need all that stuff? *All* of it?

● Check the condition of old gear: every single seam, every grommet, every zipper. If anything looks worn, send the gear back to the manufacturer and explain that you are planning a long-distance hike. Ask for a repair of the specific problem and a general "checkup" of your equipment.

● Make sure you've got all the little things:

tent stakes for your tent; the waist-belt buckle for your pack; shoelaces; all the parts of your stove.

● Think about fuel: You can't take it on planes, so you'll need to find some when you get where you're going.

● Make sure you've got the things that don't normally ride in your pack — like your hiking boots, hiking sticks, and the clothes you walk in.

● Check the bat-teries in any bat-tery-powered equip-ment.

have lots of pockets, and many of
them have a U-shaped zipper that
allows you to open the main compartment and get at any piece of gear
easily. In contrast, the basic internal-
frame pack is constructed according
to the stuff-it-in-a-duffel theory: The
bulk of your cargo goes in one big
compartment, so you need to pack
carefully in order to have access to
things you'll need during the day.
This design prejudice reflects the ori-
gins of internal-frame packs, which
hail from the world of mountaineering
and rock climbing, where you want to
stow all of your stuff inside (so it
won't be in the way, get snowed on, or
get torn off when you shimmy up a
rock) and where you need the pack to
ride as close to your center of gravity
as possible. Some internal frames do
have sewn-in pockets. (Mine has two
pockets running lengthwise down the
back, a top compartment, a panel
that can be used to separate the
sleeping bag from the rest of my gear,
and an optional front pocket where I
carry daily accessories and water.
That's plenty of organization for me.)
Other pack makers sell add-on
pouches that can be attached to the
main body of the internal-frame
pack. These tend to wiggle around a
little, but they do provide those cov-
eted compartments. For some hikers,
these modifications aren't enough, so
they hoist up their trusty old exter-
nals and hike on, more organized
than the rest of us, but perhaps not
quite as comfortable.

The author has long favored down-filled bags, but
recent improvements in the loft and compress-
ibility of synthetic fibers along with their ability to
shed moisture are forcing a re-evaluation.

SLEEPING BAGS

Possibly more
than any other
piece of equipment,
the sleeping bag that
works for you is going
to depend on the kind of
trail you're hiking and the
season you're hiking in. On
a long-distance hike, you
could be hiking through all
four seasons. On my
Appalachian Trail thru-hike, for
example, nighttime temperatures
ranged by as much as 80 degrees.
Needless to say, no single bag can be
comfortable in that wide a range, and

many hikers on mega-trails end up using various combinations of bags, liners, and bivvy sacks.

The major considerations in choosing a bag are temperature rating, whether the fill is down or synthetic, and (for a down bag) loft. A secondary concern is the shell fabric. Provided that the bag is well-made with, for instance, sturdy zippers, draft tubes, and convenient hood closures, other factors (like whether you buy a close-fitting mummy bag or a looser modified mummy) are largely matters of preference.

Temperature Ratings

Many hikers consider temperature ratings a piece of advertising fiction, and I have to admit I count myself in this category. Or maybe I'm just a cold sleeper. What I know for a fact is that even with clothes on, I can't sleep comfortably without a tent in my 20-degree bag when it's honest-to-God 20 degrees out there. Other people are different. Dan gets much colder than I do when we stop walking during the day, but he sleeps warmer and sheds clothes as soon as he zips up for the night.

Compounding the confusion is the fact that each manufacturer's measurements for temperature ratings are a little different. There is, however, consistency between different

SLEEPING COMFORT

◉ In hot weather, sleep inside a lightweight silk or nylon bag liner.
◉ In cold weather, add a vapor-barrier liner. VBLs don't let sweat escape, so they keep body heat in. By keeping your sweat away from the down, the bag doesn't get soggy over time. Using a VBL also helps prevent condensation from collecting (and freezing) on the tent walls and snowing on you in the morning.
◉ Use a bivvy sack. (For extra-cold weather only; condensation can be a problem.)
◉ In warm weather, use a light-weight fleece blanket instead of a sleeping bag. (Budget-conscious hikers can make their own: Just buy some polyester fleece and sew two seams to make a sack. Cost: about $15)
◉ If you don't have a winter bag, use two lightweight bags together for colder weather. (Note: this works best if one of them is a looser rectangular shape and the other is a tighter mummy.)
◉ Before using a down bag, always shake it out to fluff up the down and let it expand to its maximum loft. More loft means more warmth.

models made by the same manufacturer. In other words, a Northface 10-degree bag is going to be warmer than a Northface 20-degree bag. But it may or may not be warmer than a Feathered Friends 20-degree bag. Manufacturers — at least those who make high-end gear — are trying to standardize their temperature ratings using scientific measurements on a naked mannequin, but even when they figure out the protocol, you're still going to have to factor in how your body responds to cold. It's unreasonable to expect a temperature rating to account for the fact that when my husband and I are asleep in the cold, I need a warmer bag.

This is the category where the kinds of field tests performed by some of the major outdoor magazines can be most helpful, because field tests compare various pieces of equipment under similar conditions. A few companies that consistently test well include The Northface, Marmot, Moonstone (specializing in synthetic bags) and Feathered Friends. In addition, EMS and REI both make affordable quality bags.

If you want one bag to work in a multitude of three-season back-country conditions, the best choice is probably a 20-degree bag. The bags I own have comfort ratings ranging from -30 to +40 degrees, but the

GEAR TALK

THRU-HIKERS' CHOICE

In addition to the "big five," here are a few items that pop up consistently in the packs of thru-hikers:

● Headlamps: Petzl is the brand favored for serious winter use because of its extra-hardy battery and ease of use. The mountaineering model is on the heavy side but a scaled down version is available, too. Three-season hikers more typically carry lightweight Mini-Maglite flashlights or small headlamps made by REI. A headlamp means that both hands are free — a real advantage if you're cooking in the dark. You can buy a headband that turns your Maglite into a headlamp.

● Sport sandals: Teva is the most popular brand. Not only are they comfortable in camp, you can also wear them in town, or use them for river crossings. Some hikers opt for cheap imitations because they're lighter, but I like the Tevas because I've actually had to use them as emergency footwear when my boots blew out. If the Velcro closures start to stop sticking, you can hold the straps in place with rubber O-rings from your local hardware store.

continued on page 84

● Air mattresses: Therm-a-rest is the most popular brand. Thru-hikers lose body fat on a long hike, and they appreciate having the comfy padding of an air mattress between their protruding bones and the hard ground. Bring a repair kit, because they can puncture — although not as easily as you might fear.

● Water filters: Too much fuss and bother and frequent breakdowns make water filters easy winners in the category of "most vilified equipment." Many thru-hikers get rid of their filters, choosing to use iodine instead or take their chances with *giardia* (the preeminent bugaboo of backcountry water, *Giardia lamblia* is a protozoan parasite that wreaks havoc in human intestines). Unfortunately, *giardia* often bites back. Among hikers who do use filters, the PUR Hiker gets *by far* the highest marks for low weight, speed, and trouble-free long-term use.

● Socks: Thorlo field-tested its socks on the AT before bringing them to

20-degree bags are the ones most often trotted out — although if I truly expect 20-degree temperatures, not to mention colder, I take a heftier bag.

Down versus Synthetic

I used to think there was a right answer to this question, and the sleeping bags lying spread out in my attic tell the story: For years, all of the sleeping bags residing up there were made of down.

But lately, a synthetic bag has joined my feathered friends. The reason: I do lots of hiking in the rainy East, and synthetic bags are less vulnerable to a dousing. My survey of Appalachian Trail thru-hikers confirmed that synthetic bags

are the rule rather than the exception in the East. In the West, the opposite seems to be true.

With increasingly sophisticated technology, the gap (formerly wide) between down and synthetics has narrowed considerably. Down is still a little warmer per ounce, it's more compressible (that means it takes up less room in your pack), and with good care it retains its loft longer than synthetics. Synthetics are less expensive and do better in wet weather.

SHELL FABRIC Windproof, water-resistant fabrics can add extra protection against both the elements and inadvertent spills. On the weatherproof front, Dryloft (a W. W. Gore market. Cushioned in all the right places, Thorlo socks have just the right balance of wool for warmth and synthetics for strength. I would have never believed it, but I learned in the field that I can tell the difference. That is, if you blindfolded me and put a pair of regular Ragg wool socks on one of my feet and Thorlos on the other, I could tell you which was which after a couple of miles on the trail.

● Water bags: The MSR Dromedary is made of tough fabric that resists punctures, and the valve shuts reliably tight, making it easier to haul water from stream to camp — no matter how far away — without dribbling. They come in several sizes. For camp chores, the 4-quart size is most convenient.

● Walking sticks: Not everyone uses one, and even fewer hikers use two, but two-stick hikers (like me) are fanatically evangelistic on the subject of how much a pair of sticks helps with knees and balance. Leki's Super Makalus are telescoping, adjustable, and have nifty little springs that help absorb shock.

product) has supplanted Gore-Tex as a sleeping bag cover. It's not as waterproof, but it's more breathable, which is usually more important in a sleeping bag. Microfibers are tightly woven shells that offer some weather protection. Nylon and polyester taffeta are smooth and pleasant to the touch (important in something you'll be sleeping in). Ripstop nylon is more durable. Whatever your selection, look for a close weave: It's more weather resistant and it prevents down from poking through and making you look like you've slept in a chicken coop come morning.

TENTS

Hikers recognize that the less gear they carry, the happier they'll be on the trail. But the flip side of that is also true: The more gear they carry, the more comfortable they'll be in camp. Who would argue that on a blackfly-infested, mosquito-clouded snowmelt day in the northcountry, you'd be living in luxury if you had one of those house-sized tents in which four people can strike up a game of cards?

Still, no matter how many what-ifs you put into the equation, long-distance hikers still come to the same conclusion: Most are willing to risk the possible discomfort of a few nights stuck in a small shelter in order to avoid the certain discomfort of a too-heavy pack. This is especially true on the AT, where hikers often sleep in lean-tos, or on the

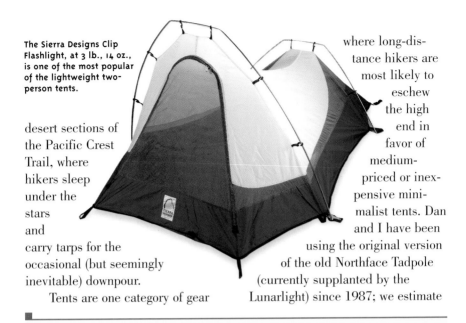

The Sierra Designs Clip Flashlight, at 3 lb., 14 oz., is one of the most popular of the lightweight two-person tents.

desert sections of the Pacific Crest Trail, where hikers sleep under the stars and carry tarps for the occasional (but seemingly inevitable) downpour.

where long-distance hikers are most likely to eschew the high end in favor of medium-priced or inexpensive minimalist tents. Dan and I have been using the original version of the old Northface Tadpole (currently supplanted by the Lunarlight) since 1987; we estimate

Tents are one category of gear

GEAR TALK
REPAIR KIT

Long distance hiking is rough on gear, and you can be guaranteed that somewhere, something is going to break. Trouble is, you can't predict where or when. Nor do you want to be hauling around a tool-shop. But a well-chosen repair kit can keep you going even when your boots delaminate, your pack frame cracks, and your stove starts coughing and spitting like a tuberculosis patient. Here's what's usually in mine.

Needles (several sizes). Thread (several weights including some I can't break with my bare hands). Wire and dental floss (be sure you have a strong enough needle with a big enough eye). Thimble. Safety pins. Duct tape (several yards wrapped around a spare pen). Tape-on strips of Velcro. Small pliers. Parachute cord. Glue (A urethane-based glue like Shoo-goo or Free-sole, or barge cement). Tweezers. Zipper headers and sliders. Adhesive patches and rip-stop tape. Spare stuff (cordlocks, buckles, buttons, shoelaces, batteries, flashlight bulb, clevis pins). Stove parts (including cleaning tools, O-rings, and instructions). Alcohol swabs (for cleaning gear before you repair it with adhesives). Hose clamps (for splinting things like tent poles and pack frames). Cigarette lighter. Pole sleeve for tent. Army knife with scissors.

that we have slept in it, singly or together, at least 1,000 times. In 1993, we bought another one, exactly the same model, at a close-out sale for $150, figuring that the old tent would wear out sooner or later. But it hasn't: Last summer on a hike in the Pyrenees (which are renowned for their fierce storms), it gave us secure and cozy shelter in some of the most impressive thunder and lightning and torrential rain I've ever tried to sleep through. This year, we're finally giving it an honorable retirement to weekend duty — but I expect it'll be around for several more seasons. In all that time, the total damage the tent has sustained includes 1 inch of split seam, one tiny tear in the tent fabric, one door zipper that needed to be replaced, and one pole that snapped. More expensive tents are available, but with performance like that, I can't think of a reason to spend more money.

Our experience seems typical on long trails, where two kinds of tents

The best shelter doesn't always mean an expensive tent. The simple tarp can be the best answer, provided you learn to use one (see page 88).

dominate: the two-pole tunnel design (such as the Sierra Designs Clip Flashlight) and the three-pole wedge design (like the Northface Tadpole; the design has since been copied by a number of manufacturers). With

(see page 88).

GEAR TALK

TENT TIPS

To get a little more room for the weight, select a tent whose inside is largely made up of mosquito netting. (A good option for warm-weather hikes. But note: These tents don't hold in as much body heat in the cold and they're useless in snow.)

Three-pole wedge tents like the Northface Lunarlight can be erected with just the rain fly and the poles. You save the weight of the tent body, but you lose bug protection.

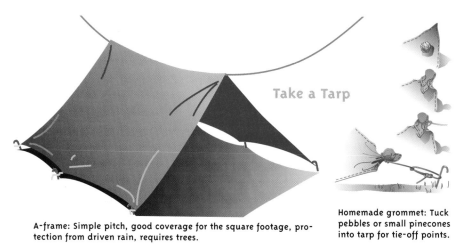

Take a Tarp

Homemade grommet: Tuck pebbles or small pinecones into tarp for tie-off points.

A-frame: Simple pitch, good coverage for the square footage, protection from driven rain, requires trees.

Modified lean-to: Good if wind direction is predictable, protection from damp ground, requires trees.

Peaked canopy: Good ventilation, protection from rain falling straight, can't handle high wind, requires trees.

Lean-to: Simple pitch, if near fire captures radiant heat, good coverage for the square footage, requires trees.

Modified A-frame: Uses sticks (or hiking sticks) for support when no trees are available.

two poles instead of three, the Clip Flashlight wins in the weight department (3 pounds, 14 ounces as compared to an average of about $4^{1}/_{2}$–5 pounds for the wedges). The wedge design is more stable in high winds and has the additional and not insignificant advantage of being free-standing. Two other manufacturers frequently seen on long trails are Eureka and Walrus.

These minimalist tents are also light enough to work for solo hikers who don't want a tarp or a modified bivvy sack. (The one-person bivvy tents on the market are prone to condensation and many of them don't offer enough headroom to eat indoors in rainy weather.)

It is worth noting that the major complaint hikers have about their tents is that they are "too small." (And the few hikers who choose bigger, roomier tents complain that they are "too heavy.") This is one of those wanting to "have your cake and eat it too" situations. Unfortunately, there's no such thing as a palatial tent that weighs 4 pounds; for that, we'll have to wait for the next wave of high-tech materials. Many of the ultra-light two-person tents are suitable only for two people who are of small stature and like each other a lot. Larger people, or people who don't want to roll over and find their face in their hiking partner's armpit, will definitely want to consider a slightly bigger (i.e., heavier) tent.

offer great air circulation in hot weather, and for the weight of one piece of gear you get shelter against both rain and sun (you'll appreciate the latter if you're traveling in a desert).

Tarps

They're light, cheap, versatile, and durable. So why don't more people use tarps? Possibly because they require a little practice to "get it right."

There is one major trick to being happy under a tarp: Learn a few different ways to put it up before you find yourself in hairy conditions.

There are several things that tarps won't do: They don't trap in warmth like tents do. They won't shelter you from bugs. And if you don't pitch them just right, they can let wind-driven rain inside. But they

STOVES

Most hikers today carry stoves if they expect to be eating hot meals. The reason: Stoves are easier than fires — on both the environment and the hiker.

You don't have to look far in a popular campground to see leftover fire rings — sometimes hundreds of them — many of which contain half-burnt tinfoil and goopy globs of garbage. In fragile alpine and desert areas, campfire scars can last for years. And in dry, windy places, forest fires can be the tragic result of a tiny little unattended campfire.

STOVE TYPES

LIQUID FUEL
(e.g., MSR Whisperlite International; MSR XGK- II; Peak I Apex II; Optimus, all models)
● Routine maintenance makes these stoves more efficient. Keep the leather pump cup oiled. Check the gaskets. Run the fuel through a filter before using it. If you're using MSR's self-cleaning shaker-

jet stoves, give them a quick shake before each use.
● In countries where white gas isn't available, look for dry-cleaning fluid.
● On multi-fuel models, check to see if you need to change parts before you change fuels (most commonly required for kerosene). Lighting kerosene is difficult, so

continued on page 90

continued from page 89

add a couple of drops of alcohol from your first aid kit to the priming cup.

● These are by far the most popular stoves on American trails and on high-mountain expeditions.

CANISTERS

(e.g., Camping Gaz; Peak I X-pedition; Primus, all models)

● Canisters are readily available in all kinds of stores near recreation areas.

● Compressed fuel is the most popular and most available fuel in some European countries.

● You can ship fuel canisters to yourself in your food drops if you specify that the package be shipped by ground (not air).

● These stoves don't work well in very cold temperatures.

● They are easiest to operate because you just turn them on and light the match.

● If you're stuck in the deep freeze, sleep with the fuel canister or use your body heat to warm it up before lighting.

● Pack out the empty canisters.

WOOD-BURNING STOVES

(e.g., Zzip Sierra Stove)

● You don't have to buy fuel — you just have to collect it.

● Above treeline or after several days of wet weather, dry fuel can be a problem.

● Keep a zipper-lock bag full of dry tinder. Once you get the tinder going, even wet wood will burn.

● Take out the batteries so they don't accidentally turn on when the stove is packed away.

● In strictly regulated no-fire zones, these stoves may be illegal because there is a risk that careless disposal of burning embers from the stove could cause a wildfire.

● The lightest choice: 1 pound for the stove and no fuel to haul around.

But there's another reason to use stoves: They're just plain more convenient. No hunting for wood. No trying to keep a match lit in a strong wind. No fussing over a wet-wood fire that won't quite

A climber bivouacs high above Palisade Glacier on Temple Crag in the Sierra Nevada, California. Among mountaineers, stoves must be as reliable as they are lightweight and compact.

burn. No dropping your mac and cheese into the fire when a supporting log crashes into the coals.

The type of stove you choose should depend on the kind of fuel you expect to be using and the season you'll be hiking in. Basically, you've got three choices. Refillable liquid-fuel stoves run on white gas and sometimes on other liquid fuels

such as kerosene, unleaded gasoline, and occasionally alcohol. Canister stoves use canisters of compressed gas (usually a combination of propane and butane), which are often available at convenience stores and campgrounds near recreation areas. And finally, there are wood-burning stoves, which use a battery to aerate a small container in which you put tiny pieces of wood — or

In a survey of 60 Appalachian Trail thru-hikers, 40 used the MSR Whisperlite stove (left), a liquid fuel model. Canister-fueled models like the two-burner Coleman (opposite) are also popular.

● THE ESSENTIAL OUTDOOR GEAR MANUAL, by Annie Getchell *(Ragged Mountain Press)* This useful volume tells you how to get the most out of your gear. Care and repair can extend the life of virtually any outdoor equipment, and a few simple tricks can make the difference between a repair that falls apart and a repair that lasts.

anything else that is burnable.

In the back-of-beyond, your biggest stove problem is likely to be finding fuel. In the United States, liquid-fuel stoves that can operate on a variety of different fuels are probably the most versatile — especially if the stove will take unleaded automobile gasoline. (Warning: auto gas burns hot, but it's not recommended for long-term use because it's a "dirty" fuel that will cause gumming up over time.)

RAIN

I t is said that the Inuit people of the Arctic have a whole vocabulary of words that describe different kinds of snow. Hikers ought to do the same for rain.

We ought to have words for cooling summer showers, and for those swollen splatting raindrops that explode just before a thunderstorm. We ought to have a word for needle-like shards that prick at your eyes, and a word for the kind of drenching downpour that makes you think you're going through the rinse cycle at your local car wash. We ought to have a word for an all-day drizzle that can't seem to make up its misty mind. And we ought to have a word

for when the rain falls sideways.

Rain is something most hikers quite sensibly try to avoid. If the weather forecast promises down-pours, you might postpone your weekend trip, no matter how much you've looked forward to it. On a long hike, however, you may not have a choice. "No rain, no pain, no Maine," Appalachian Trail thru-hikers chant as they march northward under soggy spring skies.

Is it even possible to enjoy hiking under those kinds of circum-stances? Indeed it is. Look on the positive side: You're not likely to overheat. The mosquitoes back off. Rains replenish springs. A mist-

The author and her husband, Dan, on Moss Pond along the Appalachian Trail in New Hampshire. Rain can be trying, but it also brings its simplifying beauty to the landscape. The right raingear will allow you to enjoy same.

to walk in the rain and remain both warm and dry. Sure, there's Gore-Tex: Designed to keep the rain out while letting your sweat escape, Gore-Tex comes to the hiker's wardrobe with high prices and high expectations. "Guaranteed to keep you dry" is what the ads say, nothing less. But Gore-Tex, while an immense improvement over the coated nylon that it

shrouded forest is pretty to look at.

While a positive attitude might get you through a shower or three, it starts wearing thin after, say, a water-logged week. Some skills and gear can help.

Rain Gear

Some hikers declare it can't be done — that it is, quite simply, impossible

replaced, isn't infallible. If you're working hard, it's par for the course to generate far more sweat than can pass through the pores at once.

Roland Mueser (see page 72 for more information on his survey of 136 Appalachian Trail hikers) concluded, "If you don't climb the mountain too fast and the jacket is new and loose and the storm does not last more than an hour or so and it does not rain too hard, you will do just fine" in a Gore-Tex rain suit — a far cry from "guaranteed to keep you dry." But he also concluded that Gore-Tex was the overwhelming rain gear of choice. Other products — various coatings and laminates, many of them proprietary to different companies — exist, but until recently few of them offered the same level of waterproof breathability that Gore-Tex achieves.

The typical foul weather outfit is rain pants and a rain jacket. Often, you'll find that rain pants are unnecessary because they hold in so much heat that they become too warm to walk in. In cold weather, some hikers prefer to wear long johns made of a wicking fabric like polypropylene, which keeps you warm even when it's wet. Some hikers find polypro more comfortable in those in-between cases where it's a little too cold for bare legs and a little too warm for Gore-Tex. This is certainly something to experiment with. The problem, however, is that if you intend to use polypro to walk in the rain, you need to pack along another pair of long johns for when you get into camp, so you don't save much weight by using polypro instead of rain pants. Another issue is wind resistance: Gore-Tex blocks the

WHAT TO LOOK FOR IN RAIN GEAR

A Gore-Tex rain suit (jacket and pants) can set you back anywhere from $200 to more than $500. If you're going to drop a few C-notes on rain gear, you want to be sure you're getting your money's worth. Here's what to look for:

● What makes it waterproof and breathable? Sometimes, so-called waterproof/breathable products are nothing more than a coated nylon jacket made "breathable" by adding such elements as back vents. Don't be fooled! This is not the same as Gore-Tex, which is a waterproof /breathable membrane that is bonded to the fabric. In addition to Gore-Tex, there are proprietary waterproof/breathable laminates produced by individual manufacturers. Take into consideration the reputation of the company if you're trying to evaluate a new product you haven't heard of before. (If a company like Marmot, which makes high-quality rain gear, says that its proprietary laminate is waterproof and breathable, I'll take their word for it. But if some no-name company is making the same claim, and the gear is priced so low that it seems too good to be true, I'll take a pass.) If

continued on page 96

WHAT TO LOOK FOR IN RAIN GEAR
continued from page 95

you want to know more about a product, call the manufacturer and ask if it's been reviewed in any of the major outdoor magazines.

● Simplicity of design. High-tech rain gear has, for some reason I can't quite wrap my mind around, become trendy fashion apparel on inner-city streets, giving a whole new meaning to the term "city slickers." And it's led to some startling colors and designs. As with other backpacking gear, too many gizmos and seams most often lead to problems (tears and leakage). It's better for the backpacker to choose an unfashionably bland jacket made out of as few pieces of fabric as possible than to succumb to the allure of a Joseph's dreamcoat made up of many different colors stitched together.

● Three-ply fabric. Gore-Tex isn't really a fabric; it's a membrane bonded to a fabric. Two-ply Gore-Tex consists of two layers: the outer fabric and the inner membrane. This construction requires another layer of something to go between the inner laminate and your skin, usually a lightweight liner that in my experience acts as a condensation trap — you start feeling wet the minute you work up a sweat. Three-ply fabric is a Gore-Tex sandwich: The laminate is safely ensconced between two other layers, and there's no need for that extra liner.

● Adequate length. The bottom of the jacket should cover your derriere. Extra-long sleeves allow you to pull the sleeves over your hands when your fingers turn to ice in a heavy cold rain. If the sleeves are long, be sure they have a cuff closure so they don't drive you crazy the rest of the time.

● No extra insulation. Remember

wind, polypro doesn't. And finally, there's convenience: As long as your rain pants have some sort of calf-high zipper, you can take them on and off over your hiking boots as conditions change during the day. For all alpine hiking, and anywhere else where you can reasonably predict hypothermic conditions (a combination of rain, wind, and temperatures below 50

degrees), you should have rain pants, no question about it. But in temperate summer conditions, especially below treeline, you can experiment with saving the weight and leaving the rain pants behind.

One other choice is worth mentioning. A minority of hikers prefer ponchos, some in conjunction with a lightweight windproof and water-the law of layering: Never use one item where two will do. An insulated rain jacket is only useful in the most frigid temperatures, and even then, it's not as versatile as the combination of a non-insulated jacket and a pile jacket or wool sweater.

● A comfortable, loose fit: You want to be able to fit the jacket over a couple of layers of clothing. A loose fit also helps with ventilation.

● Where the pockets are. High pockets mean that you'll be able to unzip them and get at your snacks and gloves without undoing your pack's hip belt.

● How comfortable is the hood with a pack on? This is a picky little issue, but a good fit means comfort. Try the rain gear on in the store with a pack and see how it moves once you're all strapped in.

● Ventilation. When you're working hard, you might work up more sweat than can pass through

the laminate. Design features like "pit-zips" under your arms help you stay more comfortable.

● Zipper length on pants. You need to be able to take your rain pants on and off with a minimum of fuss. Calf-high zippers will go over hiking boots (barely) but not over crampons. If you're heading to ice country, get full-length zips.

● Storm flaps. These protect zippers and other openings from wind, rain, and snow.

● Best deal for the budget conscious: Campmor's Vagabond II three-ply Gore-Tex rain pants and rain jacket. They're not pretty, and as far as features go, there are none. But I know several hikers who have gone many thousands of miles using this rain gear in extreme conditions. Total cost of the set is less than $200.

resistant jacket. Ponchos offer great ventilation, are cheap, can be used as an emergency shelter, and can protect your pack as well as yourself. But they have liabilities: In a strong wind, they'll flap around uncontrollably (solution: tie a rope around your waist) and they won't keep you warm (then again, they won't make you overheat). The lowdown: Check them

out for use on temperate below-tree-line trails in warm weather.

Rain Accessories

A few other items can help keep you and your gear dry on a rainy day. Regardless of any claims to the contrary, your pack is not waterproof, so you need a pack cover. My choice is the simplest model available, which

are fabric coverings for your shins that fit over your boots and keep the water out. They come in two heights: ankle-high (for three-season use) and knee-high (better for winter). They also keep other junk — pebbles, sand,

Walking (not singing) in the rain. On such days, take frequent short breaks to snack and drink; long lunches are fair-weather treats.

is a piece of waterproof nylon held to the pack by an elastic (or drawstring) cord. The reason: When the rain starts, I want a pack cover I can put on in 10 seconds, max. The Appalachian Trail Conference sells an innovative model that is reversible: The back side is international orange for protection during hunting season. Note: Pack covers aren't 100 percent effective — there's always some water that sneaks in somehow — but the combination of a pack cover with waterproof stuff sacks is extremely reliable.

OR (Outdoor Research) is a company that specializes in well-designed accessories for extreme weather. If you're heading out to predictably soggy climes, OR's "Seattle Sombrero" rain hat can increase your comfort about a thousand percent by keeping the rain out of your face and hair while allowing your neck to ventilate. Gaiters

scree, burrs, and cactus thorns — out of your boots and offer some protection against poison ivy, rattlesnakes, and ticks. Gore-Tex overmitts are a lightweight way to keep your hands warm: They can be worn alone or in combination with glove liners or mittens.

Packing for Rain

Deal with rain with a preemptive strike: Pack defensively. This means developing a system. Even a minor effort at organization will make it easier to find things when you really need them: in the dark, in an emergency, or when quickness counts — like when you're putting up a tent in a downpour.

Pack for convenience. Keep your pack cover where you can get at it fast — like in the top compartment of your pack — and your tent somewhere where you won't have to unpack every single thing in your pack to get at it when the time comes to make camp and at that exact second, the heavens open. Ditto for clothing: You should be able to get to at least some of your warm clothes in the flick of an eye if the weather suddenly shifts or at the end of the day, when you stop walking and start losing body heat.

Snacks and water are two other items that you need to have available. A pouch that rides on the front of your pack is the best place; that way you'll be able to eat and drink without taking off your pack and standing around in the cold.

Finally, protect everything with waterproof sacks (your warm clothes and your sleeping bag, especially), garbage bags (you can find a dozen uses for them), and plastic zipper-lock bags (for small items like food, first aid supplies, a camera, a journal, maps and guidebooks, matches and firestarter).

Walking in the Rain

Here's the goal: a comfortable steady pace that you can sustain without freezing or overheating.

In warm weather, you might not mind a gentle, cooling rain. But remember that temperatures can drop precipitously when the rain starts. What feels like cooling relief can quickly make you shiver. Unless you've been walking in a steamy summer heat wave, it's better to put your rain gear on when the rain starts, rather than waiting until later

when you're soaked and shivering.

In average summer temperatures just about anywhere below treeline, a jacket will more than do the trick, but above treeline, you're more exposed. If the temperature drops, it's time to put on more layers, the sooner the better. Don't try to tough it out. Find a sheltering rock to break the wind and add more clothes: rain pants, a light insulating layer, and a hood or a hat. (Use a baseball hat or a visor if you wear glasses: It'll keep you from wishing you had windshield wipers.)

Take time to eat and drink, even in the rain. If your hiking day usually includes long lunch breaks, you're going to need to change your strategy. Long lunches are fair-weather pleasures. Instead, proceed through the day by seizing every opportunity to stop and snack. If there's a grove of trees, stop and snack. If there's a temporary lull in the storm, use it to put some more calories into your system. (Now's a real good time for that Snickers bar and a handful of the GORP you've been saving for an energy boost.) Keep eating, especially when you're cold: You're burning off lots of energy, and constantly refueling will help both physically and emotionally. Also, remember to drink. With all that cold water coming down on you, you might not feel like putting any inside, but it's important to stay hydrated: Drinking enough helps prevent both hypothermia and altitude sickness.

In addition to your layering

Layering is key to comfort, because once you're damp it doesn't take very cold temperatures or much wind for you to become chilly and vulnerable to hypothermia. Your pack also must be protected.

system and outer waterproof shell, try the following warm-ups:

Rain pants do a good job of keeping rain out of your boots. If it's too warm to wear your rain pants, use gaiters. Either way, don't expect miracles: In a car-wash downpour, your feet will still get wet — but not as wet, and not as fast.

If your hands are freezing cold, cover them with a big zipper-lock bag held in place with a loose rubber band around your wrist. If they're still cold, sandwich a pair of socks between bag and skin.

Constantly fiddle with all those armpit vents, zippers, wrist closures, and adjustments to fine-tune your comfort.

After the rain stops, leave on your rain gear. The wind that blows out the storm is guaranteed to create an "after-rain," in which all those raindrops stuck in the trees get blown down on you. At foot level, the grasses will be wet for hours. I once survived hours of rain with dry feet, only to take my rain pants off and get soaked within minutes by wet vegetation that overhung the trail.

Don't hesitate to stop and make camp if conditions are miserable. Hypothermia is far more easily prevented than it is treated.

Rainy-Day Campsites

First things first: You need to choose a home for the night. Look for protection from wind and rain. A grove of trees is ideal, but a big rock or a bush can act as an effective wind-break, too. Check out the slope and the drainage: You want your tentsite to be a little higher than the surrounding ground. Even a couple of inches will help.

Once you've chosen a site, the real work begins: getting your tent up and your gear inside and keeping everything dry. Once it's time to make camp, all of that gear that has been riding snug and dry in your pack all day has the potential to come tumbling out. And all the while, you have to be thinking about maintaining your body heat, because when you stop walking in cold wet weather, you stop working up heat.

If you were organized when you packed, now is when you reap the benefits. Your warm clothes are in a handy place. Put them on, before you lose more body heat. Your tent is where you can get at it without exposing everything else to the rain. Take it out and pitch it, with its back to the wind, of course.

Use your pack cover (or a poncho, a groundcloth, or a tarp) to cover your gear while you're setting up camp. Once the tent is pitched, you can bring your pack inside the vestibule (if your tent has one). If you don't have a vestibule, you'll need to be sure to keep soaking wet gear like your rain jacket, pack cover, and rain pants separated from dry gear (like your sleeping bag and your warm clothes). If you've got spare garbage bags, use them to separate wet gear from dry

Pitch your tent on slightly higher ground for better drainage. And, unlike this hiker, remove wet raingear before hunkering down inside.

gear. Until you're ready to crawl into your sleeping bag, it's a good idea to leave it in its waterproof sack.

It's not good enough to just throw up the tent. You need to make your shelter tight as a drum. Stake out your tent even if it is freestanding. (Guy lines anchor the tent more securely, and a taut tent fly will shed water better than a loose one.) And make sure your ground cloth is folded, stuffed, or otherwise tucked under the edges of your tent. If it sticks out, it will collect and channel water underneath the tent floor.

Once your tent is up and your gear is protected, you can crawl in and thumb your nose at the storm.

Fending off the cold and rain. To safely cook and remain dry, use your tent's vestibule.

Take off your soaking-wet rain gear before getting in your tent and shove it in a corner of the vestibule.

Finally, if you've got a tent with some headroom, hang a clothesline: Your body heat will help damp gear to dry.

GEAR TALK

STARTING A RAINY-DAY FIRE

● Collect enough dry or dryish wood for the size fire you want before you start building the fire. Even in wet weather, there's usually a lot of dry wood around. Look in tree hollows, under rock ledges, or under bushes. Standing deadwood (or a fallen log with branches and twigs sticking out) is especially good because the wood doesn't lie on wet ground. Look also inside old stumps for dry chunks you can rip out. If a twig or stick feels wet, break it in half to see if it snaps; if it breaks with a nice firm crack, it's dry inside and will eventually burn.

● Use a firestarter. If you didn't bring any, try pine needles, birch bark, little pieces of standing deadwood, used-up pages of your guidebooks, lint from your pockets, or a candle stub. You can make dry wood by whittling a stick with your army knife.

● Once your fire is going, pile damp wood around it so it can dry out before you need to put it on the fire.

Cooking in the Rain

Once you've got your camp battened down and you've changed into warm, dry camp clothes, your thoughts will probably turn to dinner. You might want to wait out the storm for a while: Even the fiercest storm usually eases up every once in a while.

If it looks like the rain will never, ever stop, choose the easiest meal in your pack. Do your prep work — cutting, mixing, and soaking, or (in my case) tearing open the just-add-water container of freeze-dried food I carry just for this kind of weather — in the tent, before you turn on the stove. This will save fuel, keep your ingredients from getting wet and mushy, and minimize the time you spend outside.

Do not bring the stove into the tent. Dangers of cooking indoors include asphyxiation, burns, and setting your tent on fire. The priming process is especially dangerous. You can, however, stay in your tent, scoot up near the door, and reach outside to cook. Prime the stove as far away from the tent as you can reach without getting soaked. Once the stove is harmlessly chugging along, you can pull it into the vestibule — but leave the door open.

It's worth noting that if you're using one of those ultra-light, ultra-small two-person tents, and you have two people plus gear inside, cooking from inside the tent is a major exercise in patience and cooperation. There just isn't enough room for there to be any good way to do this. So if you anticipate hiking in lots of rainy

SEAM-SEALING

The stitching that joins two pieces of fabric together forms a seam. It also forms tiny little holes that are

more than big enough to let in droplets of water. Over time, the smallest seam can let in so much water that you can actually find yourself sleeping in a puddle!

That's why, when you buy a tent, you'll usually also get a seam-sealing compound, which needs to be applied to every single seam on the tent fly and to the bottom seams of the tent body. You might be tempted to skip this process. Don't! As persnickety as it

continued on page 104

SEAM-SEALING
continued from page 103

sounds, it can make the difference between a wet night and dry night.

Seal from the inside (put the tent fly on upside down and seal the inside of each seam). Two thin coats are better than one thick coat. On the rain fly, all seams get treated, including those around the company logo and the grommets. On the non-waterproof main body of the tent, you only need to seam-seal the tent bottom and the "bathtub" — the area that extends up about 8 inches from the floor.

Do the work outside on a nice day. The fumes from the compound are vile, and the sealant needs to dry. If you intend to immediately pack away the tent, dust some cornstarch on the seams before you stash it in its stuff sack to prevent the compound from sticking to other parts of the tent.

weather, you might want to consider the considerable weight of a more commodious tent. If you know how to put it up (see page 88), a tarp gives you more floor space for the weight than a tent. Another option is to take a minimalistic tent and a tarp. In horrendous conditions, use the tarp both as a gear shelter while you're making camp and as a protected kitchen. It's easier to cook under a tarp than from a prone position inside your tent.

The Next Morning

If it's bright and sunny, take your time in the morning and give your tent (and any other casualties of the deluge) a chance to dry off. Before starting out, strap anything wet to your pack — who cares if you look like a walking clothesline? — and let them dry during the day.

If, however, it's still gray or raining, you'll need to pack up wet. A soaking-wet tent is best confined to a waterproof sack or a garbage bag. Shake it out first: no need to carry *all* that extra water. You can also experiment with packing your tent at the bottom of your pack (where it won't drip all over everything) and storing your sleeping bag higher up.

Wet clothes are another problem. As unpleasant as it seems, if it's still raining there's no reason to put on dry clothes, since they'll just get wet as soon as you start hiking. Instead, wear your wet clothes (socks, too) and save the dry ones for later. Once you start walking, you won't feel the difference.

Finally, backpacking rewards the flexible approach. If the sun comes out mid-morning, stop and air out your wet gear.

WINTER

My local news channel recently broadcast a survey that concluded that cold makes more people miserable than does snow or rain, but that all three are misery inducers. I am assuming that only adults were counted in the survey; also that said adults were questioned while engaged in some hopelessly grown-up activity like sitting in traffic or digging out a stuck car. Not putting a three-year-old on a sled. Not waking up in a lean-to to watch a world turn quiet and white and clean around them. The fact that snow and cold are counted as "things that make people miserable" is telling. Among other things, it tells why comparatively few people have discovered the great joy and beauty of winter backpacking.

Still, sensible people ask the question: Why camp in the winter?

Because winter strips life down to a state of raw intensity.

Because it turns even a modest local park into place of undiscovered, magic wildness.

Because 16-hour nights let you catch up on your sleep.

Because there are no bugs, no rattlesnakes, no crowds.

Because there may be no peace like that of a winter forest.

But the survey did get one thing right: There is a vast difference between being out in the cold and

Do not venture into the backcountry in winter in a group of fewer than four. If you must split up, stay in two pairs for safety.

Thinking Winter

First things first. A winter hike requires an attitude adjustment on the part of the hiker. A winter trip isn't about mileage, or getting somewhere fast. It's about time: spending time, taking time, letting time slow to a crawl.

Nothing happens quickly on a winter hike. It takes longer to get from here to there because you've got snow underfoot and a pack on your back. Making camp takes more time, because you've got to tamp down a campsite and dig out a kitchen. Lighting a stove takes more time because you've got to deal with three layers of gloves and cold metal parts. More than anything, a winter hike is a series of tasks and adjustments, a process of adapting to an ever-changing environment.

being cold, and a cold hiker is a miserable hiker indeed. Fortunately, with a combination of thorough preparation, the right gear, and the right skills, a winter hiker can be comfortably cozy — even in the kinds of deep-freeze temperatures that usually send those survey-addicted newscasters into apoplexy.

And all of this during the shortest days of the year. In the northern United States, daylight in the dead of winter can be as little as 8 hours long. That's 8 hours to break camp, make camp, and get from one to the other. Which is why the first rule of winter is: You're out there to *be* out there, not to *get* somewhere.

You don't need to go far afield to get a hearty taste of winter camping. Even if you live in a developed, densely populated part of the country, you'll find that winter can turn a boring old close-to-home trail into a path of discovery. Staying close to home has another advantage: If the temperature drops way below your comfort level, or a raging winter storm rolls in; you'll have an easier time getting out if you know the terrain. There's no shame in calling it quits when the mercury shrinks to a tiny red pinprick at the bottom of your thermometer. After all, the point of all this is to enjoy yourself.

Finally, thinking winter means thinking safety. The extreme conditions aren't dangerous in and of themselves if you have the equipment to keep you warm and the sense to stay out of trouble. But with slippery ice underfoot and threatening clouds overhead, there's more that *can* go wrong on a winter hike, if you let down your guard. Pay attention to the weather, don't be afraid to change your plans, and try — especially in ultra-cold, high-mountain, or predictably rough-weather conditions — to go out with a group of at least four people so that even if you encounter an emergency situation and have to go for help, no one is ever alone. Don't hesitate to hunker down and wait out a storm: The best way to solve problems is to avoid them. Finally, pay attention to details like keeping snow out of

THE WINTER LAYERING SYSTEM

How many layers you need depends on the cold, how hard you work, and your body. One rule to go by: If you're comfortable standing still, you're dressed too warmly for walking.

When you get out there and get going, use all those fancy features on your clothing — the zip-pers, hoods, Velcro fasteners, and pit-zips — to continuously make small adjustments. It's amazing how tiny little adjustments can affect your comfort. The most effective way to change how warm you feel: Change what's on your head.

WICKING LAYER
● Function: To move moisture away from your skin.

continued on page 108

your boots and making sure you're adequately hydrated. If you don't believe that it's the little things that count, read Jack London's classic tale of winter mishap: *To Light a Fire.*

WINTER GEAR

One general principle (yes, you've heard it before) will stand you in good stead when looking at winter gear: Opt for simplicity. Gear with complex

THE WINTER LAYERING SYSTEM
continued from page 107

- Garments: Long johns, both top and bottom. Also used in glove liners, sock liners, and hats.
- Fabrics: Polypropylene, Thermax, and Capilene are popular synthetics. Silk is a natural wicking fabric.

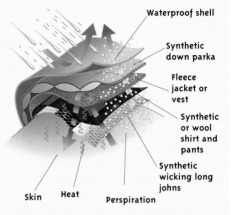

Waterproof shell

Synthetic down parka

Fleece jacket or vest

Synthetic or wool shirt and pants

Synthetic wicking long johns

Skin   Heat   Perspiration

Layering in winter

INSULATING LAYER
- Function: To keep you warm even when they get wet.
- Garments: Pants, shirts, sweaters, gloves, camp socks, hats, and jackets.
- Fabrics: Pile, fleece, and wool.
- Note: Down is also an insulating layer. I usually take a lightweight down jacket on trips when I expect temperatures below 20 degrees. This is an insulating layer only; it's not covered with a waterproof shell. That makes it more versatile. Synthetics like Lite Loft and Polarguard work well, too, and aren't as vulnerable as down to getting wet.

PROTECTIVE LAYER
- Function: To keep water and wind out and hold heat in.
- Garments: Rain pants and rain jackets. Climbing suits for mountaineering. Gore-Tex socks are now available. Gore-Tex is also used in gloves and hats.
- Fabrics: Best choice for winter is fabric lined with Gore-Tex. Note: Shells used by climbers are made of heavier fabric than three-season rain gear. But in moderate winter conditions, a rain suit is fine.

buckles and adjustments is a liability. You should be able to fasten your pack belt with your mittens on, light your stove wearing glove liners, and put up your tent fast, no matter how cold your fingers are.

Backpacks

No argument here: The best choice by far for winter is a high-capacity internal frame. You want all of your gear — especially your sleeping bag — safely ensconced in protection. Strapping things outside (as you do with an external-frame pack) takes longer with gloves on, and when you put your pack down in the snow, the gear outside ends up there too.

Another advantage to the internal frame is the lower (more maneuverable) center of gravity, which helps if you're on snowshoes, skis, or slick footway.

To select a pack, you need to consider fit and comfort (because you're going to be hauling a load) and capacity (those cubic inches, again; you need at least 5,800 of them). You may be able to use your smaller summer pack if you add on extra compartments, which are sold separately and can give you several hundred cubic inches of extra room. Be prepared: A pack loaded for cold might weigh 50 percent more than a summer-weight pack. If you can't carry that much in comfort, consider pulling a pulk, a lightweight toboggan-like plastic sled that you drag behind you.

Boots

BACKPACKING AND SNOWSHOEING Leather boots are the ticket; leave your lightweights at home. Look for sturdy full-grain leather with high ankle coverage and minimum seams. The fit should be on the generous side if you'll be wearing thicker than normal socks. The Merrell Wilderness or the OneSport Couloir are ideal because in addition to being sturdily built, they have high ankle coverage, minimum seams, and are crampon compatible.

ALPINE HIKING Plastic mountaineering boots look a little like ski boots, with an inner insulating bootie and an outer molded plastic shell. In truly frigid conditions they will keep your feet lots warmer than even the heaviest leather boots — but at a price (not only financial). These boots are stiff and heavy (a pair of Asolo's AFS Expedition boots weighs 5.7 pounds), which makes them more appropriate for kicking steps and front-pointing on crampons than for actually making mileage. New on the market is more foot-friendly footwear that tries to bridge the needs of hikers and climbers. Check out the Salomon Super Mountain boots, which combine plastic shells and leather uppers. At 4.5 pounds, these boots are lighter than traditional plastic double boots — and not any heavier than some of the all-leather hiking boots on the market.

BASE CAMPING AND DAYHIKING Shoe-paks are those felt-lined rubber

backcountry ski-packing you need a good solid leather boot that comes up over your ankle to keep you warm and give you adequate support on trackless terrain. Note: You can also strap your ski boots to your snowshoes.

Shelter

Winter tents (often interchangeable with mountaineering tents) are heavier and tougher than their three-season equivalents. Their design differs, too. First, they shed snow. With some three-season tents, you could wake up with your tent roof down by your nose because of the weight of the accumulated snow. Worse, your poles could collapse.

Before pitching your tent on snow, tamp the snow down to make a firm, even base, a blessing compared to summer's rocks and roots.

and leather boots beloved by north-country hunters and ice fishermen. With their waterproof shells and felt booties, they sort of work like double boots, but they lack the structural support to be good for lots of walking, let alone climbing. If you're carrying a heavy load a long way, you'll probably find that they don't provide enough support.

CROSS-COUNTRY SKIING Leave the lightweight touring boots at home. For

Quality four-season tents have stronger poles. The design of the tent might be a tube or a dome; often (in both domes and tubes) the poles (at least three, and usually four or more)

crisscross each other for added stability in high winds. Even so, in an all-out blizzard, you might need to help the tent do its job, because it is possible for winter tents to collapse under extremely heavy snow

A well-chosen winter campsite. High in the stormy Patagonia Range a snow drift has been used as both windbreak and site of a snow cave.

loads. If snow accumulates on the roof of the tent, and you can't knock it off by shaking the tent from the inside, you and your hiking partners will need to take turns going outside to shovel out the area around the tent, especially near the doors, and knock accumulating snow off the roof.

Winter tents are bigger — even for hikers who happily sacrifice space for weight in their fair-weather accommodations — because you need someplace to put all that extra stuff, and you need room to move around when you're tent-bound by a storm. At the same time, resist the temptation to get too big a tent: Not only does it weigh more, it takes more body heat to warm up. The smaller your tent, the warmer you'll be. Expect a winter tent to weigh considerably more than a three-season tent: Our Northface VE-25 tops the scales at just over 10 pounds (although it does sleep three plus gear). You can use your three-season tent, if it is roomy enough. A three-person three-season tent is ideal for two people plus gear in winter conditions.

Other useful winter features include large vestibules for your gear and lots of ventilation so that you won't wake up drenched in condensation. For instance, some winter tents have "windows" that open and shut by means of a drawstring cord. You also can use them as emergency exits, or lean outside to do your cooking.

Finally, winter tents need to be easy to put up. Test them with your gloves on, and then imagine doing it with fingers stiff from cold.

The Winter Tentsite

Winter gives you infinitely more tenting possibilities than summertime. First, with enough snow, you needn't worry about a water supply. Water, in frozen form at least, is everywhere.

However, the process of melting snow for drinking and cooking water is more laborious than it sounds. Snow (especially powdery, fluffy western snow) can be up to 98 percent air — which means that you have to melt many pots of snow (10 or even 20 isn't unusual) to get a single pot of water, all of which takes a lot of time and a lot of fuel. For this reason, it's preferable to camp near running water, if you can find it. Do remember, however, that even in winter, you need to treat your water.

When you choose an area for your tentsite, look for shelter. Remember to look up — not just for the usual widow-makers, but also for avalanche slopes and for trees whose branches have accumulated snowloads that could come crashing down on you in a strong wind. A grove of bushes or a huge boulder gives good shelter —

without the danger from above. Or you can make your own shelter by building a snow-wall, known as a berm. You'll also want to avoid cold spots, like the bottom of a canyon where cold air collects.

Before you can pitch a tent you need to tamp down a platform, so you don't sink into soft snow when you crawl into your tent. Tamping down is just a fancy way of saying stomping around, usually on your skis or snowshoes. In very dry, fluffy western snow, you might find that even after stomping around, the snow is still soft underfoot. You can help it to coalesce by pouring a couple of pots of water on the area, stomping around some more to make it as flat and even as possible, and then waiting a half hour or so for the patch to freeze and harden before putting up your tent. You'll also want to tamp down and dig

WINTER MINIMUM IMPACT

● Garbage. Winter white is pure and clean, but when the snow melts, the traces of your camp will be left over. It's easy to inadvertently leave garbage around in the winter because it gets covered with snow — until spring, that is, when the truth will out. So make an extra effort to pick up.

● Latrine site. The same goes for your latrine site. It's easy enough

to dig a hole in the snow and cover up the evidence of your passing with a few shovelfuls of more snow. But that only works till springtime exposes the evidence of what you thought was a pristine camp. Always use outhouses if they are available. If not, think about where you're putting that latrine. Keep it away from mapped trails and streams (or any another water source) and, if possible, look for a sheltered, hidden place.

out enough of an area around your tent for camp chores and cooking, and a path to a latrine area so you can answer the call of nature in the middle of the night without having to put on your snowshoes. If you find yourself

SNOW SHELTERS

The Eskimo people knew that snow was a good insulator: They used blocks of it to make igloos. Winter hikers use snow shelters, too, although the time these shelters take to build makes them most practical only if you're planning to spend several days camped in one place. In the shorter daylight hours of midwinter, you might find it impossible to pack up your camp, move any significant distance, make a new shelter, and set up camp. But making some kind of emergency snow shelter is an essential skill for die-hard winter hikers.

IGLOOS These semipermanent structures are made by cutting blocks of ice and laying them one atop the other in a spiral. Igloos are the most famous snow shelters, but they're also the least practical for backpacking because they take time and some amount of skill to build, and they require compacted wet

icy snow — not western powder.
SNOW CAVES This is the shelter of choice for mountaineers. The ideal location for a snow cave is on the lee side of an obstacle, like a tree or a rock, where snow tends to accumulate. You need a snow depth of at least six feet, and preferably more. The goal is to dig a tunnel into the drift, then dig up and scour out a sleeping shelf and a ventilation shaft.

QUINZHEES These are really snow caves above-ground. They are most useful in places where there is a lot of snow, but not enough for a deep drift. First you shovel snow into a man-made drift, then you dig into it as if you were making a snow cave.

Snow Cave

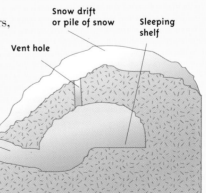

Snow drift or pile of snow

Sleeping shelf

Vent hole

Entrance

A snow cave provides snug, spacious shelter when snow conditions are right and you're planning to stay put for several days.

them and often they are shaped like a long, skinny shovel), you can use skis, ski poles, and ice axes to stake out your tent. An added benefit: Skis and axes used as stakes aren't likely to be left lying around where they can get buried and lost in new or wind-drifted snow. You can also attach your guy-lines to a "deadman" by filling a stuff sack with rocks (or snow) and burying it in the snow.

Sleeping Bags

This is simple: Get the warmest bag you think you'll need. Down is usu-ally the best choice as it is lighter for the warmth it offers and it's more compressible, two important consid-erations in the winter, since you've got so much stuff to cram into your pack. The major liability with down is that it loses its insulation when wet. But in winter, it's easy to keep a sleeping bag dry as long as you brush snow off your clothes before you enter your tent.

enjoying your architecture in the snow, you can make your camp luxu-rious by digging out a kitchen com-plete with shelves for preparing and cooking.

Stake down your tent securely — even if the weather is fair. If the weather changes during the night, you won't be kept awake listening to your storm-fly fabric crackling in the wind as though at any moment it would rip into a billion pieces. In addition to snow stakes (which are a little flatter and fatter than fair-season stakes; sometimes they have holes drilled into

Winter sleeping bags should have substantial draft tubes (which run the length of the zipper so cold can't poke through) and roomy hoods with draw-strings you can reach without turning yourself into a pretzel. Most winter hikers sleep in several layers of clothing (Boy Scout myths about naked bodies staying warm to the con-trary), so you'll want a bag that fits loosely enough that you can turn around inside it, even if you're wearing lots of layers. But resist the temptation to get too big a bag, because it won't keep you as warm.

Old-time winter hikers buy extra-long sleeping bags. Why? Because they don't sleep alone. No, I'm not talking about romance: I'm talking hardware. In a northwoods night, some of your gear needs a warm night's rest. Depending on the temperature, you might have a lot of company in there:

- Boots: Sweat will turn to ice overnight. Put them in a garbage bag and shove them to the bottom of your sleeping bag.
- Your stove: Works better when warm. You don't have to sleep with it, but at least keep it in the tent.
- Fuel: It's not going to freeze, but warm fuel works better — especially compressed propane/butane.
- Water filters: Ice clogs the filter.
- Anything battery operated: Batteries lose power in the cold. Before you declare a battery dead, put it in a warm pocket for a while and see if it comes back to life.

SLEEPING WARM

- Use your winter sleeping bag's fancy features, like the drawstring that pulls the bag snug around your face and neck. If you and your partner have zip-together bags, consider abandoning romance in favor of warmth: Sleeping solo in your own bag is warmer because you don't lose all that heat around your neck and shoulders.
- Make sure there is adequate insulation under your mattress. For most people, this means a full-length air mattress. In really cold temperatures, an extra closed-cell foam pad adds even more warmth.
- Wear a hat to bed instead of burrowing into your sleeping bag. If you sleep with your face inside your bag, condensation can collect inside the bag's insulation.
- If your tent has ventilation features like storm windows, open them to allow air circulation to whisk away the condensation that does gather.
- Vapor barrier liners hold heat next to your body. They're clammy, but warm.
- Try clenching and unclenching different muscles if you're cold. You won't work up a sweat, but you'll feel a little warmer.
- Eat or drink something warm just before you go to bed, and if there's hot liquid left over, put it in a canteen and take it inside your sleeping bag with you.
- Be sure to brush snow off your clothing before climbing into your bag. That innocent-looking dry white powder can soak your clothes and sleeping bag.

Drink something warm just before going to bed.

Camera: Cold batteries can drain; frozen film can harden and tear when you try to wind it. In deep-freeze temperatures, don't put a camera in your sleeping bag right away because condensation could fog the film. Instead, let it adjust to warmer temperatures slowly. Bring it into the vestibule first. After a while, bring it into the tent. Then, later bring it into your sleeping bag.

Water bottles: Make sure the lids are on tight.

Winter Accessories

Of all the seasons, winter is the one where a trip to your local outfitting store yields big dividends: accessories

worth their weight in warmth. In three-season hiking, most accessories fall into the category of luxuries. But in winter, well-designed accessories aren't luxuries at all.

What qualifies as well designed? First, winter clothing accessories should have a high warmth-to-weight ratio. Second, gear (and clothing, too) must be operable with a minimum of fuss: Zippers should have pulls for easy zipping and unzipping; buckles should be workable with frozen fingers. OR (Outdoor Research), in addition to making good rain accessories, manufactures a line of high-quality, creative solutions to cold-weather problems.

GAITERS Typical winter gaiters are knee high, and good ones can be fastened even if you're wearing bulky gloves. (OR's "Crocodiles" fasten with Velcro.) Gaiters keep snow out of your boots and add a few degrees of warmth to your toes. Try putting them on and taking them off with gloves on before you buy.

SUPERGAITERS These have a tight-fitting band of rubber that holds the gaiter around the sole of your boot. The net effect is something like an overboot — it keeps your feet much warmer. But the rubber is stiff and fiendishly difficult to stretch over the boot, and even when you get the gaiters in place, they have an irritating habit of sliding off. A dab of Shoo-Goo can help keep your supergaiters in place. Apply it a couple of days before you head out so it has time to set. Between trips, be sure to remove the supergaiters. The rubber exerts enormous pressure on boot soles and will ruin them if left on indefinitely. Supergaiters are worth the trouble if it's really cold outside (say, 0 degrees). For normal winter use (temperatures above 10 degrees) regular gaiters are perfectly adequate and a lot less fuss.

GLOVE SYSTEM Layering works for your hands, too. The bottom layer is an ultra-thin pair of gloves made of a wicking fabric like polypropylene. These gloves are thin enough to do most camp chores, even those that require some amount of manual dexterity, like zipping and unzipping, turning on a stove, or threading a tent pole through a sleeve. (Gloves with the fingertips cut off are also available, but I find that it's possible to do almost everything, including light a match, with ultra-thin polypro gloves.) Over the liners, use mittens and overmitts. OR makes a dedicated mitten/overmitt package. The mitten is made of pile, and the overmitt is Gore-Tex. Two other choices: Consider taking a pair of ski gloves if you'll be using an ice ax,

Knee-high gaiters (bottom); glove, overmitt systems (below); and two layer mittens (page 118) help keep warmth in, cold and moisture out.

because they enable you to change hand positions when holding the ax (mittens don't — which can lead to cramping). And a lightweight pair of fleece gloves stays warm even when wet and lets you perform most camp chores.

SOCK SYSTEMS Cold toes are one of the most common discomforts of winter backpacking — and in really low temperatures, frostbite is an ever-lurking danger. Like your other body parts, your feet will appreciate a well-thought-out layering system: The fundamentals are wicking liners and warm, insulating socks. Don't make the common mistake of wearing too many pairs of socks and cramping your foot in the boot — cramped space leads to cold toes. If you find that you routinely suffer from Popsicle toes, consider buying a pair of winter boots that are a smidge larger than your three-season boots so you can wear beefier socks and add a thicker insole (which insulates your foot better against the cold ground underneath). You can also use vapor barrier liners (VBLs; see page 119), which help retain body heat. If you use VBLs, it's likely that your feet will be damp from sweat when you get to camp. Be sure to remove even slightly damp liners and socks and change into dry camp socks. Instead of (or even in addition to) wool socks try heavyweight pile camp socks and down (or synthetic-filled) booties with a tread on the soles so you can walk around and do chores outside.

HATS & CO. No matter which part of your body is cold, the most effective thing you can do to warm it up is put on a hat. Or two. Here again, layering is key. Start with a lightweight balaclava, which will keep your face and neck warm. Add a fleece or wool hat. A neck gaiter (same idea as a scarf, but since there are no loose ends hanging down, you don't run the risk of hanging yourself on your pack) is another good addition to a winter wardrobe. Finally, the hood on your Gore-Tex outer shell will keep out the wind as well as keep in the warmth. A good rule: Always take one more head layer than you think you'll need.

COLLAPSIBLE SNOW SHOVEL Essential for winter hiking. You need it for constructing your camp, digging out after a blizzard, and avalanche emergencies. Choose a metal shovel; it is much sturdier than a plastic one.

SKI POLES Use them for balance when walking, skiing, or snow-shoeing. In camp, use them to stake down your tent. Some models can be screwed together to make an avalanche probe.

FULL-LENGTH AIR MATTRESS Your body needs to be insulated from losing heat to the cold ground. Winter campers need a full-length mattress, not a three-quarter one. An air mattress will keep you much warmer than a foam pad — but it's not overkill to carry a second closed-cell foam pad to double up the insulation.

COMPRESSION SACKS These useful stuff sacks can help you fit lots of bulky clothes into your pack.

MECHANICAL WARMING DEVICES You can buy hand and foot warmers in outdoor stores. They are little packets that produce warmth for a specified period of time when acti-

Hat layers: start with a balaclava, then add a fleece or wool hat.

vated. You can also buy socks with battery-powered warmers. Neither should be relied on for a winter trip: The packets weigh too much to be used constantly, and I've tried the battery-powered socks several times, always with unsatisfactory results. Instead, you need to be confident that your gear and clothing are adequate for the conditions. But by all means tuck a couple of hand- and foot-warming packets into your first aid kit. In an emergency, they could help prevent frostbite.

SUNGLASSES Absolutely essential, because sun plus snow equals snow-

VBLs

Vapor barrier liners are a commonly misunderstood way to add a few crucial degrees of warmth. Here's how they work:

Insulating layer keeps you warm

Vapor barrier keeps heat and sweat inside

Skin is cooled by sweating

Wicking layer holds most of the sweat

The idea behind vapor barrier liners is to keep the heat your body produces close to you, rather than letting it vent out and soak the materials that are keeping you warm. The effect: Your sweat is not allowed to evaporate, making you warmer but wetter.

VBLs are most often used as socks. They're also used as sleeping bag liners (they keep your sweat from soaking the down and add several degrees of warmth to your sleeping system) and — more rarely — as a layer of clothing.

In socks, the VBLs go on over your liner socks and under your wool socks. (Hint: If your feet are getting trashed on an unexpectedly cold day, you can improvise a VBL with a plastic grocery bag. Just slip it between your sock liners and your wool socks.)

The VBL theory seems to contradict one of the ground rules of backpacking — that being wet equals being cold. And indeed, it doesn't work for all people, and it doesn't work in all conditions. If you're a heavy sweater, you might generate an uncomfortable amount of moisture. But if you sweat moderately and keep up a slow, even pace, a VBL can be an effective tool in your winter arsenal. When you stop, however, you'll need to change into dry socks immediately.

blindness. Choose glacier glasses with UV protection and sideflaps.

COLD-WEATHER CUISINE

We usually think of calories as units of food (or fat), but in reality calories are units of heat. This takes on a different meaning in winter camping, when you use up something like twice as many calories as you do in day-to-day indoor life. Simply maintaining your body temperature when you're asleep in the cold takes more calories.

Most backpackers carry slightly heavier rations for winter, usually about 2½ pounds of food per person per day of quick-cooking, easy-to-prepare foods. The fewer steps and the less time they take, the better. Remember, you need more stove fuel in winter: Cold water takes longer to heat; the stove is less efficient because it loses heat to the environment; and you might have to melt snow for water. So avoid foods that need to simmer for 20 minutes. Also, you'll be wearing gloves, which makes it more difficult to slice and dice bits and pieces of various ingredients. My ideal winter meal is the same as my ideal rainy-day meal: anything where the directions say "add hot water and eat." Instant soup is a must-have: Not only does it warm you up, but it helps you avoid hypothermia by keeping you hydrated.

For lunch, choose foods high in calories, including fats. Foods like peanut butter, cheese, and cans of sardines are great, but they can freeze. An hour before lunch, put the containers in an inside pocket where they can soak up some body heat and thaw. Lots of experienced climbers and winter backpackers take along some butter or margarine and add it to everything from cereal to tomato sauce. Be sure you store it in a leakproof container — just in case of a sudden thaw. Quick defrosting tip: You lose most of your body heat through your head, so if you need to quickly thaw a packet of margarine, put it under your hat!

Snacks are also important for keeping up warmth and energy. Splurge on a variety of your favorites (chocolate bars, energy bars, health-food bars, cereal bars, GORP, and

---

GEAR TALK
WINTER ZIPPERS

Tie bright-colored nylon cord to zippers on packs, sleeping bags, and clothing so that you can pull them open and shut while wearing mittens. Stop cords from fraying by burning the ends with a match after you cut them.

nuts) and bring a lot. Eat when you're tired, eat when you're hungry; above all, eat when you're cold. Always keep a handful of a snack where you can get at it without even taking off your pack — and bring a few snacks into your tent at night.

Cooking Tips

● To make a fire, dig a hole in the snow. Put down a layer of medium-sized sticks as a base. Then build the fire on top of the wood. Note: The fire will sink as it burns, but the layer of sticks will help prevent the melting snow from drowning the fire, at least until the fire gets good and going. Note: The hole needs to be wide enough that snow melting around the fire doesn't put it out.

A kitchen counter carved from snow.

● Use a pad under your stove to slow down heat transfer from stove to ground and to prevent the stove from melting the snow underneath it. Three light-weight choices: a plastic placemat, an old computer mouse pad, or a square of ensolite wrapped with duct tape. These items also double as cutting boards. If you forgot a pad, try using your guidebook (protected in a zipper-lock bag of course) or a snow shovel.

● Always use the heat reflector, the windscreen, and a heat exchange if your stove is designed to work with them. Keeping the lid on tight saves fuel. Don't take the lid off every 5 seconds to see if the water is boiling.

● Compressed gas cartridges don't work well in the cold. But a sputtering cold cartridge stove can be revived by dipping the fuel canister (not the stove element) into warm (not hot) water.

● Wrap fuel bottles with several layers of duct tape. You can pull the tape off and use it as necessary. But while it's sitting around the bottle, it's doing a job: adding a layer of insulation between your fingers and the fuel bottle. Why you want this: Your fuel is the temperature of the air, which can be below zero. Touching anything that cold (either the fuel itself or the metal bottle) can cause instant frostbite.

● Keep an extra pair of glove liners with your cook kit.

● Don't waste hot water. Your spaghetti water can be used for a cup of instant hot soup. Or choose foods that require less hot water, like rice and instant mashed potatoes.

- One-pot meals require less fuel to cook, are easier to prepare, and stay hot longer.
- Insulated mugs keep hot food hot longer. Don't bring a metal cup.

SNOW TRAVEL

Snow going is slow going. The footway is slippery, and each step takes more care. More effort, too, since you're wearing those boots and packing that load.

Take turns breaking trail — even if there are only two of you and the snow is but a couple of inches deep. Walking in someone else's tracks makes a big difference. They don't have to be human tracks: Follow animal paths if they're going in your direction. Settle on a walking pace that keeps you warm without wearing you out. What you want to avoid is

WINTER WATER

SNOWMELT Always start your pot with an inch of liquid water, or the snow will scorch and taste burnt. If you melt snow over a fire, you can decant and aerate the water to get rid of the ashy taste by pouring it from one bottle to another.
MELTING MACHINE If you've got a couple of hours of sunny weather, a black garbage bag or a dark tarp can do some of the work for you. Either lay out the tarp, spread snow thinly over it, and channel the meltwater into a pot or shovel snow into a black garbage bag, close the bag, lay it in the sun, and wait for the snow to melt. This kind of snowmelt is better for cooking than drinking because it has a slightly plastic-tainted flavor.
AT NIGHT Sleep with the water you

intend to drink. If you're storing extra water for the next morning, you can stick the water bottle upside down in a snowbank. It won't freeze because the snow insulates it. Turning the bottle upside down ensures that any ice that does

working up a big sweat, then stopping for a desperately needed rest and getting chilled from quickly cooling sweat. Set a comfortable, sustainable pace and you won't have to stop as often to fuss around with adjusting layers and such. This pace is likely to be quite a bit slower than your fair-weather hiking pace, so cut back on mileage goals. Finally, pay attention to daylight; in winter you don't have much of it. By the time the sun sets (and the temperature plummets) you'll want to be all snug in your camp.

SNOWSHOES

In the last few years, snowshoeing has burgeoned into one of the fastest-growing outdoor winter activities in America. It used to be that snowshoes were wood and rawhide contraptions that hung over fireplaces in rustic northcountry lodges. Today, they've joined the recreation main-

---

form won't clog the lid. Mark the spot you've buried the bottle with a ski pole.

WATER BOTTLE INSULATORS Outdoor Research makes a fabric insulating cover for water bottles. You can use it to keep water from freezing or from getting so cold that even the thought of drinking it is painful. To keep yourself well-watered and well-warmed, try heating a bottle of water in the morning before you set out, stashing it in an insulator, and sipping on it throughout the day. Depending on just how cold it is out there, the water should stay warm for a few hours.

WATER BOTTLES Wide-mouthed water bottles are so far superior to narrow-mouthed bottles I can't think of a reason a backpacker would even consider the latter.

Wide-mouthed bottles are easier to dip into an ice-choked spring, they're easier to handle when you've got gloves on, and if you need to add a few spoonfuls of snow, you can. For winter, look for bottles with several tiers of threading: They are less likely to pop open under the stress of constantly changing temperatures.

WARM DRINKS If you pour boiling water into a water bottle and close the lid, the water inside will contract as it cools. As it does, the heat of the water softens the plastic, which then contorts and starts to collapse because of the lowered density of the cooling water. To prevent this, open the cap on your water bottle for a few seconds every 15 minutes or so to let some steam escape and equalize the air pressure.

more efficient, but the inherent beauty of snowshoeing is still its simplicity.

Why the boom? After all, cross-country skiing is faster, and for years it's been touted as the best exercise. Not only are snowshoes slower, they're a lot more work. You walk up a hill — and walk back down. No screaming downhill runs. No long lazy Telemark arcs weaving serpentines in the snow.

When hiking in deep snow use teamwork by moving in single file, with the leader breaking trail. Better yet, strap on a pair of snowshoes.

stream, complete with bright colors and materials made of something concocted in a chemistry lab. But a form of transportation that has survived thousands of years isn't going to change too radically overnight: Trendy as snowshoes have become, their shape and function remain the same. Snowshoes spread a person's weight out so she can walk without sinking into deep snow. Improvements have made the equipment

But snowshoeing offers some advantages — in addition to being a great workout. First, it's inexpensive: You can expect a good pair of snowshoes to cost from $100 to $300 — and they'll last forever. Second, it's easy to master, with a learning curve about as steep as the highest point in Delaware. Third, it opens up the backcountry to virtually anyone. In contrast, those Telemark turns skiers love to carve take years to perfect, and only an expert backcountry skier can tackle steep trails clogged with trees, underbrush, tight turns, and an under-snow obstacle course of rocks and deadfall. Opt for snowshoes, and once you get the basics under your belt (you learned to walk, didn't you?) you can go through dense forest without spending half your time in a face-plant. This is something you'll really appreciate when navigating your way with a heavy pack, because even a fine skier can become tipsy and accident-prone under the weight of a winter load.

The ease of snowshoeing makes it ideal for backpackers. But there are a few differences between day-hiking on snowshoes and heading out under the weight of a full pack.

Choosing a Snowshoe

The high-tech boom means choices: There are now snowshoes for racing, jogging, and climbing. But for the snowshoe backpacker, the most important decision is still the size of the shoe. The smaller the snowshoes, the more maneuverable they are. The larger the snowshoes, the more weight they can support. Another factor is the type of snow you'll be floating over: eastern crud or

Rocky Mountain powder? You sink less deeply into compressed, wet snow than you do in light, fluffy, dry stuff. So western snowshoers need more "float" — that is, bigger shoes. Because the winter backpacker has to factor in pack weight as well as body weight, he usually ends up in the big-footed category of snowshoes. For all-purpose trekking, the tried-and-true "Bearpaw" design is one of the most versatile.

BINDINGS Traditional snowshoes have lace-up bindings, which have the advantage of simplicity: They're less likely to break, and if they do, it's pretty easy to improvise an on-the-spot solution. This is an important advantage for the winter backpacker. Lace-ups do take a bit of practice and attention to affix them so they stay put. If you're careless, you'll end up picking up your foot and leaving your snowshoe in a snowbank, which leads to tumbling into said snowbank and then fumbling to try to reattach the straps. Practice with the bindings at

Modern snowshoes like this Tubbs model have tough, lightweight aluminum frames, durable vinyl decking, and molded plastic bindings with built-in toe cleats.

When climbing steeps on packed snow, take shorter steps and aggressively dig your toe cleats into the surface.

Backpacking on Snowshoes

Snowshoeing with a pack on isn't much different than snowshoeing without a pack, except that you will sink deeper into the snow.

● Take along a pair of ski poles for balance. Make sure they have baskets on them, or they'll sink into the snow.

● Getting up after a fall is a little more difficult with a pack on. To avoid spills, concentrate on keeping your feet just a little bit farther apart than usual so you don't trip over yourself (in time, this becomes second nature). If you do fall, the best way to get up is to roll over until you're in a crawling position, and then scramble to your feet. Practice once or twice before you set out.

● Climbing on snowshoes with a pack on is the same as climbing on snowshoes without a pack, only slower. To traverse a steep slope, kick the snowshoe into the slope and then step down, putting your weight on the side of your foot closest to the mountain. This counteracts the snowshoe's tendency to match the slope's incline. With crampons on the bottoms of your snowshoes, you can climb much steeper, icier slopes than you would think. Attack them head-on!

home to get the hang of it. The trick is to hook the front of the binding up near the toe of your boot, then lock the heel into place, then lace up the front. Then go back and forth a couple of times between the heel and the toe, making sure that they are completely tight.

Newer models have more convenient plastic bindings. I'm frankly cautious about taking anything I can't fix into the backcountry, so my advice for backpackers is to stick with the simpler lace-up systems. If you do opt for the molded bindings, be sure to try them on in the store with the boots you plan to use: Not all bindings fit all boots (especially if your foot is unusually big or small).

CROSS-COUNTRY SKIING

Cross-country skiing is more difficult than snowshoeing, but it offers a whole host of rewards to those who get the hang of maneuvering themselves gracefully with planks strapped to their feet. It's much faster than any other mode of self-propelled winter travel, enabling you to cover far more distance, and it's great all-over exercise.

Unlike snowshoeing, the rhythms of cross-country skiing don't come naturally. No one steps into a pair of skinnies and instinctively figures out the so-called diagonal stride. Being really good at cross-country skiing means having a repertoire of turns and being able to handle a variety of snow conditions. Telemark turns in deep powder and skating across a long flat field are all skills that take time to learn — and are far beyond the scope of this book.

The good news is that you don't have to be an expert to be able to use backcountry skis on a winter camping trip. If you're moderately coordinated, all it takes to begin to pick up the rhythm is a quick lesson. Add to that a couple of other skills, like stopping, turning, and getting up from a fall, and you're set to go — at least on moderate terrain. The steep stuff takes more practice. If you find yourself attracted to the idea of backcountry ski adventure, a good place to gain the necessary skills is at the nearest cross-country ski area — especially after new snowfalls. More advanced skiers might want to hone their skills on the beginner slope of a downhill ski area. Once you get the hang of turning on skis, bring your pack along for a trial run. You'll be amazed at how the added weight affects your momentum — and your maneuverability.

Ski-Packing

The first couple of times you head out for a ski-packing trip, you'll need to pick the trail carefully. Give your sense of adventure a rest and focus on your sense of survival: Look for old dirt roads to ski on, or ski trails marked "easiest." The reason: Even if you're an accomplished skier, you'll find that a heavy pack plus snow plus skis plus gravity plus unfamiliar terrain equals an initial (and sometimes terrifying) loss of control. Merely getting started can be a challenge. In deep powdery snow, it can be a major project just to get your skis on and then heft a heavy pack without falling and floundering like a turtle on its back!

Steep hills present additional challenges, especially when you have to turn to avoid a tree. Look instead for open fields and old roads with gentle grades.

Part of the beauty of winter ski-packing is going off the beaten path. Or, more accurately, going off any path. Leaving behind the nicely groomed ruts of the Nordic touring center means pristine snow, fields of white — and lots more work. The first person in line gets the brunt of it. As each person in line follows, the tracks get deeper and the going gets smoother. Take turns at the point position and be ready to switch off any time the person in front needs a break. And if you're breaking trail, don't be shy about asking to be relieved: Exhaustion leads to hypothermia.

HYPOTHERMIA TREATMENT

❶ Assemble your group and assess the situation. If you are in a frequently used area, ask other hikers for help.

❷ Get the victim in as protected an area as possible. Put up a tent or a tarp, find a windbreak, or cover the victim with a space blanket. Put down a mattress pad for insulation.

❸ Make sure the victim has a hat and, if possible, a hood or balaclava to cover the neck. If dry socks are available, cover the feet, too.

❹ A severely hypothermic person cannot warm himself: He needs an external source of heat. But forget about the old body-to-body method. Research shows that when a person becomes hypothermic, blood pools in the muscles, where it becomes acidic. Body-to-body contact warms the pooled, acidic blood too quickly and sends it back to the heart, where the resulting shock can lead to cardiac arrest. Instead, concentrate on stopping heat loss. Put the victim in warm, dry clothes. Then put him in a sleeping bag.

❺ Winter hikers should carry heat paks. Place these in the victim's armpits and groin. This method is safer than body-to-body

contact because it warms only the blood that has been circulating in major vessels.

❻ If someone else is available, have him heat up some water. If the victim is conscious, a warm drink or soup will help. If he is unconscious or semi-conscious, do not attempt to make him drink. A hot-water bottle can be put in the sleeping bag with the victim.

❼ Do NOT give the victim alcohol. Alcohol is a vasodilator, and dilated blood vessels lose heat. Also avoid drinks with caffeine.

❽ Do not allow the victim to fall asleep.

❾ Any handling of a severely hypothermic person should be extremely gentle. In the late stages of hypothermia, the heart muscle is actually chilled and any shock or jolting could cause it to arrest.

❿ Leaving a victim alone is the absolute last resort. If you must leave to get help, be sure his condition is stabilized and that he is protected from the elements.

⓫ Once a victim's condition is stabilized and his temperature has returned to normal, he MUST either hike out or be evacuated so that he can receive a full medical evaluation. The victim should NOT be allowed to continue the hike, even if he feels up to it.

Safety Tips for Ski-Packing

You don't have to be an expert to ski with a backpack, but what you lack in skill you need to make up in common sense.

When trekking over open terrain, pulling a pulk is the most efficient means of transporting the heavy loads winter camping demands.

 Ski within your limits. Especially remember that with a pack on you have more momentum and less control. Try small hills before big hills, and don't let pride (or your skiing partners) goad you into trying something your gut knows you're not ready for.

There's more than one way down a hill. If the slope looks too steep for you, look to see if it's possible to make long slow switchbacks. You can traverse the slope losing only a little elevation, and then perform either a moving turn (a stem Christie or a Telemark turn) or a standing turn (the kick-turn). Then repeat the traverse in the other direction. If the slope isn't wide enough for a traverse, try side-slipping down. Or, as a last resort, take off your skis and walk.

If you find yourself flailing out of control — simply sit. It's utterly unglamorous, and you'll be admitting to the world that you were in over your head, but isn't that a whole lot better than becoming one with a tree?

Safety goggles are essential for forest skiing.

On tricky terrain, remove the pole straps from around your wrist so that if you fall, you can drop the pole. (Having the pole attached to your wrist can cause broken bones if you fall and can't get clear of the pole.)

Internal-frame packs are mandatory. You simply can't ski in control if you've got a frame pack on and the center of gravity is somewhere up around your shoulders.

Pay attention to pace and distance. You could make great mileage one day if the snow is right and the terrain just ever-so-slightly goes downhill. After a night of snow, the return trip could take twice as long.

Choosing Your Equipment

Avoid skinny touring skis, which are the equivalent of "dayhiking" gear. These work on groomed trails or trails where you're likely to be

a challenge when you're packing a load. And these skis are fun, too, especially for Telemarkers, who ski into a base camp and then spend the day plundering the area for fresh powder and virgin runs.

Tough, high-top Telemark boots and wide, metal-edged skis with cable bindings are the way to go when cross-country skiing into the backcountry.

following in the ski tracks of others, but they're too flimsy for the backcountry, especially when you've got a pack on. They don't have edges for turning, and they don't provide enough flotation when you're carrying a pack.

For packing a heavy load (and, let's face it, any winter pack is a heavy load) you'll do far better with heavier mountaineering or backcountry equipment — skis and boots both. Like all winter backpacking equipment, skis should get you where you're going with a minimum of fuss and bother. Look for a general all-purpose mountaineering ski that floats well in deep snow and has a good glide. A new trend in backcountry skis is shorter, fatter boards that have good float and turn easily: These are especially useful for backpackers, because turns can be quite

WAXABLE OR WAXLESS? The next decision you need to make is whether to buy waxable or waxless skis. The wax (placed on the underside of the ski in the area under the foot) lets the ski grip the snow so you don't slide backward every time you try to glide forward. Different kinds of snow — cold and dry, hard and icy, or wet and goopy — react to the ski differently, so different kinds of waxes work better in different conditions and temperatures. During the day if conditions and temperatures change, you have to stop and change the wax.

Waxless skis have a sort of raised fishscale pattern under the foot where the wax would go. The fishscales grip the snow so you don't slide backward with each step. A dead giveaway of a waxless ski is the scraping sound it makes each time you glide. Waxless skis are a one-size-fits-all affair: They don't work great in any particular condition, but they always work. If the snow conditions change dramatically overnight, you just ski out: No new layer of wax to reapply, no fuss. For beginners, waxless skis are a practical choice. And backpackers, who already have enough to do to keep warm and dry in winter camping, might find it worthwhile to give up a little finesse in favor of ease of use.

SKINS If you're going into hilly terrain, you'll also need a pair of skins. Originally made of pelts, the skins were attached to the bottoms of the skis with the grain of the fur against the slope. The friction of the fur against the snow is what keeps you from sliding downhill when you are going uphill. Today skins are made of synthetics, not fur, but they still work

FROSTBITE

Unlike hypothermia, which can occur at temperatures up to 50 degrees (and, on rare occasions, even higher), frostbite requires temperatures well below freezing, so the three-season hiker is usually not at risk. But when the mercury drops below freezing, you need to be concerned with keeping your extremities — face, toes, and fingers — warm and dry. Avoid contact with cold objects (especially with metal fuel canisters), and avoid contact with liquids like water or, worse, fuel (which remains liquid no matter how cold it is). Pay attention to how your feet and hands feel. If they are numb with cold, warm them up with dry socks and mittens. If they are turning whitish and waxy, you have frostnip, and you need to take care of it before it gets any worse. If your cheeks are cold, cover them with warm hands. Hands can be warmed by putting them in your armpits. Your feet will need the help of a trailmate's stomach.

Anything worse than frostnip requires evacuation. Deep frostbite is characterized by tissue that is white and waxy, and the underlying tissue is hard — that is, frozen. You should never try to thaw the injury in the backcountry: Improper thawing can lead to infection and amputation. Deep frostbite should not be thawed until the hiker is in a place where the injury will not refreeze. Finally, forget about the old "rub-with-snow" method. Never rub a frostbitten area with anything: It can do permanent damage. As for rubbing with snow, it defies common sense, old wives' tales notwithstanding.

● COLD COMFORT, by Glenn Randall (*Lyons and Burford*) Sounds oxymoronic? Not with the right gear, the right skills, and a healthy respect for the elements.

● WILDERNESS SKIING AND WINTER CAMPING, by Chris Townsend (*McGraw-Hill*) From loading a sled to sleeping in the snow, this book tells you how to do it. It also covers navigation, blizzards, frostbite, hypothermia—and how to stay comfortable even when the temperatures drop to something that belongs in a science lab!

● AMC GUIDE TO WINTER CAMPING, by Steven Gorman (*AMC*)The Appalachian Mountain Club stomping grounds are the White Mountains of New Hampshire — home to some of the worst weather in the world. But even there, you can stay warm and enjoy winter if you've got the right gear and a little bit of know-how.

on the same principle.

BINDINGS 75-mm three-pin bindings are the traditional standard for back-country equipment. Step-in plastic bindings like the New Nordic Norm are convenient for touring, but some of them can't withstand heavy-duty backcountry use: I snapped mine in the woods behind my house. Fortunately, I only had to trudge 2 miles home. I'm glad I didn't make that mistake in the backcountry. Whichever bindings you choose, be sure they are designed for back-country use, not touring.

H I G H C O U N T R Y

A way we go to the topmost mountains," wrote John Muir about his beloved Sierra Nevada. "Many still small voices, as well as the noon thunder are calling 'Come higher.' "

Maybe you've heard them too.

Perhaps you live in Colorado, where hiking forward means hiking up. Or Arizona, where higher elevations offer relief from the desert inferno. Maybe your home is in the Pacific Northwest with its towering volcanic cones. Maybe you breathed in your first lungful of above-the-timber air in New Hampshire's White Mountains and you found it instantaneously addictive. Or perhaps you live 100 miles or more from the

nearest bump that would show up on a contour map, but across the prairie, you've heard those small voices calling. Maybe, like me, you're hooked on the highcountry.

But before you heed the voices and follow Muir up to the topmost mountains, you're going to need to add a few extra skills to your backcountry bag of tricks.

A warning is in order: While this chapter covers some skills that are the stock-in-trade of mountaineers, it is not a mountaineering primer. Technical mountaineering — using aids, glacier travel, and the like — is beyond the scope of this book. So while I cover some basic moun-

Alpine challenge: the footpath disappears under snow near Cathedral Peak on the John Muir Trail, making skill with map and compass a necessity.

Higher yet, you've paused to rest in the shade of Ponderosa pines, then, as the land becomes colder and more exposed, you've huddled on the lee side of smaller trees, bent by the wind. Eventually, the trees shrink to shrubs, the shrubs to grasses, and finally even the grasses give up, abandoning the land to hardy lichens that eke out a living among the gray granite rocks.

Welcome to the highcountry.

taineering skills like self-arrest and the use of crampons, it takes more than that to make a climber. If in your enthusiasm for high places you set your sights on glaciated summits, you'll need to take a course and gain in-field experience.

THE ALPINE ENVIRONMENT

Imagine yourself standing in Death Valley National Monument in July, where the average daytime temperature can easily top 100 degrees. Now travel a short way west — so short, in fact, that you don't even cross county lines — to the town of Lone Pine at the base of Mount Whitney. Go uphill until there's nothing left between you and the sky. Congratulations: By climbing to the summit, you have — at least as far as the climate is concerned — done the equivalent of walking to the Arctic Circle. On the way, you've seen desert give way to arid forests of piñon and juniper.

More than anything else, alpine hiking is affected by elevation. The higher you go, the more you'll be affected by three key factors. First, temperature: On average, you lose 3 to 5 degrees per 1,000 feet, which means that up on top of 14,494-foot Mount Whitney, it's going to be 43 to 70 degrees colder than down at sea level. Second, thin air: A molecule of air at high elevations is made up of the same percentage of nitrogen, hydrogen, and oxygen as it is at sea level — but at higher altitudes, there's less air in a given volume of space because there is less pressure. And that means that with each breath, you take in less oxygen. And finally there's weather: Volatile and fickle, mountain weather can change several times within a few hours, or from one side of a ridge to the other. Winds race over mountain passes and hit you with the force of a freight train. It snows in July. Thunder roars and echoes against mountain walls, booming like the percussion section of an orchestra made of Titans.

Altitude Sickness

The first thing you notice is that you're getting winded a little bit sooner than usual. You wonder if maybe it's jet lag. Or age is starting to catch up.

As you gain altitude, your heart beats faster, which you attribute to the fact that, good as your intentions might have been, you missed one too many sessions at the gym. Finally, you arrive at your campsite, altitude

A mountaineer suffers altitude headache after climbing Mount Shinn, Antarctica. Heed the early symptoms of this potentially fatal condition.

12,000 feet in the Colorado Rockies. You feel a slight throbbing in your head. Strangely enough, considering the 5,000 feet of elevation gain and

ALTITUDE SICKNESS: HOW TO KNOW, WHAT TO DO

NORMAL ACCLIMATIZING
Working harder than normal.
Pulse is elevated.
Breathing is more laborious.
WHAT TO DO
Give yourself time to adapt.
Use power breathing techniques.
Limit net elevation gain to 1,000 feet a day.
If you climb high, retreat to a lower elevation for sleeping.

WARNING SIGNALS OF ALTITUDE SICKNESS
Slight headache.
Lack of appetite and slight nausea.
Poor sleeping or insomnia.
Weird, vivid dreams.
WHAT TO DO
Take a rest day.
Do not climb higher until the symptoms go away.
SYMPTOMS OF ALTITUDE SICKNESS
Nagging, persistent headache.

continued on page 136

ALTITUDE SICKNESS
continued from page 135

Nausea; possibly vomiting.
Difficulty breathing.

WHAT TO DO

Go downhill to the last altitude at which you felt good.

FULL-FLEDGED ACUTE MOUNTAIN SICKNESS

Irregular heartbeat.
Vomiting.
Ragged breathing.
Cyanosis (blue skin coloring).
Combination of irrational behavior and impaired motor skills makes person appear drunk.

WHAT TO DO

This stage can be fatal. Go downhill immediately, even if it's the middle of the night: Pack up and get out. Note: A person in this stage must not be left alone. If you're a solo hiker, you had better have the knowledge and sense not to get into this fully preventable mess. If your hiking partner is afflicted, you've got to stay with him or her.

the 12 miles you've hiked, you're not hungry. At night, you don't sleep well, and when you do sleep, you have edgy, vivid dreams.

If, at sea level, you've got headaches and nausea and you don't sleep well, you can blame it on your boss, your spouse, MSG in the take-out food, or whatever you like. But at 12,000 feet, the culprit is clear: Blame it on the altitude.

How you respond to the shortage of oxygen depends on a lot of factors, some of which are not fully understood. Internal factors like blood chemistry seem to play as much of a role as fitness. In fact, fit people can actually be more vulnerable because they climb faster and don't give their bodies a chance to acclimate. (And they may also be more accustomed to ignoring discomfort or pushing through it.) But while doctors continue to study human responses to altitude to account for differences among individuals, one thing is perfectly clear: Most cases of altitude sickness are caused by going too high too soon. In the United States, the average edema due to acute mountain sickness (AMS) occurs at an elevation of only 12,000 feet. Most of these occur in the Pacific Northwest, where sea-level city dwellers succumb to the siren's song "come higher," but don't give themselves enough time to acclimate to the elevations of mountains like Rainier and Adams.

Part of wilderness safety is knowing when you are at risk — and when you aren't. While panting and an elevated heart rate at 12,000 feet in Colorado is doubtless due to the altitude, panting at 4,000 feet in Vermont is far more likely to be due to lack of fitness. It is not uncommon for a sea-level dweller to be slightly more winded at 4,000 or 5,000 feet than at home, but it's unusual for most hikers to be troubled by altitudes of less than 7,000 or 8,000 feet; 10,000 or 12,000 feet is a more common threshold for symptoms like headaches and slight nausea, but even that rule of thumb doesn't apply to everyone. If, for instance, you live at 8,000 feet, climbing to 10,000 feet might be nothing more than a walk in the park for you. But if you've just flown in from sea level, a jog at 7,000 feet will likely leave you a little on the woozy side. Remember, what happens to you when your body encounters thin air may well vary from the norm.

To acclimate, experts generally recommend "climbing high and sleeping low." After a day of wandering around on ridges, choose a campsite lower down so your body can recover during the night. Higher than 10,000 feet, most people find that by limiting net elevation gain to 1,000 feet a day they have enough time to acclimatize. But for those first few days plan on low mileage.

In addition to acclimatizing properly, there are four other things you can do to cope with altitude:

POWER BREATHING Power breathing forces you to take in more air per breath (and hence more oxygen). The focus should be on how you exhale, not on how (or how deeply) you inhale. Hold your hand out at arm's length. Purse your lips. Pretend your fingers are a candle and you're blowing out the flame in one sudden, short burst. That's power breathing: It actually makes your lungs take in more air. This technique is so effective that you can use it to rid yourself of a minor high-altitude headache.

DRINK WATER Blood thickens at altitude, especially if you become dehydrated. Drinking enough keeps your blood flowing and your muscles working. Pay attention, because at altitude, many people don't feel thirsty, even though they are losing more water than usual through sweat and respiration. Drink at every rest stop, and keep track of your urine: You should be urinating several times a day, and the output should be pale yellow, not dark.

PROPHYLACTIC DRUGS Diamox overrides the body's natural responses to altitude. Most hikers can acclimate without drugs, because they're not going as high as climbers and they're not gaining elevation as quickly. One exception: high-altitude hikes in a place like the Pacific Northwest where major mountains are within an easy drive of sea level. A quick weekend up-and-down in those circumstances is the kind of situation in which Diamox might be appropriate. It's a prescription drug, so you'll need to discuss this with your doctor.

GIVE YOUR EGO A REST Better yet, leave it at home. People acclimate at

talus field where the nearest shelter is several miles away — and several hundred feet down — just as a lightning bolt announces its intention to make its acquaintance with every atom in my body.

Fast-approaching dirty weather along the Pacific Crest Trail. Never underestimate the speed with which the weather can turn nasty in the mountains.

radically different rates, which reflect neither their fitness nor their strength. In addition, a climb that seemed a piece of cake a few years back might give you trouble this time around. If you have any of the symptoms, assume altitude sickness. Having altitude sickness doesn't mean you're weak or a wimp or a whiner — it means you're having a normal response to a lack of oxygen. Minor symptoms will usually go away if you simply take a rest day and sit around camp doing nothing. They will not go away if you ignore them and keep climbing. And they can be fatal.

Storms

In the interest of honesty, I have to report that there is a big difference between how I think about mountain storms in the comfort of my office, writing a chapter about bad weather and such, and how I think about them when I am standing on an exposed

In such cases, I bolster my odds by taking the few precautions that experienced mountain travelers have developed over years of exposure to the evil tempers of the gods of mountain summits. And I take great comfort in statistics: Lightning kills only between 100 and 300 Americans a year, most of whom were not hiking when they were struck.

As unhelpful as it sounds, like so many other issues of safety, the best strategy regarding lightning is to avoid it. Rarely do storms race in without any warning at all, and even when storms are sudden, they may also be predictable. The most common pattern in mountains worldwide is that storms roll in during the afternoon, by which time you should plan to be off of the ridges and safely below the timber. This advice has practical implications. For instance, if you're climbing one of Colorado's "fourteeners," you will drastically improve your safety (not to mention the view from the summit) if you start early, say at five in the morning.

But what about those times when your route keeps you high all day — or the weather does get capricious, and a storm roars though in the morning? What happens when you're stuck up there, exposed and far from shelter? In this case, what not to do is as important as what to do, because above treeline, something that looks like shelter may actually act as a lightning rod. For instance, did you know that shallow caves — which look like good shelter — are lightning attractors? And lightning doesn't always strike from the sky: It can also travel along the ground. So avoid puddles of water (an electricity conductor) and rock outcrops (they attract ground currents) and gullies (a good lightning path). The National Fire Protection Code additionally suggests staying away from exposed fields, hilltops, bodies of water, and wire fences. If you are stuck above treeline, try to at least get off of the highpoint or ridge. To further reduce exposure, crouch or kneel, but do not lie flat or put your hands on the ground (you want to minimize the contact between your body and the ground). Keeping your hands off the ground makes it more likely that even if you were to be hit by a ground current, the lightning would pass from one foot to the other — not through your body's central core to your hands and thence the ground. You can further protect yourself by standing on a coil of rope or a mattress pad, which provides insulation between you and the ground, and by getting rid of metal: your external-frame pack, your steel ice ax, or your aluminum ski poles. If someone in your party is hit by lightning, they might need to be treated with CPR, a skill that you should know how to perform.

Avoiding Ground Lightning

WRONG: On ledge on a steep incline

RIGHT: Sitting on packs

WRONG: Sitting under an overhang or in a cave

WRONG: Sitting in a depression

RIGHT: Sitting on rocks atop other rocks

Avoiding ground lightning is counterintuitive; seeking shelter can lead you to the most hazardous spots.

GEAR FOR HIGH ALTITUDE

You don't need to go out and buy a whole new set of equipment for summer forays into higher climes. The 20-degree synthetic bag that you used hiking in the forests of the East will serve perfectly well, as will your old frame pack and your fabric-and-leather boots. But if you're replacing gear with an eye toward higher elevations, you might want to consider some peculiarities of hiking high.

Boots

Ankle-supporting all-leather boots have distinct advantages on high-mountain trails, which are typically rocky and rubbly and can require boulder-hopping or scree-skiing down huge talus slopes. All-leather boots can also be used with crampons, and they keep your feet warmer than fabric-and-leather combinations if you have to cross snowfields. The stiff support of a steel shank is also more effective if you're kicking steps into an icy slope.

Tents

High-altitude tentsites tend to be windy. They also tend to be on hard, gravelly ground that can bend tent-stakes into corkscrews. Ergo, you want a stable, low-lying, freestanding tent.

The three-pole wedge design (one of the most popular designs among long-distance hikers, also called a modified A-frame) is the best choice for alpine adventures. Three crossed poles and a low-to-the-ground profile give stability. The wedge shape sheds wind. And the tent is freestanding. Several manufacturers make variations of this design: Mine is a 10-year-old no-frills Tadpole by The North Face (this model has been discontinued and replaced with the very similar Lunarlight). Wedge-shaped tents come in different sizes and weights. Some have extensive mosquito netting,

ALPINE MINIMUM IMPACT

- Don't camp on alpine grasses or meadows. Choose instead sturdy gravel or mineral soil.
- Don't make fires — even if there's enough wood (which there usually isn't). Alpine areas can take centuries to recover from fire.
- Wear camp shoes in camp to minimize your impact on fragile vegetation.
- Use campsites that have obviously been used before to concentrate impact in one place.
- If you are camping in an area where there are no signs of previous campsites, set up your tent out of sight of the trail, and leave no trace when you pack up the next morning.

giving them great ventilation and cutting down on pounds, but making them useless in all but the lightest snow. (Note: No wedge design is a good choice for heavy snow, because the squat shape doesn't shed snow well. If you think you'll be sleeping in the snow, a tube or a dome is a much better choice.) Some are larger (and therefore heavier) than others. Some have pole sleeves (greater strength); some have clips (greater ease of setup). Some tents by The North Face use the no-hitch-pitch system, in which specially designed clips keep the poles attached to the tent body when you take down the tent. This is a useful feature if you're putting up the tent in a heavy rain, because you just shake out the tent and it practically pitches itself. But keeping poles attached to the tent body limits packing flexibility. Furthermore, sleeves — not clips — are more stable in high winds and more durable over the long haul. For these reasons, many distance hikers opt for the old-fashioned sleeves.

Living on the edge. A tentsite at high altitude can require special skills and plenty of nerve. Also the ability to sleep calmly.

Dome tents are another good choice for alpine areas, although they are heavier for the same amount of floor space than the wedges. What you get in return for those extra ounces is more headroom and a shape that sheds snow. I've spent several tent-bound days in my Tadpole casting covetous glances at some less-weight-conscious friends' palatial domed accommodations, and have once or twice been grateful for

an invitation to leave my cramped quarters and pay a visit to the big house next door for afternoon tea. You'll have to make your own decision: extra weight on the trail, or extra comfort in camp.

One of the most popular lightweight tent designs — a two-pole hoop tent like the Sierra Designs Clip Flashlight — can give you headaches up high. The two poles aren't nearly as wind-resistant as the three-pole wedge or dome, and this design is not freestanding, which means a major hassle if you can't force a stake into rocky alpine ground.

Accessories

SUNGLASSES Choose high-quality glacier glasses that filter out UV light. They should also have side flaps (in a pinch, you can improvise flaps with a piece of cardboard and some duct tape). Warning: The light at altitude is especially bright, and if there is snow, sunburn of the retinas can cause temporary, but excruciating blindness.

SUNSCREEN Choose an SPF (sun protection factor) above 15. Remember, there's no shade above treeline. And pay attention: In cooler temperatures or under gray skies, you may not even be aware of an impending sunburn. Experienced climbers wear sunscreen even on cloudy days.

LIP BALM A lip balm with a high SPF factor can prevent chapped lips. It can also help prevent an outbreak of the herpes simplex virus, which is activated by strong sunlight.

TECHNIQUE

After a number of years of learning how to walk uphill, I've finally gotten to the point where I climb like a salmon swims upstream — neither easily or gracefully, but naturally, following an instinct that home is where the contour lines bunch together in craggy brown cliffs and steep mountainsides.

The key — *the* key — to hiking uphill is finding a pace you can stick with all day. For some hikers, an all-day pace is a brisk stroll. Other hikers are better served by the ungainly, stop-and-start, little-engine-that-could gait of the rest step. Either way, slow and steady will get you there. Begin-

TECHNIQUE TIP
HIGH-ALTITUDE CAMPSITES

● Choose a campsite sheltered from the wind. The above-treeline vegetation often shows you which way the wind most often blows. Pitch your tent on the lee side, or crawl in among some bushes or behind a few large rock formations. Stay away from passes because they funnel winds.

● When you're putting up your tent, weight the ground cloth with rocks so it doesn't blow away. When you get the tent up, weight it down before you try to stake it out.

● Likewise, when you spread out your gear, anything not weighted down is subject to becoming airborne.

● Even if you use a freestanding tent, always stake it down. If the ground is too rocky for stakes, you can tie the guy-lines to rocks or (if the rocks available aren't big enough) to a stuff sack filled with stones.

ners who haven't learned to pace themselves sometimes push too hard and then fall into an exhausted heap. It's far better to find a pace you can sustain for an hour or so, and then take a 10- or 15-minute break. As you gain experience your body will actually learn to climb; you may even find that you can climb comfortably without the need for a rest.

Going uphill is work, so be sure you've got enough fuel to do the job: A liter of water before a climb and a quick snack will give you that extra oomph. And if your spirits and energy are sagging midway along on the climb, stop for a quick pick-me-up. A rest and a snack won't make the mountain any smaller, but they will help you get there.

If you are hiking with a partner who is stronger or weaker than you are, the uphills are where your relationship will be put to the test. Be warned: If both partners don't respect the abilities and limits of the other person, the uphills can turn into a battlefield. Slower hikers usually feel pushed, rushed, and sometimes demoralized. Stronger hikers feel frustrated and tethered, as if their momentum is slowly being drained away. In my opinion — and it's one that is put to the test every time I hike with my husband — there is no solution to this dilemma except for each of you to go at your own pace and meet somewhere up the trail. Nagging a slow hiker to go faster doesn't result in a faster hiker; it results in a resentful, unhappy hiker. Nor is it any fun for a fast walker to have to slow down to what feels like a virtual crawl. You need to consider the different strengths and weaknesses of the members of your party when you plan your hike. The fact is, a group can only go as far as its weakest member. If getting somewhere by a certain time is a consideration, you might want to redistribute the gear to reflect the relative strength of the people in your group.

If you do split up, agree on a place to meet and make sure you both have adequate food and equipment to get there, including rain gear, water bottles, and food. Dan sometimes stays behind to give me a head start and writes in his journal for a while. That way, he gets to spend his waiting time in below-treeline comfort rather than atop a blustery pass. But if the trail is poor and might pose navigating problems, the faster hiker should go ahead. This avoids a time-wasting situation in which the slower hiker gets to an unmarked junction and has to wait for the faster hiker — who is sitting down at the bottom of the mountain taking a nap in order to give the slower hiker a head start! Also, by the time the slower hiker gets to the junction, the faster hiker may have figured out which way to go. Note: Many hikers who split up on a climb plan to meet at the top. But a windswept summit might be an uncomfortable place to wait, so you and your partner should agree that if the weather is bad, the person up ahead has the option of continuing on and down the other side until he reaches a protected place where he can wait more comfortably.

Rocks and Rolls

If you're used to well-groomed packed dirt trails, the mountains have a surprise waiting for you just above that first rocky rise. On high-mountain shoulders, trails are likely to be cairned paths through crumbly scree. Sometimes, it seems as if you're being led through a field of marbles, each of which is only waiting for you to step on it before answering gravity's call to roll downhill.

There are two kinds of high-country rock: scree and talus. Scree is the crumbling stuff that you skid down on. Talus is the bigger rock rubble — boulders and slabs — that forms a high-altitude obstacle course. Both can be nerve-racking in the same way that an earthquake is nerve-racking: Having the ground move beneath your feet is a challenge to the normal order of the universe. That's what mountains do (and perhaps why we love them): They challenge the normal order of the universe.

FOUR LEGS ARE BETTER THAN TWO

How many times have you wished that you had a better sense of balance, or more strength in your knees? A hiking stick might be the most helpful piece of "extra" gear you carry.

● Studies sponsored by the manufacturers of hiking poles conclude that over a typical 10-mile day of backpacking, hiking sticks can take up to 250 tons of pressure off of your knees and back.

● Two hiking sticks are twice as good as one hiking stick. In addition to taking weight off your knees and back, they help with balance and give you third and fourth legs when you have to descend on steep unstable rock or cross snowmelt rivers.

● Buy telescoping hiking poles: not only can they be customized to your size, they also can fit conveniently into luggage and be strapped on the outside of your pack when you don't need them. And you can adjust them to your liking for uphills, downhills, and long traverses (where you might want the uphill poles to be shorter than the downhill ones).

● Some hiking sticks can be used as a monopod for your camera. Check to see if the grip unscrews.

● Also check to see if your poles can be screwed together to make an avalanche probe.

Sometimes the best way to deal with a problem is simply to walk around it. If you have a choice, a long loop around a scree or talus slope may take a lot less time than a direct path through a jumble of rocks. But often, high-mountain terrain doesn't offer you a choice. That's when a little experience and a few tricks will help.

Climbing scree is a little like climbing a sand dune: You can work awfully hard and end up in pretty much the same place you started. But unlike sand on a dune, scree isn't very deep. You can actually kick steps into it and get purchase with the front of your boots. Even so, it's a laborious way to climb. Another choice is to try to switchback by traversing the slope and gaining a little elevation at a time. This makes the climb less steep. As you ascend, you'll probably see bigger rock chunks here and there. These can make good footholds, but test them first since they are subject to the same law of gravity that keeps trying to pull you downhill: A stable-looking rock could be sitting on an unstable layer of scree that will start to slide just as you put your foot on it.

Descending is a lot easier and a lot more fun, because you can let gravity take you. Boot skiing (or "screeing") is a combination of running, sliding, and hopping from foot to foot. Get a shuffling start and bend your knees in a skier-like stance until you start to slide. Then shift

Jumping and scrambling across a talus field, Imja Glacier, Nepal. The key to talus travel is to always look several steps ahead.

your weight from foot to foot to keep your balance and momentum.

Warning: This technique is best on an all-scree hill that doesn't have too many big obstacles to fall into. The lower your center of gravity (and the more bent your knees), the more control you will have. (This is a huge argument in favor of internal-frame backpacks for alpine hiking, because internal-frame packs have a lower center of gravity. No matter what kind of pack you use, putting heavy equipment low and close to your back will aid you in keeping your balance on unstable and difficult terrain.)

THE REST STEP

It's debilitating and demoralizing to have to stop every 50 steps, gasping and futilely looking for the end to the climb. The rest step keeps you going — forward motion is the name of the game — by giving you tiny little chances to, quite literally, rest, even as you continue to climb. What it lacks in grace, it makes up for in effectiveness. I use two variations on the rest step, depending on how I feel. (After crawling uphill for a couple of hours, I sometimes need a rest from the rest step!) Both are described below; they differ only

in when you take the rest. The first method is the one most commonly taught in climbing schools. But for some reason, I find that the second is easier to use for an extended period

VARIATION 1
1. Take a step up with your right leg.
2. Do not shift weight to the uphill leg. Leave it on the downhill (left) leg. Pause for the "rest."
3. Now shift the weight to the uphill (right) leg and simultaneously take a step with the left leg.
4. Leave the weight on the downhill (right leg) and take a momentary rest.

VARIATION 2
1. Your right leg moves forward and up; your weight stays on the downhill (left) leg.
2. As your weight is transferred to your right (uphill) leg, lock your right knee. This momentarily transfers weight from your muscles to your bones. Here's where you rest. Your left leg dangles around doing nothing. If you need to put it somewhere for balance, set the toe down somewhere in the vicinity of your right foot.
3. Move the left leg forward and up.

Talus, otherwise called a boulder field, is made up of big broken rock chunks. Moving on it can be difficult: Big rocks force you to take bigger steps (which is hard on the knees going down and requires strength going up) from one rock to the other. You also need good balance, because all the while the rocks can be moving underfoot. The key to talus travel, whether you're going uphill or down, is to always look several steps ahead. That way, if a rock starts to shift and throw you off balance, you can simply hop to the next one without taking time to think. Climbing is easier than descending: Going up, you're fighting gravity; but going down, gravity is tugging at your balance and can pull you somewhere you may not want to go. The best way to climb up is to take a diagonal route. Not only is it less strenuous than the straight-up approach, it's also safer for your hiking partners below you, who could be hit if you dislodge a loose rock.

Going downhill on talus can be frustrating, nerve-racking, and hard on the knees. Beginners usually go one rock at a time, trying always to stay balanced and in control. Or they look for a way around the rocks (unfortunately, there usually isn't one). Far easier is hopping from rock to rock in a controlled dance with gravity. Think of learning to ride a bicycle: You know that balance comes with speed, but even so, the beginning cyclist has a few awkward moments. The natural inclination of

Boulder fields can make for slow going, especially during storms as here, in the Bugaboos.

the beginning cyclist (and talus-hopper) is to wait till you have control and then add speed, but the speed is what gives you the control. To practice, try moving downhill on rocks without your pack. Keeping your knees bent, hop from one to the next. Use a side-to-side motion; it's slower and easier to control. (Side-to-side is easier on the knees, too, than going straight downhill.) Likewise, choose a less steep lateral route whenever possible. Whether you're traveling fast or slow on talus, hiking sticks help: You can use them to take the weight off your knees for big steps, to test the stability of rocks, or to fine-tune your balance on a fast descent. However, if you've got bad knees or a heavy load, or if the descent is simply too frightening to attack head-on, you may have to resort to the tried-and-true and one-step-at-a-time approach.

Whether you're traveling on scree or talus, remember that if you do lose your balance or the rock underfoot starts to slide, the best thing to do is go forward, hopping from rock to rock or between rocks until you regain your sense of control. Beginners typically try to stop, which makes things worse because in addition to being off balance, their bodies are now fighting gravity and momentum. Far better is to use quick footwork to catch up with your momentum and then, when your feet are underneath you again, start slowing down to fully regain control. Be especially careful on wet rock or on rocks with wet (read: slippery) vegetation. And finally, give your partner plenty of room. If either of you loses your balance, it may take several steps of out-of-control scrambling before you regain it.

River Crossings

Most river crossings are a dash-and-splash affair, sometimes causing consternation but rarely actual danger. Indeed, by far the most common kind of crossing is a rock-hop over an ankle-high stream. On many major trails, you'll often find bridges over water that runs deep and fast.

But during snowmelt season, all bets are off. Bridges can be washed away; streams that are gentle trickles in August can be mad torrents. Sometimes, river crossings can be dangerous indeed.

Hikers heading to high mountains in early season often assume that the biggest challenges await them high up on not-yet-melted icy slopes. But down in the valleys, the ice that melted last week — or yesterday — and poured into a fast-running stream can be even more of a problem.

Stream crossings fall into two categories: dry and wet. Dry crossings usually are simple affairs: Most often, you simply hop your way across, using a walking stick for balance. Whether it's an ankle-high

TECHNIQUE TIP
ROCK!

You're walking along minding your own business, and out of nowhere you hear someone yell "rock!" Duck and cover your head! This call means someone has dislodged a piece of rock and it's airborne. Don't try to look for the rock. When you hear the call, you've got time to do just one thing: Protect your head.

rivulet with conveniently placed rocks or a knee-deep stream with lots of big boulders within a stride of each other or a narrow watercourse bridged by a couple of fallen logs, a dry crossing means that you can negotiate it safely without getting your feet wet.

Hiking sticks can help keep your feet dry by helping you keep your balance. I use two poles, which I find essential in early-season alpine hiking. I had a firsthand look at the difference between crossing with and without sticks last summer: I got across a minor little torrent in about 10 seconds, while some fellow hikers who were stickless took 10 minutes to get across the same stream — and by the time they did, their feet were soaking wet. With sticks, you can poke at a rock to see how stable it will be underfoot. You can also use them as a third leg for balance. Gaiters can also help you cross dry: They won't keep water out of your boots if you're actually wading, but they offer great protection in the case of a quick little accidental dunking.

Watch out for wet, algae-covered rocks; they are often as slick as ice. As on talus, you can either go one slow step at a time, testing each rock for slipperiness and stability, or attack the whole obstacle course at once so quickly that you never stay on a single rock long enough to lose your balance on it. I have to admit that this isn't something you're going to be able to learn from a book. Like getting com-

Hiking along the Flathead River, Montana. A pair of sticks makes all the difference in maintaining balance during river crossings.

fortable on a balance beam, rock-hopping takes practice. In general, the fast approach is more suitable for easier crossings or for one big lunge from one solid rock to another. If the rocks are unstable and far apart, it's usually best to proceed more deliberately, one obstacle at a time.

In addition to boulders, you might be lucky enough to find a well-placed log that makes an adequate bridge — but again, watch out, because wet wood can be so slick that you might wonder if you've wandered into a figure-skating competition as you flail about on the slippery surface. It may be better to sit and scoot across rather than try to keep your balance on a slick log. Snow bridges can also provide a dry path across a stream, but they require extra caution because as each day goes by, they become a little thinner and a little less reliable — and the consequences of falling through one can be deadly. If you must cross a snow bridge, take small steps, and test each one, first with your stick, and then with your foot, before committing your weight to it. Stay away from grayish, translucent-looking snow or from bridges where the part over the water looks different in density or color than the snow nearer the banks: It's on the verge of collapsing. Finally, don't rely on someone else's week-old footprints to tell you that a bridge is safe.

Hikers will go to all sorts of lengths to cross a stream without getting their feet wet. But no matter how experienced you are, caution should rule the day: Don't attempt a dry crossing if there's a chance you could fall in. Always weigh the consequences of a misstep. Where will you end up if you slip off of that slick-looking log? If the rocks are too far apart, or the logs are covered with algae, or the stream is too deep and wide, or the consequences of a fall are too serious, you'll have to get your feet wet. And wet crossings require planning: not only where to

cross, but when.

One single rule can save you all kinds of hassles and prevent unnecessary risk-taking: If you need to cross snow-fed rivers, plan your day so as to hit the major fords as early as possible in the morning. During the night, mountain temperatures drop, and as they do, the rate of snowmelt decreases. Consequently, the water level in the streams is lower and the flow is slower in the mornings. (Downside alert: the water will be much colder early in the morning.) As the day wears on and temperatures climb, the snow melts faster and the river's flow will increase until it reaches its zenith in late afternoon.

Once you arrive at the stream, your first job is to choose a route. The safest way across is not necessarily the straight line between where the trail ends on one side of the stream and where it picks up again on the other. That path in and out of the water might be easy enough in August, when the stream is a meek, pleasant trickle. During snowmelt, the same stream might be a torrent — and the direct path impassable. Look for "social" trails up and down the banks; they may indicate where other people have crossed. Sometimes cairns will indicate a possible passage. Take the time to scout upstream and downstream for a safe passage, and don't be surprised if you have to walk quite some distance before you find it. If it is necessary to walk along the banks, check your map to see if the stream breaks into tributaries upstream. Two small crossings are usually safer and easier than one big one.

Look for calm water. White water is made when the rocks in a stream break up the flow of the water. It looks dangerous, and it is. Kayakers and canoers are taught never to stand in or try to walk through white water, and backpackers should follow that rule, too. White water can sweep you off your feet and throw you against those boulders you see poking above the water's surface — and that's only part of the problem. There are also submerged rocks that can trap your ankles. The force of water in rapids is so enormous that if you get your feet stuck and lose your balance, you could be held under and drowned in water that isn't even knee-high.

Look for the widest part of the stream, because that's where the water will be the most shallow. Be sure you have a good view of what lies downstream: If you get swept away, where will you end up? Check the map to be sure there aren't any cataracts or waterfalls or rapids just ahead. Make sure the route looks good all the way across or you might end up crossing the river almost all the way and then be forced to retrace your steps. The safest way to cross is diagonal to the current, by angling either downstream or upstream. (I prefer facing upstream and angling upstream. Fighting the current

directly seems to give me more control.) If you go straight across, the force of the current can more easily knock you off balance. Once you've identified a route, undo the hip belt on your pack so that if you do lose your footing, you can shrug the pack off and it won't hold you under. If you end up off your feet and headed downstream and you can't regain your footing, turn on your back and float feet first.

Sometimes members of a group will react to a river crossing radically differently. A hiker who happily jumps skittery, slippery boulders might freak out in thigh-high fast-running water. (And of course, the reverse is also true.) If one of your partners is having trouble with the obstacles and you're confident of your ability to negotiate them, you might offer to ferry your partner's pack across. If you're traveling with a group, you can also form a human chain. This technique is especially valuable if there's a wide disparity in the experience and confidence among the members of the group. Put the weakest hikers in the middle.

One common river-crossing myth is that using a rope ensures safety. In practice, very few backpackers are experts at handling ropes, and a rope inexpertly handled is more likely to cause a drowning than prevent one. Even an expertly handled rope may cause trouble. If you are clipped into the rope, the combination of the rope with a strong current can actually hold you underwater if you lose your balance and fall forward (the most likely scenario in case of a fall, because the weight of your pack makes you top-heavy). Your hiking partner may not be able to save you, because the force of moving water exerts enormous tension on the rope. If, however, a rope is already in place across a river, by all means use it. Don't clip in with a caribiner (here, too, you could be held under if you slip). Instead, simply hold on to the rope on the downstream side and walk across.

Always wear boots or shoes for a wet crossing. River-smoothed stones are slick and can easily trap a bare foot or twist an ankle. If the ford is easy, I usually cross in amphibious sport sandals. If there are a lot of fords, one after the other, I'll wear my sandals and carry my boots for a while so I don't have to stop and change before every single crossing. But if the fords are difficult — deep, fast, and rocky — sport sandals don't offer enough protection. If there are just one or two crossings on your route, the best thing to do is take off your socks and wear your boots across, then put on the dry socks on the other side. But if you've got a series of crossings, you might as well give up the quest for dry feet and wade right in: Most hikers lose patience with taking boots and socks on and off every 5 minutes.

Finally, and rarely, there are deep-water crossings, where the water is high enough that you'll get

your pack wet or partly wet if you wade straight through. These can be extremely dangerous, depending on the speed and temperature of the water. How you approach these crossings (and indeed whether or not a crossing is even possible) will depend on the conditions and on your comfort level (and skill and experience) in the water. If you expect to have to deal with deep crossings, it's well worth the time to pack up your gear and head out for a trial run before your trip. To protect your gear, bring along lots of zipper-lock bags, extra garbage bags, waterproof stuff sacks, a ground cloth (to wrap around your gear as an added layer of protection), an air mattress (which can help with flotation), and bungee cords (to hold the package together). Divide your gear by what can get wet (tent, stove, pots and pans, water filter, fuel bottle, rain gear, etc.) and what can't (your camera, notebook, warm clothing, down sleeping bag). The stuff that can get wet goes in the bottom of your pack; the vulnerable stuff gets wrapped in as many layers of protection as you have available and stashed at the top.

What you do next depends on the depth of the water. Some hikers try to hold the packs over their heads (or at least part of the pack over their heads). If this sounds difficult, it's because it is. Most women (and many men) don't have the upper-body strength for this kind of hauling and hefting. A much easier choice is to simply let the bottom of your pack get wet, assuming that your vulnerable gear is adequately protected and packed up high. You can also press your air mattress into service. While manufacturers of air mattresses specify that the mattresses are not approved flotation devices for humans, an inflated mattress can be wrapped around

Wet crossings like this can be dangerous unless you know the water currents and streambed you are venturing across.

a pack, secured by bungee cords, and the whole thing towed across a stream. The flotation will be enough that you can keep at least part of the pack (the part with your vulnerable gear in it) out of the water.

Finally, you might have to swim, but here's where I bow out of the advice-giving business. Swimming with a pack across a river is dangerous by its very nature, and it's impossible for a book to give adequate instructions for a situation that has so many variables and relies, in the final analysis, so heavily on the quick instincts and responses of the hiker. If your backcountry goals

include this kind of activity, work up to it by experimenting at home with different kinds of flotation devices and ways of packing your gear. In addition to an air mattress, some long-distance hikers actually pack inner tubes or life jackets if they know they'll be faced with a deep, tricky crossing. (This, however, is hard-core, even from a thru-hiker point of view. Unless you'll be crossing glacier torrents in Alaska you probably don't need to run out to look at inner tubes!) Finally, remember that retreat is an honorable option, because drowning is a very real possibility.

SNOW AND ICE

Whether or not you find yourself dealing with snow and ice is largely a matter of choice: Go high enough on a mountain early enough (or late enough) in the season, and you'll find some. In a year when the lingering winter snowpack is thick, snow can actually stick around all summer.

Alpine Equipment

ICE AX The ice ax is a multi-purpose alpine tool designed to help travelers get up, down, and across ice and snow. It can be used to chop steps, control a glissade, and act as a fulcrum for climbing, self-arrest, and self-belay. But as a backpacker, most of the time you carry an ice ax you'll be using it as a humble walking stick. While mountaineers tend to favor shorter ice axes (they are more maneuverable and more functional on the steeper slopes that mountaineers tackle), a hiker's ice ax should have a longer shaft for walking (depending on your height, 65–75 centimeters).

CRAMPONS Hikers don't usually use crampons, but in early-season hiking or in a year of exceptionally

Three-season backpackers, who don't generally need full crampons, opt for these instep crampons.

heavy snow, you might find yourself traversing steep ice slopes. If you expect to deal with seriously dangerous slopes, full-fledged crampons that fit under the entire length of your boot offer the greatest safety. (Full-length crampons may have 8, 10, or 12 points, but unless you intend to do technical climbing, you don't need front points on your crampons.) Be sure you fit them to your boots and learn how to put them on securely before you head out. Some of them are not self-explanatory and require a bit of practice, which is best done someplace other than a dangerous-looking ice slope. Make sure you have the right tools — European-made crampons frequently require a metric Allen wrench.

OTHER ICE-WALKING AIDS Three-season alpine backpackers generally don't need full-fledged crampons. Usually a guidebook, local managers, or other hikers will be able to tell you whether crampons are necessary. It's not uncommon for the verdict to be mixed: A ranger might suggest you use crampons, while fellow hikers say they got through just fine with ice axes alone. In such cases, instep crampons or creepers offer a viable compromise. Don't confuse instep crampons (which go under the instep of your boot) with step-in crampons (which are full-fledged crampons that work sort of like ski-boot bindings). Instep crampons are mini-crampons that strap under the instep of a hiking boot. Some models are extremely lightweight — they look like they might help you get to the mailbox if your front walk is iced over, but you wouldn't want to trust them to keep you vertical when you're carrying a heavy pack over a steep slope. Other models are heavier and somewhat more functional.

Finally, there are walking aids that look like tire studs for feet. The studs are inset into a piece of rubber that is shaped like the bottom of a boot, and the contraption affixes to your shoe by means of a rubber band. These can be helpful on icy trails or on terrain where you want just a smidge more security — for instance, crossing a summer snowfield that has gotten hard and icy after a night of rain. Yes, you could probably navi-

ABOUT AVALANCHES

● Know where you are at risk and go around risky areas. Avalanches tend to be found in the same places year after year. The chute will be steep and bare, usually with no trees. Avoid it!
● If you must cross an avalanche chute it's safest to do so just after there has been an avalanche, before more snow has had a chance either to fall or to begin to melt.
● Consider recent weather conditions. A series of cold nights followed by warm days is most dangerous.
● If you must cross an avalanche-prone slope, do it in the early morning, when it's still cold. This is not foolproof: On some mountains particularly prone to avalanches, you can lie awake at

night listening to them fall. Avoidance is, as always, the best strategy. Late afternoon is most dangerous.
● There is special equipment available for hikers and skiers, including a device to measure the slope of a hill, ski poles that screw together to become avalanche probes, and a transmitter to mark your position in case you're caught in an avalanche. But if you need this kind of equipment, you need to have spent some time in the field with an instructor.
● Before going across an avalanche slope, unfasten your pack belt so you can extricate yourself from your pack if necessary.
● If you are using a transmitter, turn it on.

There is only one way to learn self-arrest: Hurl yourself headlong down a steep, slippery slope, ice ax in hand.

Your topo map can give you clues about where snow is likely to be a problem. Snow accumulates in shady areas in the sheltered lee side of a mountain, as in a bowl or a cirque, and on the north sides of mountain and passes. Accumulations are far less on top of windy ridges or on very steep slopes. In late spring, snow often has frozen and thawed and frozen and thawed, so it's dense and consolidated, often with a crust on top. In the morning, this crust will be frozen solid — perfect for walking on if you have crampons, but deadly otherwise. As the day wears on, the sun softens the snow and you can kick steps into a slope that was too icy to cross in the morning. By mid- afternoon, you can find yourself breaking through the hard crust up to your thighs. Snowshoes would seem to be a solution, but traversing across springtime alpine snow often is a matter of two steps on rock, three on snow, and so on. Many alpine trails also contour around bowls and traverse steep slopes, and if the snow is hard and icy (as it often is in the spring and early summer) snowshoes are virtually unusable because of the

gate it in your hiking boots, but it would involve a lot of work kicking in steps and a few of those "if I fall, I'm going to end up 1,000 feet down there on those rocks" sorts of moments. A warning: don't try to get by with studs when you really need crampons. To evaluate which you need, consider the difficulty of the slope and the consequences of a fall.

Strategies and Techniques

Snow conditions change as you go up the mountain, they change throughout the day, and they change depending on whether you're on the cold north side of a ridge or the sunny south side. Check with rangers about snow, but realize that their information can't be up-to-the-moment — after all, the snow is melting on a daily basis. A day or so into your hike, you should have a pretty accurate idea of current conditions.

difficulty of cutting a stable edge into an icy, steeply inclined slope. And — perhaps the biggest drawback of all, especially to the distance hiker — they weigh a few pounds. You'll have to decide for yourself whether the work of carrying and hiking with snowshoes is more or less than the work of walking through deep snow without them. For the most part, the decision will depend on exactly how much snow you expect to encounter.

CROSSING ICE It might be a hassle to stop and put on crampons, but take the time. If you don't have crampons, consider where a fall would put you. If the answer is 500 feet downhill on a rockpile, do the sensible thing and detour around. If no detour is possible, wait until later in the day, when the ice or snow melts enough that you can safely kick steps in.

KICKING AND CHOPPING On ice, you can chop footholds with your ice ax. If the ice is soft, you may be able to kick in steps. Climbing, use your lower leg and kick from the knee, as straight into the slope as possible. It may take several kicks to make one step. Descending on soft ice, flex your ankle so the toe is pointed up and step down hard on the heel. When traversing, keep an eye on where you hope to end up on the other side: You want to resist gravity's ever-present temptation to pull you downhill.

SELF-ARREST Used correctly, an ice ax can help you self-arrest — that is, stop a fall. Used improperly, you might self-impale instead. The best way to learn is to cadge a lesson from a more experienced friend (or pay for one at a climbing school; many one-day introductory courses are available just about anywhere there's a hill big enough to fall down). To practice, you'll need a Gore-Tex or nylon rain or wind suit (it'll help you speed downhill faster, mimicking what really happens when you fall) and a steep slope covered with hardpacked snow (not sheer ice).

① When walking on ice, get in the habit of correctly holding your ice ax: In the uphill hand, adze facing forward. Every time you change direction on a switchback, you need to change the hand that holds the ax.

② When you fall, bring the ice ax against your chest and turn toward the ax. Dig the point into the slope.

③ Come to rest in the three-point stance.

④ Keep your upper body as close to the slope as possible.

Prepare for an ice traverse by putting all of the extra things — your camera and water bottle — in your pack. If you fall, you don't want things hanging around your neck and body, getting in the way and interfering with your mobility.

Walking on the White Stuff

POST-HOLING So named for the deep holes you leave behind, this is what you do if you left your snowshoes behind. Another thing to call it: trudging.

THE PLUNGE STEP A downhill tech-

● MOUNTAINEERING: FREEDOM OF THE HILLS (*The Mountaineers*) Now in its sixth edition, this is the classic book of mountain travel. While much of the information is devoted to technical climbing, this book also contains information about virtually any conditions you're likely to encounter when you're way up there, including lightning, storms, snow, and hypothermia.

● AVALANCHE HANDBOOK, by David McClury and Pete Shaerer (*The Mountaineers*) If you're heading into avalanche country, you need to know what to do when you get there. There's no substitute for firsthand, in-the-field training, but, as this book makes clear, you need to be thinking about avalanches long before you get anywhere near one. How do you know when you're at risk? What should you do? This book could save your life.

---

nique in deep snow or scree. The leg taking the forward step is the "plunging" leg. Lean back a little, hold your leg straight, and step down so the weight is on your heel. Let yourself slide before taking the next step. You can get into a nice rhythm, even in relatively deep snow. But resist the temptation to go too fast: If you go too fast and sink into the snow unexpectedly deeply, your leg could get stuck and your momentum could force you forward. The result could be a broken leg.

BOOT SKIING This combination of shuffling, sliding, and skiing is a fun way to get downhill fast, but you need fairly strong leg muscles to do it for long, because the trick is to keep your knees "soft." You'll go faster following someone else's tracks. A pair of ski poles helps with balance. They should have baskets so they don't get caught in the snow.

SITTING GLISSADE When your knees get too tired, it's time to simply sit and slide — what the experts call a sitting glissade. Start slowly to get a feel for how fast you can go on a given slope and still be in control. Be careful if you're wearing Gore-Tex or nylon pants; you could end up speeding out of control — and who knows into what rocks or cliffs below. An ice ax acts as a rudder and a break (but do not wear crampons; they could catch and flip you over). Wearing a pack will also slow you down. Warning: do not attempt a glissade wearing only shorts, or you risk serious skin abrasions from sliding over hard clumps of ice.

DESERTS

And just why, again, is it that you're going *there?*"

"There" was the desert, Arizona's Sonoran. The man had stopped his pickup truck as we were heading up a dusty jeep road toward Arizona's rugged, blazing Four Peaks Wilderness. He figured anyone on foot must be in trouble. What had never occurred to him is that someone would be out here walking on purpose.

Prickly, waterless, sun-scorched, scorpion-filled, rattlesnake-infested; in the words of Edward Abbey, stinging, sticking, stabbing, stinking: The desert can, indeed, be hard to love.

But imagine.

A sky that covers the earth like a planetarium dome.

A quiet that could muffle the sounds of a city, a silence as endless as time and as encompassing as the sky.

Muted colors of tan and gold and pink and purple, interrupted by the occasional flare of a sun-colored cactus blossom or the crimson fire of an ocotillo flower.

Like winter camping, desert hiking is an experience of extremes and subtleties, a trip in which time slows down until a weekend seems like a month, and a week seems to stretch out for a year. But also like winter, the desert poses some particular and memorable challenges.

Hiking on Bruneau Sand Dunes, Idaho. Experienced desert backpackers walk with the thought of water sloshing around in their brains.

The Desert Environment

First, a definition. The technical definition of a desert is land that receives less than 9 inches of rainfall a year. But for the hiker, conditions requiring desert hiking skills can occur in areas with as much as twice that amount of rainfall. Practically speaking (and throughout this chapter), desert hiking applies to situations in which you have to constantly monitor your water supply.

Water. From beginning to end, from one moment to the next, water is *the* most important factor in a hike through arid country. With enough

DESERT ACCESSORIES

Before you head into the endless sun, remember these dry-country necessities: sunglasses, sunscreen, bug repellent, bandannas, light-colored hat, extra long-sleeved clothing, long pants, tweezers (two pairs in case you lose one), a mattress that isn't an air mattress (or plenty of patches), ankle-high gaiters (for keeping prickles and burrs out of your boots), water bags and a water filter, and a comb for removing cactus joints that may attach themselves to you.

water, a desert traverse may well be one of the high points of your hiking career. But run out, and the opposite will certainly be true.

Experienced desert hikers walk with the thought of water sloshing around their brains. They know, exactly and accurately, how full their canteens are. How much they need to walk a mile. How much they'll want to drink at the top of a big climb. They know how many water sources are on their map, and which of those are likely to be reliable. And they have a plan for what they'll do when the "reliable" spring is dry.

In thinking about water, the most important question is how much do you need. Not how much does a *person* need, but how much do *you* need? People vary drastically according to physical factors: their height and weight, how much they sweat, and their level of fitness. Other factors also figure in: how far and fast they walk, whether they walk in the cooler hours or in the middle of the day, the difficulty of the terrain, mileage, elevation gain, and so on. As a starting point, figure on *at least* 6 to 8 quarts a day for cooking and drinking. From there, you'll need to modify the amount according to your body, the demands of your hike, and, especially, the temperature.

The author, Santa Cataline Mountains, Arizona Trail. In the desert, light-colored and light-weight clothes are the order of the day, and a wide-brimmed hat is a must.

PLANNING FOR WATER

Rangers often suggest that if you intend to hike in a desert you carry all of your water with you. Their motivation, I suppose, is to avoid the disastrous situation and accompanying liability of an unsuspecting hiker depending on an uncertain water source. The problem, however, is that carrying all of your water is a heavy proposition, and sometimes an impossible one, because water weighs about 2 pounds to the quart. The math is easy: At 8 quarts a day, that's 16 pounds in your pack. The distance you can cover while hauling all your water is limited.

Indeed, once you start planning a desert hike, it becomes clear that

The author drawing water from a cattle tank in the Superstition Mountains on the Arizona Trail. A filter is a necessity when relying on such sources.

what you are really doing is planning a series of hops between safe harbors, and those safe harbors are your reliable water sources. Your job is to identify likely water sources, collect as much information as you can, and have a backup plan. Or — another option — you can cache your water before your hike.

Finding Water

You'll encounter two kinds of water sources in the desert: natural sources, such as springs, seeps, and perennial streams, and man-made sources such as wells, windmills, cattle tanks, troughs, and containment dams. Neither natural nor man-made sources are 100 percent reliable: Springs can dry up.

Containment dams can be so polluted with cattle dung that the water is impossible to filter. Wells and windmills are often on private property, and they can be broken or their tanks can be sealed.

The United States Forest Service, the Bureau of Land Management (BLM), and the National Park Service are the three federal agencies most likely to manage desert lands. As a whole, National Park Service maps are more reliable and up-to-date than those of other agencies, especially BLM maps, which are often egregiously incomplete and fiendishly difficult to read.

Finding water is a treasure hunt, and like any other treasure hunt, the better your map, the richer the booty. 1:25,000-scale USGS topo maps are the best source of information. One warning: In sparsely populated and infrequently used desert areas, these maps are updated infrequently at best. A 30-year-old map won't show a road that was built 20 years ago. And the windmill you intend to rely on might be long since abandoned. Check the date of your map. If the map is more than a few years old, you should try to double-check the status of any water sources you plan to rely on by calling the management agency.

Actually, calling the agency is a good idea even if you've got a brand-spanking-new map revised just yesterday. No matter how good your map, there's no substitute for first-hand, current, on-the-ground information. In addition to the agency that manages the land, user groups like local trail clubs are good sources about water. In both cases, ask enough questions so that you get routed to *the* person (there's almost always someone) who has actually seen the water source in question. You'll know you've hit pay dirt when you find yourself on the phone with a horseman who's lived in these parts for 20 years and knows that there's always a trickle of water a few yards down from where the big tree fell across Dead Cow Draw. Be sure to ask if any springs are always reliable, no matter what, or if they dry out during part of the year. Also (this is critical) find out if it's been a dry year or a wet year. In wet years, sources deemed reliable are likely to be running, but in dry years all bets are off and you need to compensate by carrying more water or planning to hike from one reliable man-made source (like a well) to the next. Stress that you're looking for any source of water, no matter how polluted, because you have a filter.

But no matter how good your information source, never forget one sobering fact: Your life depends on finding water. Desert hiking requires a comfortable margin for error. Plan low mileage so that if one source is dry, you can go on to the next. But at the same time, you should be physically able to hike high-mileage days, in case you need to. Once, in New Mexico, we passed four dry water sources in a row and finally had to detour off our route to a house we saw in the distance, where we begged water from people whose caution, reticence, and inability to speak English convinced us they were illegal aliens. Identify several possible water sources both on your route and near it. Carry more water than you think you'll need, and make sure you've identified "bail-out" points on your map: a way to hot-tail it back to civilization if the springs are all dry. Note any cabins or houses nearby that are marked on your map: Usually houses are built near a reliable water source. And if you've left a vehicle at the place where you expect to end your hike, be sure you've got a couple of gallons of water stashed in it.

In the Field

In arid terrain, plants cluster around water sources, so look for unusual clusters of green. Typical desert plants tend to be spaced regularly. Abundant greenery tends to grow around springs. Big trees — especially cottonwoods — in a desert often signify water. Willows are an indicator, too, though not quite as reliably, because willows don't need a constant source of water, just a frequent one. If the thickets are thick and healthy-looking, chances are there's water somewhere nearby. You might find it downstream a bit or by digging about 8–12 inches into the sandy soil shaded by the thickets. Also look under big rocks, which can shade water from evaporating. Finally, look for aspens in drainage gullies. Aspens need 15 inches of precipitation a year, so in arid terrain, where there isn't enough rainfall to support them, they are sometimes found in drainage gullies where they can get water from underground.

Dry Camping

It's not uncommon for water sources in the desert to be spaced so far apart that you can't walk from one to the next in a day. Rarely, however — at least on established hiking trails — are reliable water sources spaced more than a 2-day walk apart.

One way to deal with huge distances between water sources is to plan to dry-camp. Here's the basic strategy: Arrive at your last water source before the big dry stretch in time for siesta. Drink as much as you can while you're lolling around. At the end of your break in the late afternoon, cook and eat dinner, drink some more, and walk on in the cooler evening hours, carrying enough water for the evening's walk, the night, breakfast, and the day's walk ahead. And be generous to yourself: On an extended hike, you need to be adequately hydrated throughout. Enough water for a day in the desert is still a heavy load, but it's not as heavy as it would have been if you had to carry your cooking water, too. And it breaks up the distance you have to walk the next day to reach the next sure water. When you get into camp,

WALKING ON THE WET SIDE

Sure, you know you're supposed to drink regularly and frequently, especially in the desert. But who wants to drop their pack every mile and dig out a water bottle? Now you don't have to.

● Dana Design's wet "ribs-pack" holds a water bottle right against your stomach, where you can reach it barely breaking stride. The pouch is useful for holding all those little thingamabobs you want at arm's reach: lip balm, sun-screen, bug dope, and so on.

● The CamelBak Patkeen. Your water rides in your pack (or lashed outside), and a tube for sipping lets you drink without missing a step, making this almost hands-free system the easiest yet. This system is the best choice for backpackers who do a lot of rock-scrambling because it doesn't get in the way, between you and the rock.

● Some packs have a pouch for water bottles built in. Look for an elastic mesh pouch at the side of your pack just behind your hip bones.

you can sup on cold food.

Carrying Water

Whether you're carrying water for half a day or merely 200 yards from spring to camp, you'll need a way to transport the stuff of life from here to there. Fabric water bags make the most versatile carriers because they take up almost no space when empty and only as much space as nec-

In deserts and drylands you may not need a tent for protection from rain and cold, but it's handy at holding bugs and scorpions at bay.

essary when full (as opposed to a water bottle, which takes up the same amount of space no matter what's in it). A number of different kinds are available. The best are made of rugged, heavy-duty fabric (check out MSR's "Dromedary" bags, available in several sizes). They stand up to more abuse than the older, more tra-ditional models that have a thin nylon cover and an internal plastic bladder. They also have more secure closures. Take two or three small water bags instead of a single large one: What applies to eggs in baskets applies to water in bags. If one of your bags springs a leak from, say, an accidental cactus encounter, you won't lose everything. Also, multiple small water bags are easier to stash and balance in your pack than one big one. Hint: Pack along some duct tape in case you need to perform emergency first aid on a water bag.

Desert Hiking Strategies

When most of us think "desert," we think "heat." In fact, heat is a function of both season and elevation, and deserts like the Mojave and the Great Basin are surprisingly cool. Even deserts that have earned their reputations for broiling heat only sizzle for a small part of the year. In the cooler months, some deserts offer extremely comfortable temperatures and little threat of rain. Nighttime temperatures, even in the summer, can be cool. So desert strategy number one: Hike during the cool months.

If you do decide to hike in hot desert weather, look to the plants and animals to learn survival strategies in an inhospitable environment. One thing you'll immediately notice: Nothing is moving midday when the sun shines its fiercest. Most desert animals are nocturnal, or at least crepuscular (out and about at dawn and dusk). While hiking at night isn't such a great idea (you might encounter rattlesnakes making their evening rounds), hiking in the cooler hours of dawn and dusk makes a lot of sense. In between, you'll want to find or make a patch of shade and do what the animals do: hole up for a midday siesta.

There are a few things you can do to keep your cool. Give yourself mini-cool-downs by taking a quick bandanna bath (or at least a wipe-down) when you pass a water source. Just cooling your face, your neck, and your upper chest will do wonders. When you're done washing, stick your wet bandanna under your hat and let the water dribble on your head as you walk.

Part of planning for water is planning that some of your well-laid plans will go awry. Never pass a water source without drinking, even if you don't feel thirsty. And in the morning, if you're camped by water, drink throughout your morning chores.

DESERT CLOTHING AND GEAR
Clothing

In the desert, clothing has a somewhat different function than it does elsewhere: For other hiking environments, the primary purpose of clothing is warmth. In the desert, its purpose is to keep you from getting too warm. Thus, a desert trip requires a new look at your old wardrobe.
FABRICS Although I adhere to a fairly inviolable no-cotton rule elsewhere, in the desert I occasionally allow some cotton clothing to sneak into my wardrobe. Light-colored cotton T-shirts, long pants, and long-sleeved shirts make workable desert attire. You can also try new breathable synthetics, which are even lighter in weight and wick away sweat.
LONG PANTS Most backpackers don't wear long pants for three-season hiking: In warm weather hikers prefer the looser fit of shorts, and in cooler

weather they usually use layers of warming, wicking polypropylene (or something similar) and rain pants. But in the desert a lightweight pair of light-colored, loose-fitting pants will protect skin from the heat and damage of the sun and from being clutched at, clung to, and clawed through by cactus quills and cat-claws. You might not wear them all the time, but you'll appreciate them when you need them. A new idea on the market that makes sense for desert hiking is a convertible pants-shorts combination, where the pant legs zip off to make shorts. These are great for situations where you need a quick cover-up to protect your legs from a thorny stretch of trail. If you buy these pants, be sure that the hems over the zippers are generous enough to prevent the metal from rubbing against your skin.

LONG-SLEEVED SHIRTS It might be counterintuitive that the way to stay cool in the desert is to cover up with clothing. But consider the traditional Saudi Arabian garb, which evolved as a highly practical response to desert heat: The loose layers and ventilation shade the skin and help prevent dehydration. And there's also sunburn to think about.

HATS AND HEAD COVERINGS You probably know that a hat is your best protection against winter cold. But

DESERT FOOD

● Your appetite decreases in really hot weather and heavy, fatty foods (like cheese and sausage) are likely to seem unappetizing. Foods like crackers, cereal bars, and dried fruits might seem easier to digest or at least more appealing.

● Take plenty of snacks and food that can be eaten cold. Think meltdown: Foods like cheese and chocolate can be messy in hot temperatures. If you do take them, stick them in the coolest middle portion of your pack, and — if you do find yourself camped near a cool spring — harden them up by dunking the food (in its zipper-lock bag) in the water.

● Hard candies or throat lozenges help stave off thirst if you're tem-porarily out of water.

● GORP is a great desert snack because it replenishes the salts (from the nuts) and sugars (from the raisins and whatever goodies you add to it) you've been losing to heat and exertion.

● Make sure to add banana chips to your GORP mixture, because they help replace the potassium you lose when you sweat.

● Avoid caffeinated coffee and tea: They are diuretics.

did you know the same is true in the desert sun? This is especially true for hikers who have very dark hair (which absorbs more of the sun's rays) and for balding or thin-haired hikers. A couple of things to look for: A light-colored hat reflects the sun's rays back at the sky. A hat with a brim shades your eyes as well as your head. Neck protectors (usually flaps that hang down from the back of the hat) offer additional protection to a vulnerable area. You can improvise a neck protector from a bandanna tucked under a hat. My current favorite desert hat is a light-colored synthetic hat that is lined with reflective mylar. The sides are netting, which makes for good ventilation. And a brim shades my eyes.

Boots

There's one thing you definitely don't need to worry about in choosing desert footwear, and that's whether or not it's waterproof. If you have strong ankles, you can get by with inexpensive fabric-and-leather lightweights. Forget about Gore-Tex: You don't need it, and, breathable though it may be, it still makes your feet sweatier than a fully breathable boot. Likewise, you don't need full-grain leather boots for desert hiking: The fabric-and-leather combos are cooler and lighter. Even durability is less of a factor, since some of the conditions that cause boot damage (like split seams and delamination) are at least in part aggravated by too much mud

and water. So lightweight boots with lots of seams aren't the liability they are on wetter trails. In the desert you can avoid spending a wad of money on footwear.

Lightweight advocates might be tempted to try using running shoes, but if you're going off-trail (and a lot of desert hiking is off-trail) you might get tired of prickles and thorns clutching at your ankles. In addition, desert terrain can be very rough and rocky, not to mention hot. On one desert hike, I decided to see if I could get away with using the lightest (and cheapest) boots I owned, a pair of Vasque Clarions, which are more appropriate for dayhiking than for heavy-duty backpacking. Under a heavy, water-laden pack, I felt as if the heat and rocks were boring their way right through the skimpy boot soles. Fortunately, in a fit of caution, I had packed along a spare pair of thicker socks and a pair of cushy insoles, which saved the day.

Packs

Here, too, the desert challenges conventional wisdom. While internal-frame packs are increasingly the load of choice among serious backpackers, in the desert the external frames have a distinct advantage: Because they don't hug the back quite as closely, they allow sweat to evaporate. In contrast, the close fit of internal-frame packs can lead to irritation and sometimes heat rashes. If you've got an external-frame pack, you might want to haul it out for a desert trip. If, however, you're planning a lot of bushwhacking and off-trail scrambling, you'll have to decide what's more important to you: better balance (go with the internal) or better ventilation (the external-frame pack).

A couple of notes on the care and handling of desert packs. Packcloth often comes in dark colors, which absorb heat. Pack things you want to keep cool (like a block of cheese or a slab of salami) well in the center of your pack. Also be careful when handling the pack itself: If you put it down on the ground so that the side that goes against your back faces the sun, it will absorb heat and could actually burn your back when you put it on. (The same is true of shiny metal parts.) If you set the pack down the other way, you'll need to make sure it hasn't picked up prickles, burrs, and thorns from the desert floor before you put it on or your pack could stab you in the back.

Shelter

Do you even need to bother about shelter? It's a legitimate question if you're hiking in a month in which the average cumulative rainfall is, say, a

DESERT MINIMUM IMPACT

Desert plants and animals eke out a precarious existence in dry climes. If you're going to hike in their habitat, here are a few things you can do to minimize your impact.

● Don't camp close to water sources. As in all camping, your tent should be at least 200 feet away, and not in the path of obvious game trails. Note that in some arid areas, the law requires you to camp at least 1/4 mile away from water. This helps prevent the pollution of scarce water sources. And it ensures that you won't dis-

continued on page 170

DESERT MINIMUM IMPACT
continued from page 169

turb the vulnerable animal life that depends on them.

● Take care with fences. Much arid land is leased by ranchers for grazing and is fenced for that purpose. If you must cross a barbed-wire fence, spread the strands and crawl between them. Or crawl underneath the fence. Don't climb over a fence, you'll either hurt yourself or damage the fence. The former has serious consequences for you; the latter will have serious consequences for rancher-hiker relations.

● Gates are another source of rancher-hiker conflict. Leave gates as you found them. The only exception is if the gate is open and there's a sign on it that says "Please close the gate," in which case go ahead and close it.

● No fires. Fires can leave scars that last hundreds of years in a desert.

● Cryptogamic crust is that very thin, crumbly layer of desert soil that almost crackles as you walk on it. You'll know it when you step on it, because your feet will feel like they're breaking through a hard crust like a macaroon. This fragile soil is made up of lichens and plants; once damaged, it takes a long time to heal. Avoid walking on it.

● Never wash directly in a desert water source. Too many other living things need that water, too.

half an inch. But then again, spend enough time outside and you'll find yourself being rained and snowed on in all kinds of unlikely places. Take something (if only a space blanket) that can be pressed into service in an out-of-season deluge. If you do take a tent, choose a well-ventilated one that has an inside layer mostly made of mosquito netting, or you're likely to find yourself stifling in there and going out to stand in the rain to cool off.

Tarps protect you from the sun during midday (and the sun is, after all, what you really need protection against), but they have an enormous disadvantage because they offer no respite from bugs and scorpions. Whether or not there's a bug problem depends on the season and the precipitation; you'll have to check local sources for information. One solution is to bring along an opaque ground-cloth to protect you against the sun and the unheard-of, unlikely, but almost always possible rainstorm, and a bug shelter (usually involving mosquito netting and some lightweight poles) for comfort.

Sleeping Supplies

Dry air and cloudless skies don't hold heat once the sun goes down, so at night desert temperatures drop precipitously. In the summer, of course, even a dramatic drop merely brings the temperature into a comfortable range. But before you go out in other seasons, you'll want to check average nighttime temperatures to make sure you have a warm enough bag.

Tarps are the ticket for shade, as these hikers in Big Pine Canyon, Sierra Nevada, California, demonstrate.

Air mattresses are a risky proposition in the desert, because there are jillions of cactus needles lying in wait to wreak their havoc. If you're the kind of person who can sleep like a log even if your bed happens to be a log, opt for a non-inflatable, indestructible closed-cell foam pad that won't fizzle the minute it's introduced to a cactus. If your sleeping comfort runs more along the lines of "The Princess and the Pea," go ahead and take the air mattress, but bring a patch kit. (Do remember, however, that before you can fix a puncture hole, you have to find it, and the best way to do this is to immerse the entire mattress in a pool of quiet clear water and look for escaping air bubbles. Readers will note that there is a lack of pools of quiet clear water in mattress-piercing cactus country.) Fortunately, even a leaky punctured air mattress provides about as much comfort as one of those old ensolite pads — although at more than double the weight.

● DESERT HIKING, by David Ganci (*Wilderness Press*) Sure, you prefer dry weather to wet weather. You like bright blue skies without a trace of clouds. But what about really dry weather? How do you stay cool and hydrated? How much water do you need and where do you find it? What about special gear and clothing? This book is a primer for desert hikers, with basic how-to information as well as descriptions of the unique flora and fauna you're likely to encounter.

HYPERTHERMIA AND DEHYDRATION

When hikers head out to the dry-lands, they tend to be more concerned about rattlesnakes than heat. The opposite should be true. While you're likely to run into only a few rat-tlesnakes, the twin dangers of dehy-dration and hyperthermia are lurking at every turn. A desert sun can be implacable as it burns its way across the sky. Take advantage of shade wherever you find it: A 5-minute break under a cottonwood tree or in an abandoned building, or a quick dive into a tank full of water, can bring down your body temperature.

And, at the risk of being a bore on the subject: Drink. Drink early, drink often, drink again. Don't wait till you're thirsty. Never pass a water source, and drink as much as you can. Don't worry if you feel like a barrel rolling down the trail: You'll sweat it off soon enough. Electrolyte-replacement drinks help prevent and treat dehydration (they're used by rangers at Grand Canyon National Park's first aid stations). If you're not carrying a drink mix, you can impro-vise one by putting one teaspoon each of sugar and salt into a liter of water. At the end of the day, drink some soup before dinner.

Like hypothermia, hyperthermia is insidious: By the time you realize you've got it, you're already in trouble. Learn to recognize the symp-toms of heat exhaustion (lightheaded-ness, nausea, headache, clammy skin, and a rapid pulse) and heat stroke (high temperature and dry — not sweaty — skin). Treatment for both includes drinking, cooling off, and resting (preferably in the shade: if necessary string up a ground cloth between whatever's available — tent poles, packs, a fence, or a handy plant — and lay the victim under-neath). Heat stroke is potentially fatal, so you need to bring down body temperature at once. The best treat-ment is a rubdown with clothing soaked in cool water.

FOREIGN
TRAVEL

It might be a global village out there in cyberspace, but when you're covering ground at 2 miles an hour, the world is no village. To the contrary, the world remains a marvelously, miraculously disorganized, multifaceted, ever-surprising, inconsistent mix of people, history, wildlife, culture, and geography.

Backpacking abroad is one of the best ways I know to satisfy both a love of backpacking and a curiosity about other places and cultures. The two activities — sightseeing and backpacking — complement each other marvelously. Imagine spending a week on an African safari — and finishing it off with hikes on Mount Kenya and Kilimanjaro. Or vacationing by hiking from village to village in the French Alps, sampling gourmet food and local wine, and exploring thousand-year-old churches in villages that aren't in any guidebooks. As far as meeting people goes, you can expect to encounter not only local folks, but other adventurers — people from all walks of life and dozens of countries.

But the very richness of the choices can be daunting. So can the logistics, like the prospect of deciphering a foreign train and bus system when you don't speak the language and maybe can't even read the alphabet. Fortunately, lots of people have gone before you, and they've left a trail full of information in their wake.

Passports and Visas

Most countries require Americans to have a valid passport. Applications are available at post offices, courthouses, and county seats and require proof of citizenship (a birth certificate or naturalization papers), a photo ID, two current photographs of yourself, and the $55 fee. First-time passport holders are required to apply in person; renewals can be done by mail, which takes about a month. Passports are good for 10 years, but if during that time you travel so much that you run out of room for visa and entry stamps, you can have additional pages added to your passport.

Before you head to foreign shores, make two photocopies of your passport. Leave one at home with a friend and keep the other with you, separate from the original. Having these copies will expedite paperwork should your passport be lost or stolen.

In addition to passports, some countries require visas, tourist permits, or trekking permits. Visas can usually be applied for in advance; some countries also permit you to apply when you arrive at the airport. If you opt to do this, be sure you know the country's entry requirements, which might include having photographs of yourself, additional identification, a certain amount of money, or a return ticket home.

Visas can be good for a single entry into a country or for multiple entries. Some countries have confusing rules: Kenya, for instance, issues a single-entry visa, but it is valid for multiple entries if you are traveling in Uganda or Tanzania. If you go farther afield, you must reapply for a new visa to reenter the country. To add confusion to confusion, the rules frequently change, especially in less developed countries: What was true when your guidebook was written may not be true when you take your trip.

If you're planning a trip to several countries, you might find it worth the fee to engage a visa service

TRAVEL TIP

Smile and say "all you can eat"! It's well worth the 5 minutes and few dollars to get a bunch of passport-sized photos of yourself. These come in handy for visa applications as well as for spur-of-the-moment changes in plans (you need a visa to go to a different country), emergencies (you lose your passport), or such documents as ski lift tickets or rescue insurance.

East meets west, trekking in Nepal. The method for carrying a load is one of many differences between cultures.

agency to handle getting your visas for you. The fee varies depending on what service is being provided. Your travel agent can give you information.

Another good information source is the U.S. State Department, which publishes consular information sheets that include information about visa requirements, medical alerts, safety, and a host of other issues you'll want to know before you go. Phone: (202) 647-5225.

FINDING INFORMATION
Guidebooks
Guidebooks are available for virtually every nook and cranny of the world, but the variety stocked by your local bookstore may be more appropriate

for sightseers than backpackers. A local outfitter with a decent selection of books is a better place to start.

If you don't live near a bookstore, try catalog shopping. One of the most comprehensive guidebook catalogs is the Adventurous Traveler Bookstore, available both in print, call (800) 282-3963, and on-line (www.AdventuresTraveler.com). It contains hundreds of guides and maps to places you can't even spell, and the friendly, knowledgeable staff will make recommendations if you tell them what you're looking for.

If you plan to divide your time between backpacking and sightseeing, good all-around guides are published by Lonely Planet and Bradt. Both send their intrepid authors to the back-of-beyond, and they publish information that is useful for adventure travelers going off the beaten path. The more standard guides like those published by Frommer's and Fodor's are good for big cities, but they frequently ignore the cheaper lodgings preferred by backpackers, and they don't have as much information about out-of-the-way places. You'll also need a hiking guide to the specific area in which you want to backpack, because the standard guides are usually too general to meet backpackers' needs on the trail.

Finally, don't forget your local library. It's a less expensive option, especially if you're "just browsing." Even a small rural library can help you via the interlibrary-loan system.

Hiking Clubs

Some of the major hiking and conservation organizations such as the Appalachian Mountain Club or the Sierra Club offer international trips.

In addition, members of your local hiking club may have some personal experience with the areas you're interested in. Abroad, alpine clubs exist in every European country, including Denmark, which has nary a hill, let alone an alp. Just as in the United States, the range of hiking clubs in other countries spans the gamut from informal little groups to huge organizations that publish trail guides, manage backcountry huts and refuges, or run hiking trips (some of which you may be able to join). Guidebooks often have information about how to contact such organizations.

Commercial Outfitters

Even if you're not interested in a guided trip (if you are, see page 191 for information on choosing an outfitter), commercial outfitters who run trips to distant places are a good source of preliminary information, if only because their trip descriptions might give you some ideas about places to visit and routes to explore. In addition, most outfitters provide an equipment list. You'll find the names and addresses of dozens of outfitters in the back of travel, outdoor, and conservation magazines. Write to several of them for information; you'll find that their prices and services vary widely.

Maps

Here's where things get interesting! Finding the right maps for your trip can be as much of an adventure as the trip itself. Some countries have well-organized mapping agencies that produce maps specifically designed for hikers. (France is an example. Its Series Bleu maps are 1:25,000 scale and include information about the nation's 100,000-kilometer system of trails, backcountry refuges, hiker hostels, and

The author and her husband find a superbly sheltered tent site near Mintos Hut, about 14,000 feet up Mount Kenya, Africa. The trees are giant lobelias.

natural points of interest.) Other countries are notorious for producing inaccurate, out-of-date maps that can't manage to locate towns (let alone trails) on the correct side of a river. (In Nepal, for instance, many maps used by trekkers are based on surveying and cartography that date back to the British raj in India.) Sometimes maps are produced by private agencies, sometimes by governments.

The kind of map you'll need depends on how well marked the trails are. If the trails are in good shape, you'll probably be satisfied with a scale of 1:50,000. If you expect to have to do a lot of navigating, a 1:25,000 map is better (but you'll need a lot more of them, which means added expense and weight). Don't be surprised if your international maps come in a variety of scales; in some countries, even maps produced by the same agency can vary in scale from one map to the next.

To find maps, start with the resource listings at the back of your guidebook. In addition to Adventurous Traveler Bookstore, try MapLink in Santa Barbara, California (805) 965-4402. Finally, once you arrive at your destination, it's worth a trip to a local backpacking store or the local English-language bookstore (if these exist).You might find maps that were impossible to dig up by telephone and mail order.

Hack before you Hike

In using the Internet, the biggest challenge isn't getting advice — it's evaluating the source of the advice. Is the person on the other end a Mount Everest veteran, a kid goofing off, or a know-it-all who really doesn't? Advice from others always needs to be filtered through your own research, preferences, and experience. The same goes double in cyberspace.

Chat rooms and bulletin boards are probably most useful in the preliminary stages, when you're "just looking." If someone out there seems particularly well informed, you can send specific requests and questions via e-mail. More useful are the growing number of Web pages sponsored by hiking organizations. Check out GORP (Great Outdoor Recreation Pages; http://www.gorp.com), which has links to major hiking organizations. You'll also find that national parks, wilderness areas, government agencies, and others have home pages on the Web. You can even locate and order hiking guides on your computer through companies like Amazon and Adventurous Traveler Bookstore.

Travel Agents

Your travel agent will be able to help you out with plane reservations, major hotels, train schedules, and information about passports and visa services. But don't expect much assistance when it comes to the one- and two-star hotels listed in your Lonely Planet guide and the tiny towns that don't show up on any maps. Travel agents work on commission, and tiny, inexpensive hotels don't pay. Ditto goes for hiking trails, hostels, and national parks.

MONEY

Do what millionaires do with money: Diversify your portfolio!

TRAVELER'S CHECKS You lose a little bit on traveler's checks when you buy them (and again when you change them), but they offer a margin of safety you just can't get with cash.

(When traveling in remote areas, don't expect a refund for lost checks to be handled as efficiently as it is in a television commercial. And be sure you keep those annoying receipts and a list of which checks you cashed when and where. Having that information will drastically improve your chances of getting a quick refund.) In addition to checks in dollars, your bank may sell traveler's checks in foreign currencies (usually Swiss francs, German marks, or English pounds), which are useful if you're traveling in Europe.

In some less developed countries, clerks at a tiny rural bank may be suspicious of traveler's checks they're not familiar with, so stick with the major mega-companies like Citicorp, Barclays, and American Express. (It's also not a bad idea to have two kinds of traveler's checks just in case. In extremely remote places, the rules sometimes seem arbitrary and illogical; I've been stuck on more than one occasion with the "wrong" kind of traveler's check.) As far as denominations go, figure on changing at least $100 at a time (to minimize the cost of any per-transaction fees; plus, as a backpacker, you're heading out to places where you may not be able to change money, so you need a little extra in reserve). Bring a supply of smaller denominations along for convenience and flexibility.

FOREIGN CURRENCY If possible, buy some foreign currency before you leave home. Your bank may offer this service, although you may have to arrange for it a day or two in advance. You can also purchase major foreign currencies at American airports. The exchange rate is generally usurious, but it's well worth the convenience of landing in a strange country with cab fare in your pocket. Ask for a supply of smaller denominations so you don't end up having to give the bus driver the equivalent of a $50 bill. The more remote your destination and the lower its per capita income, the smaller the bills should be.

CHANGING MONEY Check your guidebooks or gossip with other travelers to find out where to get the best exchange rates. In many places in Europe, for instance, hotels and railway stations offer poor rates and banks the best, but even among banks, rates can vary. In some countries, hotels offer the same rates as banks.

And then there's the black market. The black market operates in many less-developed countries, which often control their currencies and require you to change money only at banks and official locales. Sometimes, when you arrive you must declare how much cash you're carrying. When you leave, you can be asked to present your receipts for money that you've changed, and the numbers are supposed to add up. In reality, countries with controlled currencies may have a thriving black market, usually street-corner money changers who offer rates higher than the official government rate. But before you jump in to seize a bargain, be aware that changing money on the black market is illegal (although it may be tolerated to different extents in different countries). It also diverts hard currency from the government (which needs tourist income) into the hands of the shadier element of local society. Also consider that countries that regulate their currencies tend to be the sorts of places where you don't want to get up close and personal with the judicial system. If you do use the black market, don't be surprised to find that money changers have strong preferences for certain denominations of currency and traveler's checks. These preferences change from country to country and from year to year, so it's best to bring along several denominations.

BANKCARDS Bankcards give you the best exchange rate (the interbank discount rate) and good protection against theft. Chances are your ATM card is part of at least one internationally used network: Check to be sure. You also need to be sure that your PIN code is four digits. And if you use an alphanumeric to remember your pin code, take the time to memorize the numbers — foreign keypads usually do not have letters. Try to plan ahead a little and get a sufficient chunk of money for a few days each time you use a foreign ATM machine, since regardless of the amount you take out you have to pay a fee (usually around U.S. $5). You can also use credit cards to get cash (assuming you have a cash-advance

MISCELLANEOUS THINGS THAT CAN BE VERY, VERY USEFUL

Your foreign repair kit needs to be bulkier than its domestic equivalent, because you can't fall back on 800-number calls to manufacturers. Remember, even in densely populated, highly developed western Europe, it may be difficult to find basic supplies if the trail runs through teeny little towns in relatively remote areas. In addition to your normal supplies, be sure you have extra duct tape, extra zipper-lock bags, and extra batteries for anything you really want or need to use.

A few other things to tuck into your pack: cigarette lighters (several: they make good gifts), matches (foreign matches are junk), extra film, garbage bags, toilet paper, personal medical and sanitary supplies, and water-purification pills.

line of credit and a PIN number). But these can be expensive, since, in addition to the fee, you'll have to pay high credit card interest on the advance. ATMs in other countries aren't exactly the same as the ones you're familiar with back at home: It may take several false starts and a little bit of swearing before the machine deigns to give you money, especially if the directions are written in a language you don't speak!

FOOD AND EQUIPMENT
Packing and Carrying

With all of their straps and buckles, backpacks practically beg to be abused by baggage handlers. An external frame with a sleeping bag strapped to the outside is an invitation to disaster. A duffel bag can thwart both thieves and the thugs who use your luggage as a punching bag. Get one big enough to handle all the extra stuff — hiking boots, walking sticks, etc. — that you have to lug along. Since carrying a fully loaded duffel from one end of an airport to another is a bit of a chore, consider buying one with wheels on one end. Otherwise, buy a cheapie and drag it along behind you until it falls apart.

Once you get where you're going, mail the duffel or drop it off in person to the hotel where you'll be staying at the end of your hike. (Make this reservation in advance,

The author tries a trumpline on for size near Annapurna, Nepal. She quickly returned to her familiar shoulder straps.

and ask if the hotel will hold a box for you.) For shipping the duffel, I pack along a flat shipping box, into which I also put my street clothes, any extra gear that doesn't make the final cut (there's always something), and a few supplies that I'll appreciate having at the end of my hike, especially if I'm going to spend a few days playing at being a big-city tourist.

Point Lenana (16,300 feet), one of the three summits of Mount Kenya, Africa.

If you insist on going duffel-less, you can decrease the likelihood of a pack-mangling disaster by first taking off anything removable and then tightening and tying whatever straps are left. Don't leave the waistband dangling: Take it off or, if that's not possible, buckle it tight around the pack. Same for the shoulder straps (but remember to note any adjustments that have been made to fit your back). You can also swathe your pack in garbage bags, duct tape, and rope, which not only makes the package safer from mangling, but also discourages petty larceny. But realize that it's possible that you'll be asked to undo all of this when you arrive at your destination and go through customs.

As far as the contents of your pack are concerned, expect that anything that can spill will spill — even

if the pack isn't thrown through the air by an 800-pound gorilla. Changing air pressure in the plane's baggage compartment can cause liquids to explode, so be sure to pack spillables and oozeables (peanut butter, shampoo, toothpaste) into two layers of zipper-lock bags.

Food

The idea of culinary adventure takes on a whole new meaning when you're trying to purchase supplies for a 5-day hike in a two-aisle grocery store in a country where you don't speak the language and aren't familiar with the food. You wouldn't head out into the backcountry at home with unfamiliar products that you don't know how to prepare, but abroad you may not have a choice.

Bringing food from home works

for a short hike. What you gain in convenience you lose in adventure, but you can take time off in town for your taste buds to go exploring. If you'll be out for a longer amount of time, you'll probably have to resupply in whatever towns there are. A flexible stomach is definitely an asset! Still, you might want to carry along some basic supplies with which to confront a shopping disaster. (Some suggestions: a couple of freeze-dried meals, some instant soups, quick-cooking noodle soups, miso, bouillon cubes, and your favorite spices.)

If you speak the language (or can make anything resembling an attempt to do so) ask about local foods and how to prepare them: People all over the world are delighted to share their national cuisine with visitors.

Stoves and Fuel

A few airlines combine caution with ignorance and come up with the erroneous conclusion that stoves are "flammable" and so cannot be accepted as luggage. (Without fuel, stoves are as flammable as a screwdriver, but you can't argue with policy — no matter how erroneous — where airline safety is concerned.) Call your airline, because this is definitely not something you want to deal with at the last minute at the airport.

Gas, of course, is flammable, and it's illegal to take it on a plane (the fine can be up to $25,000). So finding stove fuel is a project you'll need to undertake after you arrive in a foreign country, before you can start your hike. Check to see what your hiking guide says. In the absence of more specific information, a multi-fuel stove is probably the best choice. But don't be impressed with third-hand tall tales about how somebody's stove cooked up a five-course feast on a pint of Jack Daniels. While multi-fuel stoves can take a variety of fuels (white gas, unleaded automobile gasoline, aviation fuel, and kerosene, to name a few), the fact is they don't run on everything. And some of the fuels they do run on (like aviation fuel) are not exactly common items in a remote mountain town in the middle of nowhere. You'll probably end up using kerosene (which in some stoves requires changing a part) simply because it's most readily available. Test any new fuel before you head out.

Also check to see if there is a strong local preference. In France, for instance, hikers overwhelmingly (by a margin, as far as I could tell, of something like a million to one) use French-made Camping Gaz stoves, and replacement canisters of bottled gas are available everywhere. But it is almost impossible to find white gas, even in camping stores that sell stoves that require it. Petroleum-based dry-cleaning fluid or white spirits might do the trick, depending on your stove, but it's not always available in more remote places. And don't count on auto fuel: During our hike of the French and Spanish Pyrenees, we didn't go into any towns that were big enough to have a gas station (and the gas station we did visit before the beginning of our hike was unable to sell us gas because of local regulations concerning how gas could and could not be sold).

HEALTH

The health precautions you need to take depend on your destination. For western Europe, you'll merely want a few "just-in-case" items for your first aid kit. For more exotic destinations, you can expect to encounter more exotic challenges to your health, so you'll need to pack a first aid kit that is up to the job, and you may need to undergo a series of vaccinations.

Before you go anywhere, check your first aid kit. If it's the one you've been hauling over hill and dale for the last two years, make sure the adhesive on the moleskin still adheres and the cotton bandages aren't gummed up with two years' worth of trail dust and grime.

The federal Centers for Disease Control, (404) 639-2573, will provide up-to-date information on vaccine requirements and other medical recommendations (including yellow fever and cholera shots, if you're going into affected areas; boosters for tetanus, typhoid, measles, mumps, rubella, and polio; shots for meningitis and hepatitis; and pills for malaria). Visit your doctor at least 6 months before your trip, because

depending on where you are going and for how long, you may need to have several different shots, and some of them can't be taken simultaneously. In addition, you need to start taking certain medications — like malaria prophylactics — a couple of weeks before your departure.

Discuss where you're going and for how long with your doctor. In the case of malaria, for instance, there are several different drugs available, and your trip's length and destination will affect which one your doctor prescribes. Be sure your doctor understands that you'll be hiking independently in places where medical help may not be available (not taking a packaged tour) and ask about other drugs for emergencies, specifically, a general antibiotic, a prescription-strength painkiller, an anti-diarrheal, and a drug called Flagyl (it cures giardiasis, which does not respond to general antibiotics). Any prescription drugs you carry with you must be clearly labeled. A letter from your doctor on official stationery is even better. Keep even innocuous over-the-counter pills in their original containers: You don't want your stash of aspirin to arouse the ire of a jittery, 17-year-old border guard wielding an automatic weapon in the middle of a country where human rights and due process are foreign concepts.

Learn the side effects of all medicines in your kit. For example, on one trip, I decided to take my malaria pills every morning before breakfast so I wouldn't forget. Trouble was, I didn't realize that these pills needed to be taken after eating, not before — and they made me so nauseated I threw them up. I later met someone else who had made the same mistake — and had contracted malaria as a result.

Another common side effect: Antibiotics (which are a component of some malarial prophylactics) may increase your sensitivity to sunlight, so you'll want to wear a brimmed hat and plenty of sunscreen.

HEALTH INSURANCE Check to find out if your policy covers international locations. Most do not, so you'll want to purchase some sort of additional protection. The International Association for Medical Assistance to Travelers (417 Center St., Lewiston, NY 14092) provides a list of doctors abroad who meet the organization's qualifications and speak at least one language (often, but not necessarily English) other than their native tongue.

DENTAL HEALTH This is not something you want to risk dealing with abroad. If you are a dentist-phobe, like me, just think of the consequences of a tooth gone bad in a place where most people over the age of 20 don't have any teeth. Have a checkup before you go.

FIRST AID KIT In addition to your normal backpacking supplies, you'll need sufficient quantities of any medicines you usually take, prophylactic drugs for malaria (depending on your destination, of course), and

some iodine for purifying water. You should also have a pocket medical guide.

AIDS If you're traveling into areas where you can't reasonably expect safe, Western-style medical care, bring along an AIDS protection kit, which includes sterile needles and rubber gloves (available from Safariquip, The Stones, Castleton, Sheffield, S302W4, England; telephone, 01433 620320). Know which blood type you are and which blood types your traveling companions are: You may be able to donate blood for each other in an emergency. AIDS is epidemic in some areas, and in some countries blood used for transfusions is not routinely tested.

IN EMERGENCIES If you need to see a doctor, check your guidebook or the local tourist office. In remote areas, a Western missionary station or a police station may be able to help. Even the most basic phrasebook contains a "seeing the doctor" chapter, so take it with you.

TRANSPORTATION

In all the traveling I've done, I have never rented a car in a foreign country. True, I'm not fond of driving on the "wrong" side of the road, especially in countries where the horn is used instead of the brakes. But the real reason is that in other countries — unlike our own — usable public transportation actually exists beyond the big cities.

Fording a stream in Nepal. In developing countries, transportation gets interesting — and slow; it took the author about an hour to make this crossing. The solution: Go with the flow.

time indeed. In Nepal, I once hiked 100 miles because I didn't want to face the alternative: a cliff-hanging 12-hour bus ride back to where I started from.

If all else fails, ask the clerk at your hotel. He talks to his sister's husband whose cousin has a car, and after a little back-and-forth (agree about the price before you set out!) you're off. Be aware, however, that this mode of conveyance can be less than luxurious if the driver decides he wants to invite along a couple of friends, family members, one or two babies, and a chicken.

In Europe, trains and buses can get you virtually anywhere, and the Eurailpass program and other similar programs offer a variety of economic packages. A printed schedule is available through your travel agent, or via telephone. Bus service is also available between many small towns not served by rail.

In developing nations, transportation gets a bit more interesting. In places where public services are not available, entrepreneurial drivers fill the need by loading up vans and buses with passengers to various destinations. Be aware that schedules may be a courteous fiction devised to soothe the neurotic time-keeping needs of foreign visitors, with no bearing on when the bus or train will leave and even less on when it will get there. And that can take a long

CROSS-CULTURAL CHALLENGES

We Americans aren't much good at foreign languages. Not only that, we're convinced that we don't have to be — after all, everybody speaks English, right?

Wrong.

Good news and bad news on the language front: Lots of your fellow adventurers will speak at least a little English. European trekkers in Asia, for instance, regardless of their language, routinely address each other using English as a sort of common denominator. But the people who live in the small rural towns and villages you will be passing through — the person who rents you a bed, the person behind the counter at the grocery store, or the waiter at the local restaurant — are about as likely to speak English as their counterparts in a rural Appalachian Trail town are to speak French or German.

Learning a little bit of the local language engenders goodwill and smooths your way. Go ahead and try: The only thing in your way is that awkwardness you're going to feel the first few times you open your mouth and something weird comes out. You'll be amazed to learn how much you can communicate with only a couple hundred words. You might not be able to express your theories of life, but you'll be able to find food and shelter, tell people what you're doing, and ask for help. And the fact that you're making an effort will be appreciated by the people you're dealing with, which generally means they'll bend over backwards to help you.

Choose a traveler's phrasebook over a dictionary. The phrasebook will have the basics and will give you whole sentences, which is what you need to get food and shelter. At first, you'll want to stick with no-frills conversations. Ask yes-or-no questions (seeing as "yes" and "no" are probably the only answers you'll under-

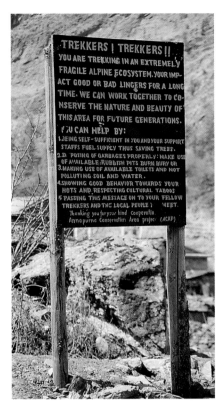

Walking softly is not the invention of the American environmental movement, as this sign in Annapurna Sanctuary proves.

stand). Stick with it, and after a little time and effort, you might be startled to open your mouth and hear another language coming out.

Cultural Sensitivity

When in Rome. . . . You know the rest.

The introductory remarks to most guidebooks catalog major cultural practices and taboos. Read them to learn how to avoid giving inadvertent offense. Many cultures are far more traditional than ours, with unwritten

Thorong-la, Nepal (17,800 feet). This is a group of trekkers the author and her husband formed on the spot to hike the 250-mile Annapurna Circuit together.

trees to tourists' need for wood, which is used to boil up hot showers and cook meals. Cultural collision between rich outsiders and subsistence villagers has created social tensions, not only between tourists and locals, but among families whose value systems are challenged by an influx of wealth that glitters but cannot be gotten. Children surround visitors with outstretched palms begging for more of whatever the last visitor gave them. It's not easy to know what to do when confronted with the obscene disparity between Western wealth and Third World poverty. Your guidebook may have suggestions for how you can minimize your impact and show respect for the culture in which you are a visitor. Our guidebook to Nepal, for instance, suggested packing in stove fuel, told us where to go to see a local exhibit on environmental issues, and described simple things we could do to avoid offending anyone at religious sites.

rules of behavior that everyone (except the unwitting tourist) understands. It should go without saying that visitors should learn the basics of local etiquette and respect religious symbols and traditions.

You should also be aware of your impact on the local culture. Even the generous-hearted impulse to give presents and pennies to children can have long-term, devastating effects. Nepal might be the worst example of this: In the 30 years since tourism has invaded that country, the word "Nepalmed" has been coined to describe what has happened. Too many tourists have put pressure on local resources, like fuel and food. A country already suffering from deforestation has lost even more of its

SAFETY

Solo travelers meet more people, have more adventures, and learn local languages better than couples or groups. But solo adventurers also take a lot more risks than travelers with partners. Especially in developing countries (and even more especially for women), solo travel is best attempted only by very experienced travelers who know a little bit of the language and the culture. Leave an

Mother and son trekking by Buddhist chölten, Khumbu, Nepal.

itinerary, and check in with someone back at home as often as possible.

What if you've polled all your friends and no one, simply no one, wants to take that bicycle trip across Mongolia? One option is to look for a partner when you get where you're going. Some cities (Cuzco, Peru; Kathmandu, Nepal; Nairobi, Kenya) act as sort of staging grounds for expeditions into the bush." A close-to-the-ground travel guide will tell you in which hotels independent travelers gather and where to leave (or read) notes advertising for a travel or trekking partner.

Women

In some cultures, some men seem to think that it's perfectly acceptable to follow, harass, proposition, and even harm solo female travelers. It's depressing to have to admit that having a male traveling companion makes a huge difference in comfort level — and in some cases safety. I've traveled alone, I've traveled with my husband, and I've compared notes with fellow female travelers. I've found that the experience of traveling accompanied by a man is completely different from the experience of traveling alone. I certainly don't advocate staying home, but I'd be ignoring reality if I didn't admit that the world continues to throw more obstacles and dangers in the path of female travelers than their male counterparts. Women travelers — especially young women — are safer in groups, and safer still in groups with men.

The hints and cautions are the logical ones. Wearing loose-fitting dresses and skirts, or lightweight cotton pants and a long-sleeved shirt, shows respect for more traditional cultures. Be aware of your surroundings. Don't give strangers information about your plans and whereabouts. Stay in a place where you can lock or jam the door shut. (You can bring along both locks and door jams.) Wear a wedding band.

Theft

Big cities pose more danger of theft than rural areas. Still, the contents of your backpack might well cost more money than the local people will see in a year. Little locks can deter nimble fingers (you won't be able to lock every part of your pack, but you can affix locks to a couple of zippered compartments), but the best defense is vigilance. Keep your valuable documents and the bulk of your money tucked away out of sight in a money belt. Keep a small amount of money in a more accessible purse or fanny pack worn in front.

Youth hostels in big cities can be rife with theft, but in more rural areas, they are safer. In addition, in some countries there are hiker hostels, designed not for roaming bands of kids, but for adults who are traveling by foot, bicycle, or skis. In this like-minded company, you're less likely to have a problem. But if you are sleeping in a public place

(a refuge, a shelter, a hostel) wear your money to bed.

Do be especially careful on city streets, particularly in cities that have a reputation for petty theft, and in areas frequented by tourists (train stations, pedestrian shopping malls, the subways, major attractions). People who make their livings fleecing tourists are good at what they do, and, after the fact, you may be stunned at the "obviousness" of the ploy you fell for. Thieves assume that if they create a disturbance, your first instinct will be to help or to check out what's happening. You can foil them by keeping your wits about you. Ignore the person who shoves a newspaper under your chin, or the person who drops a handful of change on the ground, or the person who begs extremely aggressively. When approached in an unusual manner, get immediately defensive and firmly hold on to your purse or wallet and other belongings. Before helping a stranger, make sure you're not leaving yourself vulnerable (a common ruse is for a thief to pretend to fall; his partner makes off with your wallet while you stop to help).

Guided Treks

If it's all starting to sound just too complicated, there is another, albeit more expensive option. However, it's one preferred by many experienced travelers. The guided trek appeals to people who want the emphasis of their journey to be more on "vacation" than "adventure" or to people who just don't want (or don't have time) to plan the trip themselves.

Guided trips fall into two general categories: those offered by commercial adventure travel companies, and trips offered by nonprofit organizations, clubs, and universities. Trips offered by nonprofits are not necessarily less expensive than commercial trips, but they often include expert commentary by traveling scholars or scientists.

An option for the "somewhat adventurous but not quite ready to be independent" is to arrive in a country and make arrangements to join a tour while there. The best places to find these outfitters are in smaller cities near the area you plan to explore. Often they will have storefront offices in tourist districts. Check your guidebook for recommendations, because the services provided by local companies in developing countries are uneven. Nonetheless, they offer three advantages: If you're on a budget, they are considerably less expensive than tours purchased at home. You can use local outfitters to "test-drive" the terrain: Choose a short outing both to check out the service and to see whether or not you really need a guide, a translator, and a porter. And these services may be a good choice if you are generally independent but

10 QUESTIONS TO ASK A GUIDED TOUR OPERATOR

⬤ How many years has the company been in business?
⬤ Can you check the company's references with former trip participants?
⬤ What kind of training do the guides have?
⬤ Do the guides speak the language?
⬤ What kind of accommodations will you be using?
⬤ What services are provided? (For instance, on a raft trip, do you float down the river in queenly comfort, or are you

expected to row the boat yourself? Do you put up your tent and cook your meals, or do porters carry lounge chairs so that you can sit around while someone else does the work?)
⬤ How many people will be on your trip?
⬤ What kinds of arrangements does the company have for dealing with medical emergencies?
⬤ What equipment is provided and what do you need to bring?
⬤ What does the company do to ensure that its trips are run in an environmentally and culturally sensitive manner?

A trekker in Annapurna Sanctuary below Annapurna South.

would like to see something (mountain gorillas in Uganda, for example) where you really do need the services of a guide for a few days.

Whether or not you go on a guided trip is your decision. Certainly, you give up some element of adventure for, as new as the experience might be to you, the fact that the trip is planned and has probably been run before takes it out of the realm of true adventure. Then again, adventure isn't necessarily what it's cracked up to be (although it always makes for great stories after the fact). The unexpected can be both a delight and a distress in adventure travel. On a guided tour, you'll have less of both kinds of happenstance.

You'll also have companions.

How you feel about this is up to you. You might make friendships that last a lifetime. You may come back with stories about impossible co-adventurers that last a lifetime.

PART III

LONG
TRAILS

When I was a kid, I played the globe game. I expect you've done it, too: You've closed your eyes, spun a globe, put down a finger, and promised yourself that someday you'll go where you land. If I ever keep all those promises, I'm going to be spending a fair part of the next few decades floating around in the Pacific Ocean.

Think of this part of the book as the globe — except there's no Pacific Ocean to fall into. Just a list of fabulous trails and wildernesses to explore: The Grand Canyon. The Appalachian Trail. Yellowstone National Park. The Wonderland Trail around Mount Rainier. The John Muir Trail through the High Sierra.

By its nature, this part can't be more than a sampling. When you start looking at all the trails the world has to offer, you find more miles than a single pair of feet could tread in many lifetimes — and to describe them all, you'd need more words than a single book could contain.

To narrow down the possibilities, I've looked for paths that offer a wide range of experiences and environments in the Untied States. I've backpacked many of these trails myself, and I have hiking friends who have done others. When I couldn't verify the status and description of a trail through firsthand hiker information, I talked to trail managers in person.

Each listing contains an information source, usually a park or forest supervisor's office or, in cases where a long trail crosses through different jurisdictions, an umbrella trail-maintaining organization. Most of the guidebooks and resources listed are readily available through Adventurous Traveler Bookstore; call (800) 282-3963. In addition, the Internet is becoming a major source of trail information that even a technologically challenged dinosaur like me can use. Check out GORP (http://www.gorp.com) which has links to many trail organizations and land management agencies as well as online sources for maps and guidebooks. Adventurous Traveler Bookstore should be your first stop for guidebooks and maps. And both the national forests and the national parks (along with many state parks) maintain Web sites.

One caveat: Like so many other programs administered by government agencies, trail budgets are shrinking. Not all of the trails listed herein are completed. Trails range in character, marking, passability, and skills required to safely hike on them, and conditions change from year to year. On one extreme, the Appalachian Trail is a connect-the-dots sort of trail, marked in some places almost from tree to tree. On the other extreme, managers of some wilderness areas are actually taking down trail markings or allowing them to fall into disrepair to "preserve the wilderness experience." (Many hikers, however, believe that this makes wildernesses less safe and puts them out of bounds to hikers of average ability.) Finally, there are unfinished trails where guidebooks — if they are available — describe a route that may involve bushwhacking, open ridge walking, or linking together degenerating forest service roads (which may or may not be mapped). I have avoided including so-called trails that are merely disappointing conglomerations of high-grade roads open to cars, four-wheel drives, and ATVs, although portions of unfinished North American long trails fall into that category. In the case of unfinished trails, mileages are approximate.

These listings are intended to guide you in identifying trails that you might be interested in and to convey as accurately as possible their status as of this writing. Before setting out on a hike, talk to the trail organization, other hikers, and local land managers to get up-to-date information about trail conditions, challenges, and dangers.

THE NATIONAL TRAILS SYSTEM

The 1968 National Trails System Act established federal support and protection for a network of trails of superb "scenic, recreational, or historic value." These categories generate some confusion. National recreation trails, for example, are not necessarily good backpacking trails. They tend to be close to urban areas and they may use bicycle paths or even highways for much of their route. Indeed, some of them — like the 2-mile-long Freedom Path in Boston — are entirely paved urban paths. Nor are the national historic trails necessarily trails — at least not if you accept a typical backpacker's definition of a trail: a cut marked footway through undeveloped terrain. For example, the goal of the Lewis and Clark National Historic Trail is to locate and sign all of Lewis and Clark's campsites. But how you get from one to another is more likely to be via road or river than it is via trail.

Even among national scenic trails — the trails most hikers think of when they hear the word "trail" — confusion exists. The condition, degree of completion, blazing system, and maintenance vary dramatically from one to the next, and so does the experience a backpacker must have.

In addition to these three categories, the National Trails System recognizes "side" or "connecting" trails that link up with larger trails. In theory, at least. These trails are supposed to offer access, links, and alternatives to the existing system. But the system is not yet complete, and the idea of federally designated connecting trails is enjoying a 30-year infancy. So far, only two have been certified into the system.

This chapter lists all eight national scenic trails, but describes in some detail only the six that currently offer a lengthy quality backpacking experience. Of those six, only two — the Appalachian and Pacific Crest trails — are completed (inasmuch as a trail can ever be said to be completed).

To exist, trails needs support from volunteers at the community level, especially in remote areas with low population densities. The successful models of the AT and PCT are difficult to copy in the wilds of Wyoming. You can help: Adopt a trail as your personal project. Get on the mailing list. Volunteer for a work trip. Congress created these trails on paper — but it is up to hikers and backpackers to put them on the ground.

APPALACHIAN NATIONAL SCENIC TRAIL
Running 2,160 miles from Georgia to Maine, the Appalachian Trail was originally conceived as a refuge from encroaching urban blight. Founder Benton MacKaye believed Americans needed rural respite from "the crowded East, a chain of smoky beehive cities." He wrote those words in 1921, which makes you wonder what he'd have to say about the East Coast landscape today.

A mere four years after MacKaye proposed his grand idea for a trail connecting the highest mountain in the Northeast (Mount Washington) to the highest mountain in the Southeast (Mount Mitchell), volunteers had formed the Appalachian Trail Conference. (The trail later grew beyond the original idea and now runs from Georgia to Maine.) They've been cutting and maintaining the trail ever since: Arguably the jewel of the national scenic trails, the Appalachian Trail boasts a volunteer force that contributes as much as 140,000 hours of work in a single year. In 1937, the trail was completed (meaning that it followed a continuous marked route from end to end), although, at the time, much of it ran along country roads and through private lands at the sufferance of landowners. Since then, the goal of the Appalachian Trail Conference has been to establish a permanently protected trail, whenever possible surrounded by a 1,000-foot-wide natural corridor. As of this writing, less than 40 miles remain unprotected. The 1,000-foot corridor will be more difficult to achieve. While in some places it is a reality, in others (most notably in the populated mid-Atlantic states where land values are astronomic and development creeps toward the mountaintops as certainly as a glacier creeps down a mountain slope) it remains a far-off dream.

Traditionally, AT thru-hikers "walk with spring," heading north in late March or early April from the trail's southern terminus atop Springer Mountain, about 70

Appalachian Trail

miles northwest of Atlanta, Georgia. Hikers take an average of 5½ to 6 months to complete their journey, which puts them atop Maine's highest point, Katahdin, during peak autumn foliage (and, occasionally, during early winter storms).

The Appalachian Trail follows a ridgeline route through 14 states. Elevations range from near sea level (where the Bear Mountain Bridge crosses the Hudson River in New York) to 6,642-foot Clingman's Dome in Great Smoky Mountain National Park along the North Carolina–Tennessee border.

The southern and northern segments are the wildest. In the South, hikers walk through mountains named for mist — the Great Smokies and the Blue Ridge — and climb to spectacular views from occasional balds, which are open summits covered with blueberries and rhododendron. Virginia has the most mileage of any state — nearly a quarter of the total, including the Shenandoah National Park. The middle Atlantic states are lower and more populated, but the trail here offers a quality backpacking experience that is surprisingly pastoral, especially when you consider that you can sometimes look from the trail to the skyscrapers of Manhattan. In New England, the trail rises again, climbing to the rugged peaks of the White Mountains, the leg- and lung-busting climbs of western Maine, and finally, the hiker's holy peak, Katahdin, whose name comes from the Abenaki Indian language meaning "greatest mountain" or, according to Thoreau, "highest land."

The AT attracts some 3 million hikers a year, perhaps because information and maintenance are so reliable. It also attracts the most long-distance hikers; by some estimates, as many as 2,000 people a year attempt to hike the whole trail. Northbounders who travel with "the pack" develop a close-knit, small-town-like community atmosphere, taking on "trail names" instead of their real ones.

Much of the trail from Georgia to Vermont can be walked any time of year, although winter hikers need to be prepared for cold temperatures and snow, even in the southern Appalachians. In northern New England, deep snow and frigid conditions make travel impossible unless you have mountaineering skills, and sometimes even if you do. Information: Appalachian Trail Conference, P.O. Box 802, Harper's Ferry, WV 25425; (304) 535-6331.

PACIFIC CREST NATIONAL SCENIC TRAIL

With the passing of the National Trails System Act, the Pacific Crest Trail joined its older Appalachian cousin in the national trails system. Like its eastern counterpart, the Pacific Crest Trail is a south-to-north mountain trail. But it offers a decidedly western twist on the idea of long-distance hiking: big vistas, big mountains, and big distances between roads and towns.

It's longer, too. Running 2,638 miles from the small Mexican-American border station at Campo, California, to British Columbia's Manning Provincial Park, the trail passes through California, Oregon, and Washington. And it offers more variety: On its way, it crosses six of the seven life zones found in North America, from southern California's scalding desert valleys to 13,180-foot Forester Pass in the Sierra Nevada. It dips to near sea level to cross the Columbia River, then climbs to the shoulders of the great volcanic cones of the Pacific Northwest — Mount Adams, Mount Hood, and Mount Rainier — passes through wet, lush, and ancient forests, and reaches its grand finale in the craggy, remote North Cascades.

The trail is marked and completed; it is described in a two-volume guidebook published by Wilderness Press (Berkeley, CA).

The PCT is designed to be passable for hikers and livestock, so the footway is generally easier than that of the Appalachian Trail. But the trail presents other challenges to long-distance hikers. The longer distances between towns require heavier packs between resupplies. And the hiker faces more extremes in conditions and climate.

The typical routing is northbound, starting in mid to late April. Hikers immediately confront the heat of southern California's deserts and the logistical problems of managing their water supply when the distances between sources are sometimes 2-days apart. But starting any sooner doesn't work because right after the desert is the great, jutting obstacle of the High Sierra, where hikers must cope with treacherous snow slopes atop high mountain passes and swollen streams in the valleys. After the Sierra, there's a period of good weather and easier trail, where hikers need to make big miles — averaging about 20 a day — in order to reach the north Cascades before winter does. Information: Pacific Crest Trail Association, 5325 Elkhorn Boulevard #256, Sacramento, CA 95842; (888) PCTrail.

CONTINENTAL DIVIDE NATIONAL SCENIC TRAIL

The youngest and longest of the three great north-south trails, the Continental

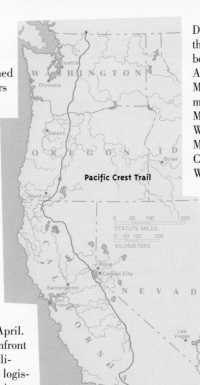

Pacific Crest Trail

Divide Trail begins at the Mexican-American border station near Antelope Wells, New Mexico, and runs 3,100 miles through New Mexico, Colorado, Wyoming, Idaho, and Montana. It crosses into Canada at Glacier-Waterton Lakes International Peace Park.

On its way, it passes through 25 national forests and 3 national parks, as well as through Indian reservations, wilderness areas, and BLM lands. The range of terrain is similar to that of the Pacific Crest Trail, climbing from the small part of the Chihuahuan Desert that ranges into New Mexico to the great peaks of the Colorado Rockies.

The CDT is a trail-in-progress. Estimates are that roughly 2,000 miles are complete, most of those in Colorado and Montana. In northern Wyoming, good, usable, and often spectacular trails wind through the Wind River Range, the Bridger-Teton Wilderness, and Yellowstone National Park, but most of these segments are not yet marked with the official CDT logo. In southern Wyoming, the route follows old unmarked roads and requires both map-reading and bushwhacking skills. In New Mexico, local interests and politics have delayed decisions about routing the trail, and many thru-hikers, frustrated with the lack of information available during the planning process and the lack of water on the route, give up and follow paved roads. However, given enough time and patience, it is possible to put together a stunning backcountry route through New Mexico.

Whether to go north-to-south or south-to-north is a problem for the few thru-hikers who actually challenge the trail each year. No matter which way they go, they'll have to cope with both left-over snow and ice slopes from the previous winter and accumulating new snow, once winter starts to come again.

The CDT is currently suffering growing pains, and its integrity is being threatened by competing user groups. Bicycle groups want access. Horsepackers want the route to stay low and safe rather than climb to the exposed above-treeline slopes of alpine Colorado. The Forest Service (the agency charged with managing the trail) too often chooses a route for reasons of expediency rather than aesthetics. And the public discourse process threatens to drown the planning and implementation of a simple hiking trail under a barrage of paperwork and comments, many of which reflect commercial concerns. Nonetheless, the CDT presents possibly the wildest, most challenging, and most remote hiking opportunity in the National Trails System. Information: Continental Divide Trail Society, 3704 N. Charles Street #601, Baltimore, MD 21218; (304) 235-9610. Continental Divide Trail Alliance, P.O. Box 628, Pine, CO 80470; (303) 838-3760.

FLORIDA NATIONAL SCENIC TRAIL

The National Trails System really does have a trail for everyone. If you don't like to climb and you think winter camping is a symptom of insanity, the Florida Trail is the answer to your backpacking prayers. It's the only national scenic trail to pass through tropical and subtropical climes. And as for climbs, this may be the flattest trail in the country with an average grade of less then 1 percent.

The trail follows the general arc of the state, staying mostly in the less populated center. Starting at Big Cypress National Preserve in the south, it passes through a variety of ecosystems, many of them wet: ink-black cypress swamps, saw grass and salt marshes, wetlands, lakes, swamps, and — at the western terminus at Gulf Islands National Seashore — the shoreline of the Gulf of Mexico. When the trail does climb, hikers are treated to sandhill prairies and pine forests. Winter and spring are prime hiking seasons.

About 800 miles of Florida Trail's anticipated 1,300 miles are currently completed. The longest completed contiguous stretch runs 300 miles, from north of Orlando to the Apalachiola River. In other parts of the state, the trail is more of a patchwork of segments on public lands; to complete the trail, the Florida Trail Association needs to solve land easement

problems involving entities as diverse as large cattle ranches, the U.S. Department of Defense, and regional water management districts. The Florida Trail Association has come up with an interesting approach to the private land/public use dilemma: Only members of the Florida Trail Association have permission to hike and camp on private property. Thus, the complete guidebook to the trail is sold only to FTA members, although another guide to the Florida Trail's route through public lands is available to everyone.
Information: Florida Trail Association, P.O. Box 13708, Gainesville, FL 32604; (800) 343-1882.

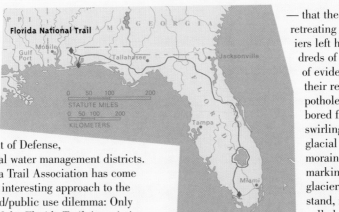

Florida National Trail

ICE AGE NATIONAL SCENIC TRAIL
Until about 10,000 years ago, a sheet of ice, sometimes as much as 2 miles thick, covered the northern part of North America. When the glaciers retreated, they left their mark on the land. Mountain hikers, of course, are used to seeing the handiwork of glaciation: the sculpting of mountains, the gouging of cirques, the lateral moraines of rubble and debris.

So it might come as a surprise to hear that the relatively flat dairy-product state of Wisconsin is called the "Outdoor Museum of the Ice Age." But it is here — on a trail whose maximum elevation is only 2,000 feet — that the retreating glaciers left hundreds of miles of evidence of their reign: potholes bored from swirling glacial silt, moraines marking the glaciers' last stand, ridges called eskers made of ground glacial debris, and a forest buried until 10,000 years ago by ice.

The trail starts in Door Country, a peninsula that combines the charm of an old New England village with the wind-brushed cold shores of northern Lake Michigan. On its curving 1,000-mile path across the state, the trail follows the glacial moraines, which mark the limits of the glaciation, and links together nine units of the Ice Age National Scenic Reserve. It is the only long-distance trail devoted to a single geological event.

The Ice Age Trail is half completed, with nearly 500 miles of existing trail open to hikers and bicyclists, 225 of which have been certified as finished according to the standards of the National Trail System. Hikers wanting to do the entire trail must link together existing trail segments with county roads. The most

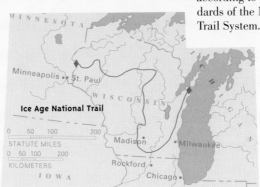

Ice Age National Trail

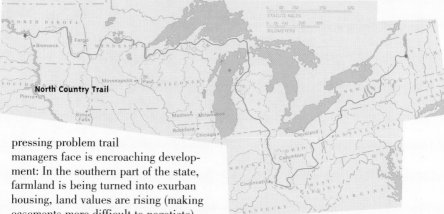

North Country Trail

pressing problem trail managers face is encroaching development: In the southern part of the state, farmland is being turned into exurban housing, land values are rising (making easements more difficult to negotiate), and the character of the terrain is losing some of its rural character. Information: Ice Age Park and Trail Foundation, Inc., P.O. Box 423, Pewaukee, WI 53072; (414) 691-2776.

NORTH COUNTRY
NATIONAL SCENIC TRAIL

It's the longest of the nation's long trails, but no one knows just how long. Originally estimated at some 3,200 miles, current estimates of the route range as high as 4,400 miles — and as many as several hundred more miles may yet be added. However long it is, the Northcountry Trail, running from the Adirondack Mountains of New York to the sea of grass in North Dakota's prairie, is indeed a behemoth. Between mountains and plains, it crosses Pennsylvania, loops around the state of Ohio, traverses both the "palm" and the "thumb" of mitten-shaped Michigan, and wends its way through the cold lake country of Wisconsin and Minnesota. About 1,300 miles have been certified as complete by the National Park Service, and another 1,300 are usable and open to the public.

Unlike the other great long-distance trails, which have a north-to-south orientation, the North Country Trail runs east-west. Only a handful of hikers have challenged its entire length in a single hike.

And for good reason: Too long, too cold, still incomplete, this trail is the distance equivalent of a round-trip on the Appalachian Trail, in parts without trail markers or guidebooks.

Even fanatic long-distance backpackers have second thoughts about a trail that, with no great change in latitude and no eyepopping highcountry views, stays largely in the same eco-zone. The Northcountry Trail does not have the dramatic variety of the great north-south trails, but it has an astonishing amount of diversity, nonetheless — both cultural and ecological. Historic sites like old forts, restored fur trading posts, covered bridges, pioneer homesteads, Revolutionary War sites, and canals remind the hikers of a pioneer past. As for the landscape, it includes Adirondack peaks, Great Lakes shorelines, forests of the coniferous, deciduous, and old growth varieties, popular suburban parks, wetlands, waterfalls, glacial moraines, and the headwaters of the Mississippi (which you can walk across), and the Makinack Bridge (which you can't — foot traffic is permitted only one day each year; the other days, a police van shuttles hikers between Michigan's upper and lower peninsulas). And also sand dunes, gorges, farmland, and the prairie of North Dakota, so vast and featureless that trail managers have installed posts at 500-foot intervals to help hikers find their way. Information: North Country Trail Association, 3777 Sparks Drive SE #105, Grand Rapids, MI 49546.

NATCHEZ TRACE PARKWAY NATIONAL SCENIC TRAIL

The Natchez Trace more appropriately could be considered a national historic trail. The landscaped parkway, which runs 450 miles from Nashville, Tennessee, to Natchez, Mississippi, commemorates a path that began as a Native American trail and was later used by explorers, boatmen, military men, and traders; 110 miles have been selected for development as hiking trails.
Information: Natchez Trace Trail Conference, P.O. Box 1236, Jackson, MS 39152.

POTOMAC HERITAGE NATIONAL SCENIC TRAIL

If this trail is ever finished, it will extend from Washington, D.C., to western Pennsylvania. Although this trail is in the most preliminary stages of planning, existing segments include the Laurel Highlands Trail of Pennsylvania, the Allegheny Highlands Trail, the 18-mile Mount Vernon Trail in Virginia (a paved bike path that starts at George Washington's home and follows the Potomac River; no camping — you'll need a hotel reservation), and the 184-mile towpath of the Chesapeake and Ohio Canal. These 184 miles are a flat, lovely walk on a dirt towpath that starts in downtown Washington and passes by the Great Falls of the Potomac River, Harpers Ferry, countless locks, and the historic Paw-Paw Tunnel. The towpath contains established campsites with piped water, but is frequently severely damaged due to flooding, so check before you try to hike it.
Information: Potomac Heritage Trail Association, 5229 Benson Avenue, Baltimore, MD 21227.

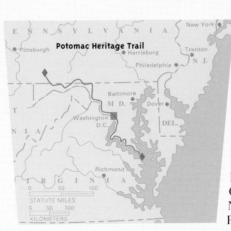

OTHER LONG TRAILS

PACIFIC NORTH-WEST TRAIL

This 1,100-mile trail-in-the-making connects the Continental Divide in Glacier National Park with the Pacific Ocean at Olympia National Park. Passing through seven national forests and three national parks, the trail runs east-west through Montana, Idaho, and Washington. Although not yet completed, the trail benefits from active volunteers who are experienced long-distance hikers; trail workers hope to someday have the trail included in the National Trails System. More than 20 people have managed to thru-hike the trail so far, usually starting in late June in Glacier National Park and reaching the ocean in late September. A guidebook (available on CD-ROM) describes the official completed route and offers suggestions for viable connecting routes for the sections where trail is not yet connected. You need map and compass skills, a tolerance for blackflies and mosquitoes during the early weeks, and a sense of adventure.

Information: Pacific Northwest Trail Association, P.O. Box 1048, Seattle, WA 98111.

ARIZONA TRAIL

One of the newest additions to the roster of long-distance trails, the 750-mile Arizona Trail is primarily a dry-country trail, running from the Mexican border at the Coronado National Monument to the Utah border just north of the Kaibab National Forest.

It's one of the most exciting new trails in the country, not only because of its length, but because of where it goes: The sky-island mountain ranges of the Coronado National Forest, where a 4,000-foot gain of elevation takes you from saguaro to snow. The San Francisco Peaks, sacred to Native Americans and home to 12,633-foot Humphrey's Peak, the highest point in the state. And, of course, there's the Grand Canyon itself, where the Colorado River etches its mile-deep gorge through 2 billion years of geology.

Although it has only been 12 years since trail founder Dale Shewater scouted and proposed a route for the trail, the AzT now boasts 250 miles of signed, completed trail, 270 more miles of trail open to the public, and 255 miles of trails in planning. The goal is to have the trail complete by the year 2000. Nonetheless, with some planning, it is possible now to hike the entire route. Challenges include route-finding, water shortages, and brutal desert temperatures during the warm months.

About 70 percent of the trail passes through Forest Service land, and another 15 percent through national park and BLM lands. The rest goes through a combination of state, county, and privately owned parks and parcels. The trail is divided into 44 sections, called "passages," which go from trailhead to trailhead and are, when complete, marked with a variety of Arizona Trail posts, blazes, brands, and emblems. Many of the completed passages (and some of the trail's best hiking) are in the Coronado National Forest in the south of the state. As each passage is completed, the Arizona Trail Association prepares an information sheet containing a trail description, access information, a basic map (adequate for planning, not hiking), a profile map, a list of resources, and notes regarding signage, trail conditions, and maps. These sheets are available from public land management agencies or the Arizona Trail Association. Information: Arizona Trail Association, P.O. Box 36736, Phoenix, AZ 85067; (602) 252-4794.

COLORADO TRAIL

The Colorado Trail is an example of what local hiking enthusiasts can accomplish. This 470-mile trail from Denver to Durango traverses some of America's most spectacular high-mountain scenery.

These are the Rocky Mountains we're talking about. The Colorado Rockies. So expect to climb sometimes 3,000 feet at a time. Expect to feel the sharp cold bite of a gulp of alpine air. Expect thunderstorms in the afternoons and carpets of snowmelt flowers underfoot, fields of purple columbine, crystal clear tarns the color of ice under gray skies, and the startling aquamarine of a snowmelt lake.

The Colorado

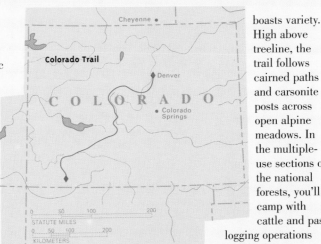

boasts variety. High above treeline, the trail follows cairned paths and carsonite posts across open alpine meadows. In the multiple-use sections of the national forests, you'll camp with cattle and pass logging operations and old mines. Lower down, the route follows both trails and roads and is open to mountain bicyclists and sometimes ATVs. The use of old jeep and snowmobile routes gives the Colorado Trail an accessibility that is unique among high-mountain trails. The Colorado Trail Foundation, in fact, runs "sagwagon" trips in which vehicles carry hikers' gear from one campsite to the next. At the same time, the character of the hike is more wilderness than not: Although plenty of people enjoy the trail, there are enough good campsites to afford peace, solitude, and a real sense of wilderness. Some of the trail can be cross-country skied in the winter months — but research this carefully, because unless you're an expert some of the trail is definitely out of bounds to skiers! Information: Colorado Trail Foundation, P.O. Box 260876, Lakewood, CO 80226.

OHIO TRAIL

To fit a 1,250-mile-long trail into a state

the size of Ohio, there's only one thing to do: run it in a giant circle. The Buckeye Trail is the only trail to circumnavigate a state. Ohio is densely populated, so you won't find much pure wilderness here. But you'll find more diversity than you might expect and you'll discover, perhaps to your surprise, that Ohio is not flat.

Fort Smith State Park across Ozark National Forest to the Buffalo National River, the Ozark Highlands Trail is a relatively undiscovered trail that offers year-round hiking. Peak times to hike are spring and fall. April through June, you'll see the riotous celebration of a southern spring, with redbuds, flowering dogwoods, and azaleas in bloom. In fall, the hardwoods

The trail is designed for multiple use — open to horses and bicyclists as well as hikers — and sometimes it follows country roads and rail trails. The best way to do this trail might actually be to take to a bike on the roaded sections, then ship the bike ahead and walk when the trail goes into forests like the ones you'll find in Wayne National Forest and Hocking Hills State Park (considered one of the trail's highlights). The Northcountry Trail follows the Ohio Trail for part of its route. Historic sites, covered bridges, monuments commemorating the state's history, and remnants of the old Miami and Erie Canal round out the hiker's experience. Information: Buckeye Trail Association, P.O. Box 254, Worthington, OH 43085; (614) 861-1854.

put on their own polychromatic show. Winters can be cold (by southern standards; there doesn't tend to be much snow). Summer is the off-season: hot and humid. But the trail's abundant water — creeks, streams, rivers, and seasonal waterfalls — offers respite. The trail is well blazed, and camping is allowed anywhere.

This is a trail with ambition: Trail building continues downstream. The eventual goal is to link up with Missouri's Ozark Trail (about 100 miles of which are finished) and form an uninterrupted 1,000-mile trail to St. Louis. Information: Ozark Highlands Trail Association, 411 Patricia Lane, Fayetteville, AR 72703; (501) 442-2799.

OZARK HIGHLANDS TRAIL, ARKANSAS, AND OZARK TRAIL, MISSOURI

Currently running 180 miles from Lake

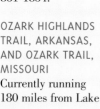

JOHN MUIR TRAIL, CALIFORNIA

John Muir Trail

For most of its length, the JMT is contiguous with the Pacific Crest Trail's route through the High Sierra. Whatever you call it, it may be, mile for mile, the most scenic mountain trail in America. Starting atop (yes, on the actual summit; how you get there is your affair) 14,494-foot Mount Whitney, the 211-mile-long trail connects Kings Canyon and Sequoia National Parks with Yosemite National Park. En route, it crosses a spectacular series of 11,000-, 12,000-, and 13,000-foot passes and the John Muir and Ansel Adams Wildernesses.

This is a summertime trail (unless you've got heavy-duty skiing/mountaineering experience). The high passes tend to be snow-clogged until early July and by late September new snow is starting to fall. It's also a popular trail, especially with groups, which may explain why the resident black bears think of humans as walking delicatessens. You can expect nightly raids on your food bags if they aren't properly hung — and even then, some of the bears show astonishing creativity in their attempt to snatch a mouthful of your mac and cheese. You can foil them by hanging your food or (better) using the bear-proof food storage boxes provided by the park service.

Two other challenges: Fording streams in early summer can be a bit of an adventure (and sometimes quite dangerous) if it's been a snowy winter. And resupply is difficult because of the distances between roads: From the top of Mount Whitney, the JMT doesn't hit a road for some 140 miles. The guidebook has some suggestions for side trails and backcountry outfitters that will hold packages, but be warned: Heavy loads are a common sight in the High Sierra. Permits are required.

Information: Pacific Crest Trail Association, 5325 Elkhorn Blvd. #256, Sacramento, CA 95842; (888) PCTrail. Inyo National Forest Wilderness Reservations, P.O. Box 430, Big Pine, CA 933414; (619) 938-1136 or (888) 374-3773.

WONDERLAND TRAIL

Part of the fun of climbing a mountain is seeing what's on the other side. But there's another way to get there, and it's the route taken by the Wonderland Trail: circumambulation.

This 93-mile trail surrounds what is arguably the most impressive peak in the contiguous 48 states. Rising 14,411 feet above sea level, Mount Rainier dominates the skyline for miles in every direction.

Wonderland Trail

This dormant volcano is covered with 27 glaciers and countless rushing streams and waterfalls, and the loop takes hikers through every life zone in the park. A full 97 percent of the park is managed as wilderness, and the Wonderland Trail takes you right through the middle of it, from towering old-growth forests to the edges of glaciers, up and down and back again, 20,000 feet worth of climbing.

Because of its towering height, Rainier attracts incoming Pacific moist air, and even when the sky is blue elsewhere, its summit is often shrouded in clouds. August is the driest month. The park service recommends 10–14 days for the loop, but that assumes a pace as slow as the mountain's glaciers (which actually sounds like a wonderful way to explore the wonderland). But if you're into big mileage and you're fit, you should be able to do the trip in less than 10 days.

Information: Mount Rainier National Park, Tahoma Woods, Star Route, Ashford, WA 98304; (360) 569-2211. Rainier Mountaineering Inc., June through September, Paradise, WA 98398; October through May, 535 Dock Street, Suite 209, Tacoma, WA 98402. Other information: Mount Adams — Mount Adams Ranger Station, Gifford Pinchot National Forest, 2455 Highway 141, Trout Lake, WA 98650; (509) 395-3400. Mount Hood — Mount Hood National Forest, 2955 NW Division, Gresham, OR 97030; (503) 668-1400.

LONG TRAIL

One of the venerable old-timers of the long-distance hiking system, the 265-mile Long Trail is the first of the state-long border-to-border footpaths. Running

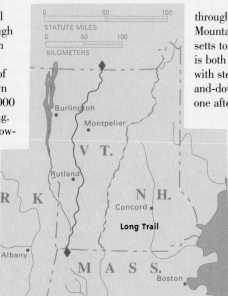

through Vermont's Green Mountains from Massachusetts to Canada, this trail is both lovely and difficult, with steep, straight-up-and-down climbs lined up one after another like a series of giant hurdles.

From the Massachusetts border to Sherburne Pass (near the Killington ski area), the Long Trail is contiguous with the Appalachian Trail; the split occurs near Sherburne Pass, just north of the Killington ski area. Guides and maps are kept up-to-date by the Green Mountain Club. Guidebooks also contain information about connecting side and loop trails.

A system of hiker shelters, or lean-tos, dots the route. These shelters are available (some for a small fee) on a first-come, first-served basis. Hikers are advised to carry a tent or a tarp in case the shelters are full when they arrive.

The best times to hike the trail are summer (after early July, when the black-flies abate) and early fall (when temperatures are cool and hikers walk through some of the most famous foliage in the country). Spring is mud season (some of the trail is officially closed during the spring to try to prevent erosion). And winter puts this northcountry mountain trail into the deep freeze.

Information: Green Mountain Club Inc., Route 100, RR1, Box 650, Waterbury Center, VT 05677; (802) 244-7037.

SOURCES & RESOURCES

MORE LONG TRAILS TO EXPLORE

When I was a kid, I played the globe game. I expect you've done it, too: You've closed your eyes, spun a globe, put down a finger, and promised yourself that someday you'll go where you land. If I ever keep all those promises, I'm going to be spending the next few decades floating in the Pacific Ocean.

Think of this section of Sources & Resources as the globe — except there's no Pacific Ocean to fall into. Just a list of fabulous trails and wildernesses to explore. By its nature, this section can't be more than a sampling. When you start looking at all the trails the world has to offer, you find more miles than a single pair of feet could tread in many lifetimes — and to describe them all, you'd need more words than a single book could contain.

WILDERNESS AREAS AND NATIONAL PARKS

The wilderness areas of the United States, protected under the Wilderness Act of 1964, are defined as areas in which human presence is transitory. The definition has some exceptions: Grazing, for instance, is permitted in wilderness areas, as is some mining. Official wildernesses exist in both national parks and national forests. In addition to designated wildernesses, there are large tracts of roadless wild areas that meet the definition of wilderness, even if they haven't been legally designated as such.

When planning your trip, remember that wilderness areas, national parks, and national forests may be contiguous to one another. Trails often jump across jurisdictional boundaries. Users of wilderness trails should

expect some variation on the subject of trail markings. In almost all national parks and in some wilderness areas, permits are required for overnight camping.

DENALI NATIONAL PARK AND PRESERVE, ALASKA

Alaskans don't believe in hiking trails. In Alaska, the backcountry starts at the trailhead with the decision of which way to go. Sometimes you can follow old roads; sometimes you'll be making your own way. Sometimes, you'll be walking on barren tundra where you can see for miles; other times you'll be face-to-leaf with an alder thicket that blocks your path, clutches at your clothing, and wraps its rubbery branches around you and refuses to let you pass. Climb a little higher, perhaps step-kicking a path up steep scree, and you'll quickly leave all that pesky vegetation behind: Treeline here is only 2,500 feet! Alaska is a place where you carry your map, wear your compass around your neck, and use them often. A GPS wouldn't hurt, either. It's also a place where you learn to go easy on the mileage. This is big country.

Denali: The Great One. The mountain, of course, all 20,320 feet of it. But Denali National Park could make claim to the same name. At 6 million acres, not including adjacent and less crowded Denali State Park (which itself contains more than 300,000 acres), it's larger than Massachusetts. Hiking season runs from May to September, although in May you can expect leftover snow to block your route now and again. Late September starts getting cold and snowy. Midsummer is the most crowded.

Special bear canisters (5 pounds empty) are available free at park headquarters (along with a video telling what to do and what not to do in bear country). As for the mosquitoes, there's a reason they call them the Alaskan state bird: Bring plenty of DEET. Information: Denali National Park and Preserve, P.O. Box 9, Denali National Park, AK 99755; (907) 683 2294.

OLYMPIC NATIONAL PARK, WASHINGTON

Washington's Olympic mountains contain some of the most important temperate rain forest in the world, with 300-foot trees that can reach 8 feet in diameter and sometimes more-so. Look for old-growth forests of Douglas fir, western red cedar, and sitka spruce.

Fog-shrouded Olympic National Park is managed with wilderness values in mind. If you're lucky and quiet, you could see mountain lions, elk,

marmot, black bear, and the elusive spotted owl. Mount Olympus is the highest point, at 7,965 feet above sea level-and in this case, take the phrase "above sea level" literally, because the Pacific is right there below you. Hundreds of highcountry lakes and some 60 glaciers round out this diverse landscape. And 140 inches of annual precipitation tells you all you need to know about the weather. Bring good rain gear, because you're going to need it. Information: Olympic National Park, 600 East Park Ave., Port Angeles, WA 98362; (360) 452-0330.

HIGH SIERRA WILDERNESS COMPLEX, CALIFORNIA

(Includes Kings Canyon and Sequoia National Parks; Yosemite National Park; John Muir, Ansel Adams, and Golden Trout Wildernesses; Sequoia, Sierra, and Inyo National Forests.)
Taken together, these forests and parks offer a wilderness area to get lost in for as long as you can carry food. It can be more than 250 miles between roads. And here's what's best: the place in which you're going to lose yourself contains muscle-soothing hot springs, clear clean mountain tarns, views that take you to the other side of heaven, and Mount Whitney, at 14,494 feet the highest mountain in the 48 contiguous states. The Pacific Crest Trail (here known also as the John Muir Trail) is the most popular long trail, but there are dozens of others, many of them virtually untrod. One of my favorites: the 75-mile east-west High Sierra Trail. Resupply options are few and far between, although a few backcountry lodges on the outskirts of the wilderness will hold packages for hikers. Permits are required. Information: Inyo National

Forest Wilderness Reservations, P.O. Box 430, Big Pine, CA 933414; (619) 938-1136 and (888) 374-3773.

BOB MARSHALL, GREAT BEAR, AND SCAPEGOAT WILDERNESS COMPLEX, MONTANA

These three areas and the roadless areas immediately adjacent form a wilderness complex of more than 2,500,000 acres in northwestern Montana. This land of soaring peaks and plunging canyons is one of the most ecologically complete mountain wildernesses in the Lower 48, with populations of grizzly bears, gray wolves, bighorn sheep, mountain goat, and elk. Its most famous geological feature is the 1,000-foot-tall, 22-mile-long limestone escarpment known as the Chinese Wall.

The "Bob," as it's known to anyone who has been there even once, is the biggest single component, with more than 1,000,000 acres of wilderness, and it has a huge network of backpacking and horsepacking trails. Glacier National Park is directly to the north.

The snow-free season is July and August; snow comes to the highcountry in September and, by October, it sticks. The trails can be muddy (and buggy) in early season, in part because of the snowmelt and in part because groups of horsepackers churn up the trails. The best month is probably August. Information: Lewis and Clark National Forest, 1101 15th St. North, P.O. Box 871, Great Falls, MT 59403; (406) 791-7700.

YELLOWSTONE NATIONAL PARK, WYOMING

Yellowstone and the surrounding wildernesses and national forests form what is known as the Greater Yellowstone Ecosystem, the largest substantially intact temperate ecosystem on earth. Yellowstone's unique combination of spectacular geology (more geysers, fumaroles and paint pots than anywhere else on earth) and wildlife (you might see moose, elk, buffalo, coyotes, black bear, grizzly bears, and wolves) makes the 3,400-square-mile park one of the most famous landscapes anywhere, and a World Heritage Site, along with other wonders like the Great Pyramids and Versailles. Surprisingly, the backcountry is not particularly crowded; perhaps because there's so much else to see near the park roads. But the park is 99 percent undeveloped-which means that most of its wonders are out of range of the roads. This is grizzly country, so take standard precautions (the rangers will instruct you when you get your permit).

The southern extension of the Greater Yellowstone Ecosystem takes you into another pristine hiking area, the Wind River Range (part of the Shoshone and Bridger-Teton National Forests). With the biggest glaciers in the Rockies south of Canada, glacial streams that carry sediment-laden milky waters down to the Green River, and its boulder fields, cirques, and shimmering lakes, the Wind River Range must surely rate as one of North America's most beautiful places for mountain hiking. Early September is the best season: The crowds are gone and the weather still holds. Information: Yellowstone National Park, P.O. Box 168, Yellowstone National Park, WY 82190; (307) 344-2160. Bridger-Teton National Forest, Pinedale Ranger District, 210 W. Pine St., P.O. Box 220, Pinedale, WY 82941; (307) 367-4326.

COLORADO WILDERNESS AREAS
Colorado has more than 30 designated wilderness areas. If I tried to describe them all, you'd read the same words over and over: sky-scraping peaks, spectacular views, alpine lakes, quaking aspen, purple columbine. But you can't go wrong with the following four.
● Collegiate Peaks Wilderness. So called because its major peaks take the names of major universities (look up to the lofty heights of Harvard, Columbia, Oxford, Princeton, and Yale). This 160,000-acre wilderness includes 8 peaks over 14,000 feet, 105 miles of hiking trails, and 40 miles of the Continental Divide.
● South San Juan Wilderness. This wilderness lies south of Wolf Creek Pass, the "bear-cat of mountain passes" (so named because of how hard it was to cross this pass in the early days of roads and cars; the small ski area at the pass gets more snow than any other ski area in the country). Characterized by high tundra, sweeping vistas, and solitude, elevations range from 8,000 feet to over 13,000 feet.
● Weminuche Wilderness. Managed by the Rio Grande and San Juan National Forests, it includes more than 500 miles of hiking trails, nearly 450,000 acres of wilderness, three peaks higher than 14,000 feet (Mount Eolus, Mount Windom, and Sunlight Peak), and the headquarters of the San Juan River and Rio Grande, each sent to different oceans by the Continental Divide. An average elevation of 10,500 feet make the trails here some of the highest in the contiguous states. Information: *Exploring Colorado's Wild Areas*, by Scott Warren. The Mountaineers, 1001 SW Klickitat Way, Suite 201, Seattle, WA 98134; (800) 553-4453.

GILA NATIONAL FOREST, NEW MEXICO
Together the Gila Wilderness and the Aldo Leopold Wilderness encompass some 700,000 acres of designated wilderness. They also offer some of the best hiking in the Gila National Forest; much of the rest of the forest is managed for multiple use, especially grazing and timber. In the wilderness areas, the hiking trails are well marked and mapped, and it's possible to connect various trails to make loops of different lengths. Elevations range from 6,000 feet to more than 10,000 feet at the top of Mogollon Baldy, so you'll be climbing through a variety of eco-zones, from piñon-juniper drylands to the climatic equivalent of Canada's Hudson Bay.

One of the region's spectacular hikes is the 10-mile trip upstream from the confluence of Sapillo Creek with the Gila River. The river — usually no more than knee deep — is framed on each side by steep cliffs which force the trail to switch from one side of the river to the other some 40 times (bring amphibious sport sandals). Information: Gila National Forest, 2610 N. Silver St., Silver City, NM 88061; (505) 388-8201.

GRAND CANYON NATIONAL PARK, ARIZONA
Grand Canyon National Park encompasses more than a million acres, and it offers a hiking experience unique in all the world. Hiking trails in the canyon are divided into levels. Three major so-called corridor trails are crowded with day-hikers, mule-trippers, and tourists. The second- and third-level trails are more rugged and less well maintained, and require navigation skills.

Rangers recommend that beginning canyon hikers get

their feet wet (so to speak) by trying out one of the corridor trails: the Bright Angel or the South Kaibab on the South Rim and the North Kaibab on the more remote North Rim. Do both in one trip and you've gone "Rim to Rim." This 3-day, 2-night, 24-mile hike involves (if you go northbound) 5,000 feet of elevation lost and 6,000 feet of elevation gained and is one of the world's classic hikes. Getting a permit for it can be a hassle, since camping slots are extremely limited in the established campsites. Either plan well in advance or be prepared to wait it out for a walk-in opening. And listen to the rangers when they tell you how much water to take: They respond to some 400 medical emergencies a year, mostly due to dehydration and the heat.

Once you've gotten the hang of desert canyon hiking, you might want to strike out, away from the pack. The Grand Canyon's longest trail is the Tonto Trail, which follows, more or less, the flat shelf of the Tonto Formation and runs parallel to the Colorado River below the South Rim.

Spring is the peak season for canyon hiking. The springs are full from snowmelt (or at least as full as they ever get) and seasonal streams are most likely to be running. Summer is hot, sometimes dangerously so. Winter is comfortably cool and the least populated season of all, but it can be dry. Winter access is possible by auto only on the South Rim. Information: Grand Canyon National Park, P.O. Box 129, Grand Canyon, AZ 86023; (520) 638-7888.

BIG BEND NATIONAL PARK, TEXAS
The name refers to the great U-turn the Rio Grande makes in southwest Texas. As 97 percent of the acreage is Chihuahuan Desert, this is dry country, home to coyotes and jackrabbits and rattlesnakes. The other 3 percent is what makes this park unique among deserts. The thin green thread of the river creates a riparian zone, and the sky-island Chisos Mountains poke into the clouds to an elevation of 7,835 feet (a full vertical mile above the desert floor). This combination of mountain, riparian zone, and desert gives Big Bend enormous ecological diversity; more than 400 species of birds have been sighted here. (If you're a dedicated birder, spring is the best time to go.)

Old-time Big Bend hikers strike out cross-country once they are certain of their skills and the amount of water in their canteens. For beginners, there is an extensive network of hiking trails. Most of the rain falls in late summer, which is a lousy time to be visiting, since ground temperatures can reach 180 degrees. In winter, temperatures can drop below freezing-but they can also reach a balmy 80 degrees. Park literature laconically states that the nearest hospital is at Alpine, 108 miles away. Information: Big Bend National Park, P.O. Box 129, Big Bend National Park, TX 79834; (915) 477-2251.

FRANK CHURCH-RIVER OF NO RETURN WILDERNESS, IDAHO
The Frank Church-River of No Return Wilderness is the largest wilderness in the Lower 48. And with elevations climbing from 2,000 feet to 10,000 feet, it's got a fair claim on the title of most diverse, too. The hiking is challenging: Trails can climb and descend thousands of feet in just a few miles.

Known for a large population of mountain lions, the wilderness is also home to the lion's smaller cousin, the lynx, as well as moose, bighorn sheep, mountain goat, elk, mule, and whitetail deer. Smaller predators such as marten, fisher, coyote, red fox, and wolverine also live here. A network of backcountry roads provides some access to parts of the wilderness. There are also several backcountry airstrips (which is unique in wilderness areas) served by charter companies based in local communities. Information: The Wilderness is located in the Challis, Salmon, Nez Perce, Payette, and Boise National Forests in Idaho and in the Bitterroot National Forest in Montana. *Trails of the Frank Church River of No Return Wilderness* (Margaret Fuller; Signpost Books).

WHITE MOUNTAIN NATIONAL FOREST, NEW HAMPSHIRE
It is the highest, most fragile terrain in the Northeast and offers the most significant arctic-alpine hiking experience east of the Rocky Mountains. And it's not easy. Hiking on many White Mountain trails is more akin to rock-scrambling than walking. Going a mile on Garfield Ridge can take you an hour, especially if the trails are slick with rain.

The weather is notoriously, almost gleefully, unpredictable. Mount Washington's summit (6,288 feet) holds the world record for the highest-recorded land windspeed: 231 miles per hour. It can snow any day of the year, and unprepared hikers die here (most often from hypothermia or from falling) with astonishing, tragic frequency — even in August.

A system of backcountry huts run by the Appalachian Mountain Club offers hearty meals and accommodations in bunkhouse rooms, but the price is as steep as some of the trails. The reward: You don't have to carry a tent, air mattress, stove, and food over all those rocks. For the hardy, tentsites and lean-to spaces are available for a nominal fee, although in peak season they fill up early in the day.

Do yourself a favor and plan low mileage — a 10-mile day here is the equivalent of 20 miles on easier trails. Information: White Mountain National Forest, Federal Building, Lanconia, NH 03246. Or Appalachian Mountain Club, 5 Joy Street, Boston, MA 02108; (617) 523- 0655.

ADIRONDACK PARK, NEW YORK

New York's Adirondack Mountains contain 6 million acres, almost 4 million of which are privately owned. But environmental regulation has a 100-year-long history here. The result: carefully controlled development and one of the most unique preserves in the United States. The region boasts large tracts of wilderness, including the High Peaks area, which contains 5,344-foot Mount Marcy (New York's highest peak) and Lake Tear of the Clouds (which lies at 4,300 feet and is the source of the Hudson River).

Perhaps the area's best-known trail is the 133-mile Northville-Lake Placid Trail, which was built in 1922 and is one of the oldest recreational hiking trails in America. The trail winds through hardwood forests of beech and maple and passes a series of loon-laughing lakes without ever gaining enough elevation to make you break a sweat. Beware of early summer: The blackflies are fierce. The very active Adirondack Mountain Club publishes guidebooks and runs educational programs for backcountry users. Information: Adirondack Mountain Club, 814 Goggins Road, Lake George, NY 12845; (800) 395-8080.

BAXTER STATE PARK, MAINE

Mount Katahdin was a holy place to the Abenaki Indians who lived there, and it's a holy place to Appalachian Trail hikers who walk 2,160 miles to stand on the wind-swept rocky summit of this towering monadnock.

Katahdin was a holy place to former Maine Governor Percival Baxter, too, who dealt with political indifference the direct way: Piece by piece, he bought up the wilderness and donated it to the people of Maine on the condition that it be kept forever wild. Today, Baxter State Park is one of the most fervently managed wild places in America. Wilderness lovers appreciate the lack of motor homes and tourist stands, but they sometimes find the camping regulations overly strict and complain that the rules-and-regulations park staff violates the spirit of freedom that is part of the outdoor experience. Administrators steadfastly hold to their vision for the park — and their rules. Perhaps as a result, Baxter State Park is indeed one of the most beautiful and wild places in the East. But if you want to see it, get your permits early. Information: Baxter State Park Reservation Clerk, 64 Balsam Drive, Millinocket, ME 04462; (207) 723-5140.

INTERNATIONAL HIGHLIGHTS

The globe is filled with hiking trails to satisfy all tastes, from rain forests to mountaintops, from beaches to deserts. This list only scratches the surface of what's available.

COPPER CANYON, MEXICO

Copper Canyon. 25,000 square miles. Every time I go to the Southwest, I hear rumors. A canyon bigger than the Grand. Millions of untouched acres, accessible only by a winding

mountain railroad. An area not completely mapped. La Barranca del Cobre in the Sierra Madre.

Copper Canyon puts a different spin on the definition of wilderness. No roads, uncharted, hard to get to (it took 90 years to get the train line built) — that's wilderness. But it's also inhabited, which contradicts our American perception of wilderness. You'll have to judge for yourself. The inhabitants are Tuhanamara Indians who practice subsistence farming. These are the people, incidentally, who are famous for running 100-mile races.

Backpackers traveling in Mexico have occasionally run into problems with bandits, so you should take appropriate precautions: Use traveler's checks instead of cash, pack old gear, not your shiniest hippest new stuff, and travel in groups. Lodges at the top of the canyon can provide rooms and meals, and guides can be hired if you are so inclined. Information: *Mexico's Copper Canyon: A Hiking and Backpacking Guide*, by John Fayhee; available from Adventurous Traveler Bookstore.

HIMALAYAN TREKS, NEPAL

Nepal offers the most accessible trekking experience in the Himalayas. Although adventure travel companies run guided treks, the truth is you can simply get on a plane and figure things out as you go (unless you're heading into exceedingly remote parts of the country). The major walking routes are well established. Accommodations and food are available in rustic tea houses, so you don't need to carry a heavy pack. Of course, for a price, you don't have to carry a pack at all: You can join a tour with a guide or hire a porter to carry your load for you. The difference in cost between independent trekking (less than $10 a day) and a guided service (can cost up to $100 a day) might make the decision for you. Everest Base Camp. The trek to Everest Base Camp is physically the most difficult of the popular Nepal treks, because the route runs perpendicular to the lay of the land. That means you'll be climbing ridge after ridge and then descending into valley after valley. And don't forget, these are Himalayan ridges; an elevation of 12,000 feet means you're standing in the foothills.

The most sensible access to this trek is to take a bus from Kathmandu to Jiri, and then start walking.

Trekkers in the Annapurna region, just north of Nepal's second largest city of Pokhara, have three choices. The entire circuit around the Annapurna Massif takes about 20 days and includes a climb over snowy 17,800- foot Thorong-La ("La" is the Nepali word for "pass"). There is also the option of a shorter trek to Jomson. The Jomson trek runs through the Kali Gandaki Valley, which is one of the deepest gorges on earth: If you look down at your feet, you might see a kaligram-a 2-million-year-old fossil of ancient shells, left over from the time when these mountains were under the seas. Above you — nearly 5 miles above you — tower the walls of the Annapurna Massif and, in full view, the fierce face of Dhaligari. Finally, the Annapurna Sanctuary can be tacked on to either the full circuit or the Jomson Trek. This walk takes you into the snowy cirque of Annapurna Base Camp, surrounded by rumbling avalanches, grumbling glaciers, and the unclimbed summit of Macchupuchare, Nepal's sacred, forbidden peak.

Information: *Nepal (Travel Survival Kit)*, by Richard Everist and Tony Wheeler (Lonely Planet Publishers).

TRANS-PYRENEAN TRAILS, FRANCE

France offers a well-developed system of long-distance hiking trails. Each route is different in character. Some, for instance, spend more time in towns and along paved roads, and some offer wilderness experiences on challenging footpaths. Most of the long routes are numbered and are referred to with the "GR" (for "grand randonne," or big hiking route) followed by the number.

Trans-Pyrenean routes. For backpackers with a love of wilderness, the trans-Pyrenean routes are probably the most rewarding. This least populated part of France and Spain contains western Europe's largest remaining wilderness (including a small and highly endangered population of the European brown bear, related to our grizzlies). The highly serrated ridges of the Pyrenees form the Franco-Spanish border from the Atlantic to the Mediterranean. This approximately 600-mile-long mountain trek is characterized by steep, difficult climbing and such an intense variety of mountain scenery — glaciers, multi-thousand-foot rock faces, lakes, and giant cirques — that you might find yourself rubbing your eyes once in a while.

There are three sea-to-sea routes and hundreds of short, interconnecting variants, all mapped and also described in guidebooks published in both English and French. The GR-10, known as a "lower" route stays entirely in France and offers trekkers the chance to stay in hiker hostels or simple village hotels almost every night. But this doesn't mean it's easy. After each descent to a

village, the trail climbs back again into the mountains: Climbs of 3,000 feet are a matter of course. The HRP (High Route of the Pyrenees) stays high, as close to the border as possible, spends time in both France and Spain (as well as the tiny principality of Andorra), and drops into villages only occasionally. It requires more navigation and alpine skills, because the route is not consistently marked. But even here, creature comforts are sometimes available: Hikers can buy cheese from local shepherds and sip local wine at backcountry refuges. The GR-11 is the Spanish equivalent of the GR-10. It's a little more rugged and less predictable than the GR-10. Information: *Pyrenean Trail GR-10*, by Alan Castle and *Pyrenean High Level Route*, by Veron (Cicerone Press); both available from Adventurous Traveler Bookstore.

INCA TRAIL, PERU

The Black Andes, they call these mountains, in contrast to the higher, snowy, cloud-piercing giants of the Cordillera Blanca. Really they're green, not black, a misty, somber, wet green. When the fog parts, the ruined city below shifts into focus. Machu Picchu. As you look at the lost city of the Incas, veiled by mist, you will understand in a way you never have what it means to worship the sun.

Most trekkers spend a few days in the ancient Incan city of Cuzco, seeing the sights and acclimating to the 11,000-foot altitude. From Cuzco, a bus runs to Ollantaytambo, the end of the road. You can take the train from here to Machu Picchu, or you can walk the Inca Trail.

Political unrest made this path unsafe for several years in

the late 1980s and early 1990s. Check with the U.S. State Department. You may feel more comfortable if you are able to form a small traveling group—chances are you'll meet like-minded people in Cuzco. In addition, guided treks are available. Information: *Backpacking in Peru and Bolivia*, by Hilary Bradt, Petra Schepens and Jonathan Derksen (Bradt Pubs.).

FJORDLAND NATIONAL PARK, NEW ZEALAND

Fjordland National Park on New Zealand's South Island contains several fine hiking paths, including the famous Milford Track. Rustic backcountry huts are available for "trampers." The South Island gets 200 inches of rain a year: Bring Gore-Tex. Best months to go: December through March.

Milford Track. Being called the "finest walk in the world" is a double-edged sword for a hiking trail, if only because it draws the crowds. So many, in fact, that trail managers encourage hikers to join organized treks (which can be very expensive). Only a limited number of so-called freedom-walkers are given permits to tackle the 32-mile-long trail independently, and reservations should be made as far ahead as you can possibly plan. However you go, what you'll see is well worth the effort: This mountain walk lives up to its billing, with craggy views, glaciers, water-falls, fjords, and rainbows.

Hollyford Track. With only about one-tenth the hiker traffic of its more famous cousin, the 35-mile Hollyford explores the lower elevations of the park, staying mostly at sea level. It starts in the Southern Alps and follows the Hollyford River to the Tasman Sea. You'll see more waterfalls than you can count, views of 8,000-foot and 9,000-foot peaks, thick lush vegetation

unique to New Zealand, and, if you're lucky, seals and dolphins up close once you reach the coast. Information: *New Zealand Handbook* by Jane King (published by Moon Publishers, available through Adventurous Traveler Bookstore).

CIRCUMNAVIGATION OF MOUNT KENYA, KENYA

Sitting almost astride the equator, Kenya's highest point is from a distance dominated by the horizontal vastness of the African savanna. It's when you get up close that the mountain reveals its many-faceted character.

The lower slopes of the dormant volcano are green and rainy, dotted with small, family-run banana plantations. On the trail, you'll see the spoor of elephants and cape buffalo. Climbing higher, you reach bamboo forests higher than your head, clattering and clacking as they sway in the wind.

Like any mountain, Mount Kenya changes as you climb, but in Africa, the alpine world has a fantastical character, with forests of giant lobelia and scur-rying little hyraxes.

A few primitive huts are operated by the Mount Kenya Alpine Club; some are open to tourists/climbers, and others are reserved for members. The out-house at Austria Hut — at 15,700 feet, the mountain's highest hut — gets my vote for the best view from an outhouse in the world.

The mountain has three summits, only the lowest of which (Point Lenana, 16,300 feet) can be reached by back-packers. For the two higher peaks (17,300 feet), you need rock-climbing skills and ropes. A spectacular backpacking trip takes the long way around the mountain, circumnavigating all of the high peaks. The loop takes about a week, depending

on how fast you acclimate. Warning: The combination of high altitude and accessibility makes Mt. Kenya one of the world capitals of acute mountain sickness. Take time to accli-mate. Information: *East Africa International Mountain Guide* (published by Cordee) and *Mountain Walking in Africa: Kenya* by David Else (published by Cicerone) are both available through Adventurous Traveler Bookstore.

WEST COAST TRAIL, BRITISH COLUMBIA, CANADA

Located on the southern west coast of Vancouver Island, British Columbia, this craggy coastal trail is one of Canada's most popular. Wide sandy beaches, rainy Pacific forests, and dramatic headlands combine to challenge the hiker with arduous trails and views well worth the effort. In addition, you'll walk past evidence of the region's vibrant and colorful cul-tural history: old lighthouses, prospecting sites, and the remains of old settlements, mis-sions, and offshore shipwrecks.

Because of the popularity of this 50-mile hike, a reservation system is in effect to preserve the unique environment. The trail is officially open from April 15 to October 15. While not prohibited, hiking during the off-season is discouraged because of the combination of arduous trail and the likelihood of bad weather. Information: *West Coast Trail and Nitinat Lakes* by Tim Leadem (guide-book published by Sierra Club of Western Canada, available from Adventurous Traveler Bookstore).

OTHER RESOURCES

What's next? Get some gear, pick a location, plan your trip. Following are organizations to contact, more books to read, and ideas about acquiring equipment.

LEADING HIKING CLUBS

AMERICAN HIKING SOCIETY
P.O. Box 20160
Washington, D.C.
703-255-9304
fax: 703-255-9308
Write or call for the society's complete list of affiliated clubs to find the one nearest you.

APPALACHIAN MOUNTAIN CLUB (AMC)
5 Joy Street
Boston, MA 02108
617-523-0636
fax: 617-523-0722
Almost 55,000 members; the club offers numerous hiking programs from 2-5 days; also publishes many excellent guides to the outdoors.

APPALACHIAN TRAIL CONFERENCE (ATC)
P.O. Box 807
Harpers Ferry, WV 25425
304-535-6331
Helps coordinate maintainence of the 2,000 mile Appalachian Trail; excellent source of current information on hiking activities.

COLORADO MOUNTAIN CLUB
2530 West Alameda Avenue
Denver, CO 80219
303-922-8976

CONTINENTAL DIVIDE TRAIL ALLIANCE
P.O. Box 628
Pine, CO 80470
303-838-3760

CONTINENTAL DIVIDE TRAIL SOCIETY
3704 N. Charles Street #601
Bethesda, MD 21218
410-235-9610

FLORIDA TRAIL ASSOCIATION (FTA)
P.O. Box 13708
Gainesville, FL 32604
904-378-8823

GREEN MOUNTAIN CLUB
Route 100, Box 650
Waterbury Center, VT 05677
802-244-7037
Coordinates up-keep and protection of and publishes guide to the Long Trail, which runs the length of Vermont and includes many shelters.

KEYSTONE TRAILS ASSOCIATION
P.O. Box 251
Cogan Station, PA 17728
717-322-0293

THE MOUNTAINEERS
303 Third Avenue, W.
Seattle, WA 98119
206-284-6310

NEW YORK-NEW JERSEY TRAIL CONFERENCE
232 Madison Avenue, #908
New York, NY 10016
212-685-9699

PACIFIC CREST TRAIL ASSOCIATION
5325 Elkhorn Boulevard
Suite 265
Sacremento, CA 95842
800-817-2243

PACIFIC CREST TRAIL CONFERENCE
P.O. Box 2040
Lynnwood, WA 98036
503-686-1365

POTOMAC APPALACHIAN TRAIL CLUB
118 Park Street, S.E.
Vienna, VA 22180
703-242-0693

WASHINGTON TRAILS ASSOCIATION
1305 Fourth Avenue #512
Seattle, WA 98101
206-625-1367

TOUR OPERATORS

In addition to regional trail associations, these organizations and tour operators offer hiking programs, or can recommend other sources to you:

BACKCOUNTRY
P.O. Box 4029-A114
Bozeman, MT 59772
406-586-3556
fax: 406-586-4288
Offers a catalog of trips and free information packets on how to query outfitters.

BACKROADS
1516 5th Street, Suite A200
Berkeley, CA 94710-1740
800-462-2848
fax: 510-527-1444
Considered one of the foremost active travel tour operators in North America; write or call for full-color catalogs.

ECOTOURISM SOCIETY
P.O. Box 755
North Bennington, VT 052757
802-447-2121
Keeps an eye on the environmental viability of programs others sponsor.

HOSTELLING INTERNATIONAL-AMERICAN YOUTH HOSTELS
733 15th Street N.W. #840
Washington, D.C. 20005
202-783-6161
fax: 202-783-6171
American and European group programs for all ages.

MOUNTAIN TRAVEL SOBEK
6420 Fairmont Avenue
El Cerrito, CA 94536
800-227-2384 or 510-527-8100
fax: 510-525-7710

NATIONAL AUDUBON SOCIETY
950 Third Avenue
New York, NY 10022
212-979-3000
The Audubon Society and its local chapters sponsor a wide variety of programs. Call for your nearest chapter's offerings.

THE NATURE CONSERVANCY
1815 North Lynn Street
Arlington, VA 22209
703-841-5300
Overseas 1,100 wild preserves and safeguards millions of acres. Ask for your local chapter information.

SIERRA CLUB
730 Polk Street
San Francisco, CA 94109
415-981-8634
This esteemed environmental group has 56 chapters & publishes an annual guide to family outings in its house publication, Sierra. Current information on trips is available by calling 415-923-5630.

STUDENT CONSERVATION ASSOCIATION (SCA)
P.O. Box 550
Charlestown, NH 03603
603-543-1700
fax: 603-543-1828
Places students in volunteer positions with government outdoor agencies.

OUTDOOR ADVENTURE SCHOOLS
These leading educational organizations are considered the best in the field:

NATIONAL OUTDOOR LEADERSHIP SCHOOL (NOLS)
Dept. R
288 Main Street
Lander, WY 82520
307-332-6873
NOLS trains future guides, year-round, even for college credit, all over the world.

OUTWARD BOUND
Route 90
R2, Box 280
Garrison, NY 10524
800-243-8520
Almost all Outward Bound participants consider their experiences with the school far more than an outdoor adventure. — the learning experience is often spiritual as well. With 31 schools worldwide OB is a school staffed by experts, with a solid reputation for safe and professional wilderness courses.

FIRST AID TRAINING
For first aid and cpr classes call the American Red Cross and ask for local chapter information:

AMERICAN RED CROSS NATIONAL HEADQUARTERS
431 18th Street N.W.
Washington, D.C. 20006
202-737-8300

MAGAZINES
The established outdoor magazines can both thrill and lend assurance to novice adventurers. They are chock full of techniques, recommendations, and usually ample sections with advertisements for outfitters, schools, and trips.

BACKPACKER
Rodale Press, Inc.
33 East Minor Street
Emmaus, PA 18098
Subscriptions: 800-666-3434
You can also read this popular outdoor magazine on your computer by sending to America Online for the software, 8619 Westwood Center Drive, Vienna, VA 22182-9806. Backpacker's annual guide to equipment is a must.

OUTSIDE
Mariah Media Inc.
400 Market Street
Santa Fe, NM 87501
505-989-7100
Subscriptions: 800-678-1131
All active outdoor sports, practically invented adventure travel, environment, annual gear guide. magazine to help families considering trips in the great outdoors.

WILDERNESS TRAILS MAGAZINE
Wilderness Trails, Inc.
712 Satori Drive
Petaluma, CA 94954
707-762-8839
A mix of adventure and environmentalism.

THE INTERNET
Trail surfing? Tune in to http://www.trailside.com on the web and find answers to all your Trailside questions. In addition to detailed descriptions of all the Trailside TV episodes — 78 in all — click trhough to the experts, locations, maps, and gear you need to make your own adventure.
    Whether you're a hiker, biker, canoeist, or snowshoer, another good place to explore is GORP, the Great Outdoor Recreation Pages (http://www.gorp.com), full of information on gear, books, attractions, feature articles, and links to other web sites of interest.

BOOKS
If you like to read or feel better easing slowly into this new venture, here are some suggestions. In addition to "Best-Bet Reading" recommendations found at th end of each Chapter.

BACKPACKING TECHNIQUES & CONCERNS
Backpacker's Handbook, Chris Townsend. $14.95. Ragged Mountain/McGraw Hill.

The Backpacker's Photography Handbook: How to Take Great Wilderness Pictures While Hiking, Climbing & Skiing, Charles Campbell. 1994. $19.95. Watson-Guptill.

Everyday Wisdom: 1001 Expert Tips for Hikers, Karen Berger. 1997. $16.95. The Mountaineers.

Knots for Hikers & Backpackers, Frank & Victoria Logue. $4.95. Menasha Ridge.

FOOD & COOKING
Gorp, Glop, & Glue Stew: Favorite Foods from 165 Outdoor Experts, Yvonne Prater & Ruth D. Mendenhall. 1981. $10.95. Mountaineers.

The *NOLS Cookery: Experience the Art of Outdoor Cooking*, National Outdoor Leadership School Staff. 1991. $6.95. Stackpole.

The Well-Fed Backpacker, June Fleming. 1986. $9.00. Random House.

Wild Foods Field Guide & Cookbook, Billy J. Tatum. 2nd ed. 1985. $8.95 Paper. $7.95. Workman.

WOMEN IN THE OUTDOORS

The Outdoor Woman: A Handbook to Adventure, Patricia Hubbard & Stan Wass. 1992. $14.95. MasterMedia Limited.

WINTER CAMPING & WILDERNESS SURVIVAL

AMC Guide to Winter Camping, Stephen Gorman. 1991. $12.95. Appalachian Mountain Club.

Harsh Weather Camping in the Nineties: Secrets, Suggestions, Tips & Techniques, Sam Curtis. 1993. $12.95. Menasha Ridge.

Wilderness Skiing & Winter Camping, Chris Townsend. 1993. $17.95. McGraw-Hill.

Winterwise, a Backpacker's Guide, John M. Dunn. 1989. $12.95. Adirondack Mountain Club.

WHERE-TO GUIDES & TRAIL GUIDES

The Active Travel Resource Guide, Dan Browdy, ed. Ultimate Ventures, $19.95. The latest edition lists 85 organizations and the tours they offer, dates, prices, and all.

Appalachian Mountain Club guides and maps. Compact books to carry with you when hiking in New England, with great pull-out maps.

Appalachian Trail series, published by the Appalachian Trail Conference, with guides and maps to the great trail.

Camper's Guide to U. S. National Parks, Morava and Little. Gulf. Two volume set on camping opportunities, including hike-in. $18.95 each.

Climber's and Hiker's Guide to the World's Mountains, Michael Kelsey. 3rd ed., $34.95. Kelsey Pub.

The Complete Guide to America's National Parks, $14.95. Fodor's Travel Publications.

Hikers Guide to series: popular guides to favorite regions of the U.S.

Lonely Planet: a wonderful series of guides for travelling and trekking abroad.

100 Hikes series, published by the Mountaineers as guides to the Northwest.

Software: Best Foot Forward databases, with guides to trails in five states, are available from: Grizzlyware
16837 N.E. 176th Street
Woodinville, WA 98072
800-258-4453

HIKING SOME OF THE PLACES MENTIONED IN THIS BOOK

Along the Colorado Trail, John Fielder & M. John Fayhee. 1992. Westcliffe.

As Far As the Eye Can See, David Brill. 1990. $14.95. Rutledge Hill.

Journey on the Crest - Walking 2600 Miles from Mexico to Canada, Cindy Ross. 1992. $21.50. Peter Smith.

The Thru-Hiker's Handbook 1995, Dan W. Bruce. $10.95. Center for Appalachian Trail Studies.

Uncommon Places, David Muench. 1991. $39.95. Appalachian Trail Conference.

Walking the Appalachian Trail, Larry Luxenberg. 1994. $16.95. Stackpole.

Where the Waters Divide: A 3,000-Mile Trek Along America's Continental Divide, Karen Berger & Dan Smith. 1997. $17.95. Countryman.

MAP & COMPASS

Be Expert with Map & Compass: The Complete Orienteering Handbook, Kellstrom, Bjorn. U. S. Geological Survey & Orienteering Services. 1994. $15.85. Macmillan.

Compass & Map Navigator: The Complete Giude to Staying Found, Michael Hodgson. 1997. $14.95. ICS Books.

The Outward Bound Map & Compass Book, Randall, Glenn. 1989. $8.95. Lyons & Burford.

Staying Found: The Complete Map & Compass Handbook, June Fleming. 2nd ed. 1994. $10.95. Mountaineers.

SAFETY & FIRST AID

Field Guide to Venomous Animals & Poisonous Plants, Steven Foster. 1994. $22.95. Paper $15.95. Houghton Mifflin.

First Aid for the Outdoors: The Basic Essentials, William W. Forgey. 1988. $5.99. ICS.

Hypothermia, Frostbite & Other Cold Injuries: Prevention, Recognition, Pre Hospital Treatment, James A. Wilkerson, et al, eds. 1986. $11.95. Mountaineers.

*Medicine for Mountaineering &
Other Wilderness Activities,*
James A. Wilkerson, ed. 4th ed.
1992. $16.95. Mountaineers.

Medicine for the Backcountry,
Buck Tilton. 2nd ed. 1994.
$12.99. ICS.

*Mountaineering Medicine: A
Wilderness Medical Guide,* Fred
T. Darvill, Jr. 13th rev. ed. 1992.
$5.95. Wilderness Press.

NOLS Wilderness First Aid, Tod
Schimelpfenig & Linda Lindsey.
1992. $12.95. Stackpole.

*Rescue from the Backcountry:
The Basic Essentials Of,* Buck
Tilton. 1991. $5.99. ICS.

Standard First Aid, American
Red Cross Staff. 1993. $6.00.
Mosby-Year Book.

MAIL-ORDER
SOURCES OF BOOKS
ADVENTUROUS TRAVELER
BOOKSTORE
P.O. Box 64769
245 South Champlain Street
Burlington, VT 05406
800-282-3963 or 802-860-6776
fax: 800-677-1821
*E-mail: books@atbook.com;
on the World Wide Web —
http://www.gorp.com/atbook.htm
— search their full selection of
3,000 titles by keyword. Largest
supplier of worldwide adventure
travel books & maps.*

BACKCOUNTRY BOOKSTORE
P.O. Box 6235
Lynnwood, WA 90836-0235
206-290-7652
*Books and videos on all outdoor
activities, as well as knowledgeable staff.*

MAIL-ORDER
SOURCES OF MAPS
Libraries are a good place to
start for maps. Your local outfitters will also carry some. We
recommend a fascinating book,

The Map Catalog, edited by Joel
Makower, 1992, $18.00, Vin-
tage Books. This invaluable
source describes the wide range
of maps published and where to
order them. Trails Illustrated is
a series published by a group of
the same name, with topographical maps for major parks and
mountains in the U.S. The
Delorme Atlas/Gazeteers have
large-scale maps of most states
with trails and campsites.

You can order topographical
maps from the following government agencies. Hikers in the
western half of the country may
also wish to contact their
regional Bureau of Land Management for maps of 3,600 miles
of marked trails. Also, try your
state department of natural
resources, state parks, or transportation authority.

MAP DISTRIBUTION
U.S. Geological Survey
Box 25286, Federal Center
Denver, CO 80225
800-USA-MAPS
Publishes a list of current maps.

OFFICE OF PUBLIC INQUIRIES
NATIONAL PARK SERVICE
Room 1013
Washington, D.C. 20240
202-208-4747
*Maps and folders for national
parks, forests, seashores, and his-
torical sites.*

U.S. FOREST SERVICE
Public Affairs Office
2nd Floor
Auditors Building
14th & Independence Avenue,
S.W.
Washington, D.C. 20250
202-205-1760
155 national forest maps.

MAIL-ORDER
SOURCES OF FOOD
ADVENTURE FOODS
Route 2
Whittier, NC 28789
704-497-4113

ALPINE AIRE
P.O. Box 926
Nevada City, CA 95959
800-322-MEAL

BACKPACK GOURMET
P.O. Box 334-C
Underhill, VT 05489
802-899-5445

INDIANA CAMP SUPPLY
125 East 37th Street
P.O. Box 2166
Loveland, CO 80539
303-669-8884

MOUNTAIN HOUSE
Oregon Freez Dry, Inc.
P.O. Box 1048
Albany, OR 97321
800-547-4060

TRAIL FOODS
P.O. Box 9309-B
N. Hollywood, CA 91609-1309
818-897-4370

UNCLE JOHN'S FOODS
Box 489
Dept B994
Fairplay, CO 80440
800-530-8733

MANUFACTURERS
OF EQUIPMENT
Who makes the gear you need?
A great many manufacturers,
most of whom will send you a
catalog and/or product information and a list of dealers if
you call. Some sell from their
factories.

ASOLO FOOTWEAR
400 dealers; no factory sales
139 Harvest Lane
Williston, VT 05495
802-879-4644
boots

BIBLER TENTS
40 dealers; factory sales
5441-D Western Avenue
Dept BG
Boulder, CO 80301
303-449-7351
tents; stoves; sleeping bags

CAMP TRAILS/JOHNSON WORLDWIDE ASSOCIATES
no factory sales
1326 Willow Road
Sturtevant, WI 53177
800-848-3673
packs; tents; sleeping bag; outdoor gear and clothing

CAMPING GAZ/SUUNTO USA
2,000 dealers; no factory sales
2151 Las Palmas Drive
Carlsbad, CA 92009
619-931-6788
stoves; water filters

CAMPMOR, INC.
retail store, catalog sales
28 Parkway
P.O. Box 700
Saddle River, NJ 07458
800-525-4784
full line of outdoor gear

CARIBOU MOUNTAINEERING, INC.
1,800 dealers; factory sales
P.O. Box 3696
Chico, CA 95927
800-824-4153
packs; sleeping bags

CASCADE DESIGNS, INC.
1,000 dealers; no factory sales
4000 First Avenue S.
Seattle, WA 98134
800-531-9531
packs; sleeping bags; sleeping pads

CLIMB HIGH
600 dealers; factory sales
1861 Shelburne Road
Shelburne, VT 05482
802-985-5056
packs; stoves; sleeping bags; full line of outdoor gear & clothing

DANA DESIGN
180 dealers; factory sales
1950 N. 19th Street
Bozeman, MT 59715
406-587-4188
packs

EASTERN MOUNTAIN SPORTS (EMS)
55 retail stores; no factory sales
One Vose Farm Road
Peterborough, NH 03458
603-924-6154
full line of outdoor gear & clothing

EUREKA!/JOHNSON WORLDWIDE ASSOCIATES
see Camp Trails/Johnson Worldwide Associates

FABIANO SHOE CO.
factory sales
850 Summer Street
S. Boston, MA 02127-1575
617-268-5625
boots

FEATHERED FRIENDS
50 dealers; factory sales
2013 Fourth Avenue
Seattle, WA 98121
206-443-9549
sleeping bags & repairs

GARUDA
34 dealers; factory sales
P.O. Box 24804
Seattle, WA 98124-0804
206-763-2989
tents

GENERAL ECOLOGY, INC.
no factory sales
151 Sheree Blvd.
Exton, PA 19341
800-441-8166
water filters (First Need)

GREGORY MOUNTAIN PRODUCTS
factory sales
100 Calle Cortez
Temecula, CA 92590
800-477-3420
packs

JANSPORT
5,000 dealers; no factory sales
14411 Airport Road SW
Everett, WA 96204
800-552-6776
packs; sportswear

KATADYN
400 dealers; no factory sales
Geneva Road
Brewster, NY 10009
800-431-2204
water filters

KELTY, INC.
800 dealers; no factory sales
1224 Fern Rfidge Pkwy.
St. Lois, MO 63141
314-576-8069
packs; tents; sleeping bags

LEKI-SPORT USA
60 Earhart Drive
Williamsville, NY 14221
716-633-8062
hiking poles

LOWE ALPINE SYSTEMS
400 dealers; no factory sales
P.O. Box 1449
Broomfield, CO 80038
303-465-0522
packs

MARMOT
240 dealers; no factory sales
2321 Circadian Way
Santa Rosa, CA 95407
707-544-4590
sleeping bags; outdoor sports outerwear

MERRELL FOOTWEAR
1,200 dealers; no factory sales
P.O. Box 4249
Burlington, VT 05406
800-869-3348
boots

MOONSTONE MOUNTAINEERING
500 dealers; no factory sales
5350 Ericson Way
Arcata, CA 95521
800-822-2985
sleeping bags

MOSS, INC.
300 dealers, no factory sales
P.O. Box 577
Camden, ME 04843
207-236-0505
tents

MOUNTAIN SAFETY RESEARCH/MSR
1,200 dealers; factory sales
4225 Second Avenue, S.
Seattle, WA 98134
800-877-9677
stoves; water filters

MOUNTAINSMITH, INC.
350 dealers; factory sales
18301 W. Colfax, Bldg. P
Golden, CO 80401
800-426-4075
packs

THE NORTH FACE
450 dealers; no factory sales
999 Harrison Street
Berkeley, CA 94710
800-447-2333
packs; tents; sleeping bags, outerwear

ONE SPORT, INC.
350 dealers; no factory sales
1003 Sixth Avenue S.
Seattle, WA 98134
800-826-1598
boots

OPTIMUS/SUUNTO USA
see *Camping Gaz/Suunto USA*

OSPREY PACKS
125 dealers; factory sales
P.O. Box 539
Dolores, CO 81323
303-882-2221
packs

PATAGONIA
retail and catalog sales
P.O. Box 8900
Bozeman, MT 59715
800-336-9090
outdoor sports clothing

PEAK I/THE COLEMAN CO.
factory sales
P.O. Box 2931
Wichita, KS 67202
800-835-3278
packs; stoves; sleeping bags

PUR
900 dealers; factory sales
2229 Edgewood Avenue, S.
Minneapolis, MN 55426
800-845-7873
water filters

RAICHLE MOLITOR USA, INC.
no factory sales
Geneva Road
Brewster, NY 10509
800-431-2204
boots

RECREATIONAL EQUIPMENT INC./REI
41 dealers; no factory sales
P.O. Box 1938
Sumner, WA 98390-0800
800-426-4840
full line of outdoor gear & clothing

SIERRA DESIGNS
800 dealers; factory sales
1255 Powell Street
Emeryville, CA 94608
800-736-8551
tents; sleeping bags

SLUMBERJACK
3,000 dealers; no factory sales
P.O. Box 7048A
St. Louis, MO 63177
800-233-6283
sleeping bags; sleeping pads

STEPHENSONS-WARMLITE
1 dealer; factory sales
22 Hook Rd.
Gilford, NH 03246-6745
603-293-8526
packs; tents; sleeping bags; sleeping pads

SWEETWATER, INC.
600+ dealers; no factory sales
4725 Nautilus Ct. #3
Boulder, CO 80301
800-557-9338
water filters

TECNICA USA
no factory sales
19 Technology Drive
West Lebanon, NH 03784
603-298-8032
boots

THERM-A-REST
see *Cascade Designs*

VASQUE
no factory sales
314 Main Street
Red Wing, MN 55066
612-388-8211
boots

WALRUS
150 dealers; factory sales
P.O. Box 3875
Seattle, WA 98124
800-550-8368
tents

PHOTO CREDITS

INDEX